WHEN THE
STONES
SPEAK

WHEN THE STONES SPEAK

*The Remarkable Discovery of
the City of David and What Israel's Enemies
Don't Want You to Know*

DORON SPIELMAN

**CENTER
STREET**

New York Nashville

Center Street
Hachette Book Group
1290 Avenue of the Americas, New York, NY 10104
centerstreet.com
@CenterStreet/@CenterStreetBooks

First edition: May 2025

Center Street is a division of Hachette Book Group, Inc. The Center Street name and logo are registered trademarks of Hachette Book Group, Inc.

The publisher is not responsible for websites (or their content) that are not owned by the publisher.

Center Street books may be purchased in bulk for business, educational, or promotional use. For information, please contact your local bookseller or the Hachette Book Group Special Markets Department at special.markets@hbgusa.com.

All photos unless otherwise indicated are courtesy of the author's personal collection.

Library of Congress Cataloging-in-Publication Data

Names: Spielman, Doron, author.
Title: When the stones speak : the remarkable discovery of the City of David and what Israel's enemies don't want you to know / Doron Spielman.
Other titles: Remarkable discovery of the City of David and what Israel's enemies don't want you to know
Description: First edition. | New York : Center Street, 2025. | Includes bibliographical references and index.
Identifiers: LCCN 2024054361 | ISBN 9781546009252 (hardcover) | ISBN 9781546009276 (ebook)
Subjects: LCSH: Propaganda, Anti-Israeli. | Excavations (Archaeology)—Jerusalem. | Jews—History. | Jerusalem—Antiquities. | 'Ir Dayid (Jerusalem) | Jerusalem—History.
Classification: LCC DS109.8.C54 S65 2025 | DDC 933/.442—dc23/eng/20250121
LC record available at https://lccn.loc.gov/2024054361

ISBNs: 9781546009252 (hardcover), 9781546009276 (ebook)

Printed in the United States of America

LSC-C

Printing 1, 2025

To my wife, Sarah, thank you for this amazing journey.

Contents

Contents

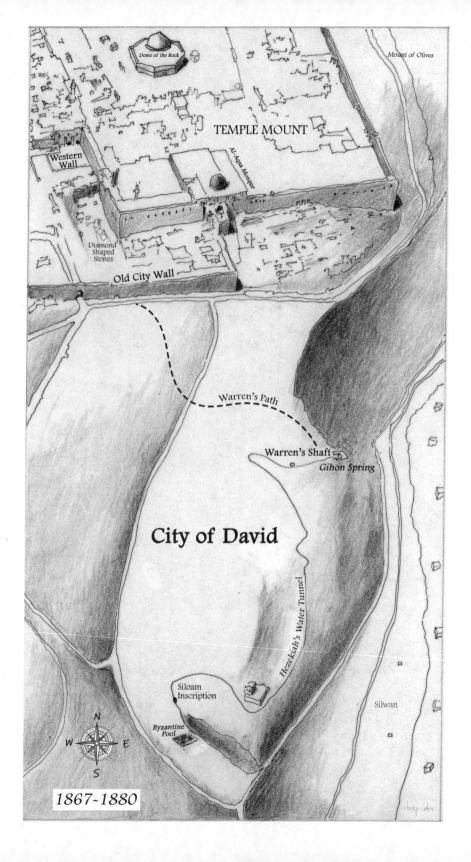

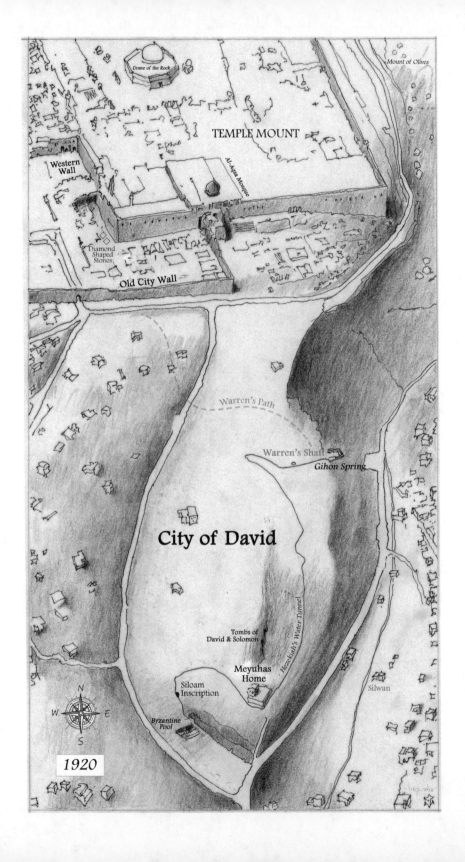

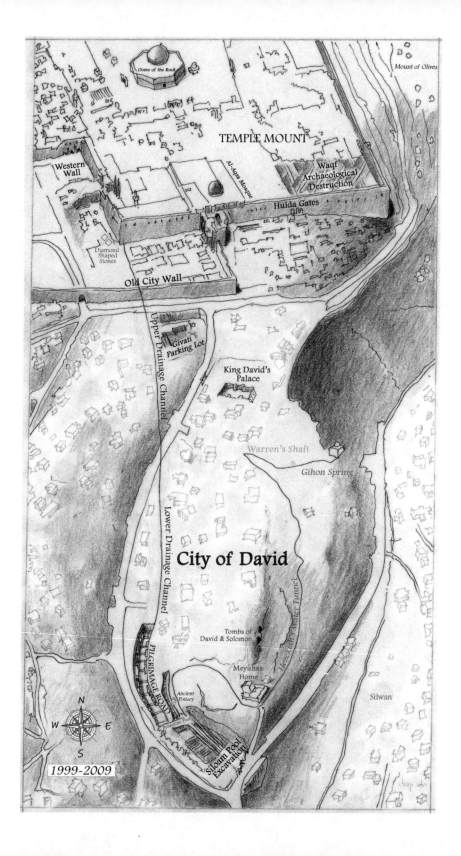

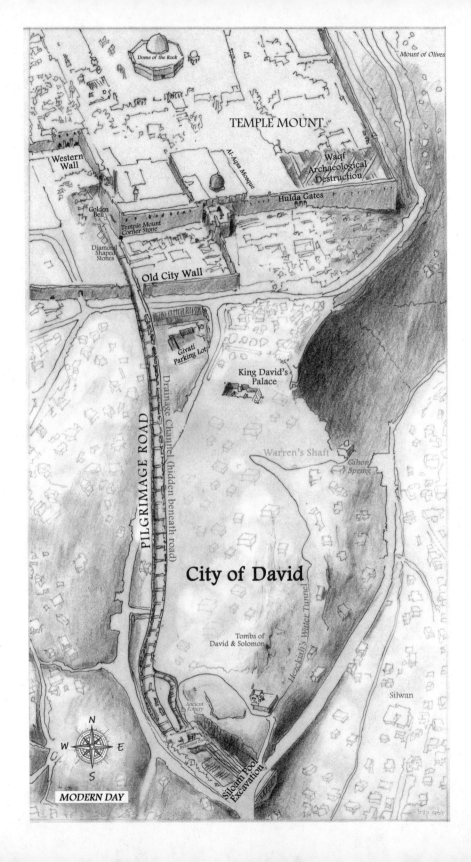

Preface

Just south of the Old City of Jerusalem is an even older city, the original Jerusalem, known then—and again today—as the City of David. The stones of the City of David tell a story even older than the stones of the Old City. They tell a story that goes back beyond the Ottoman era, beyond the medieval and Byzantine periods, beyond the Roman Empire, beyond even Ancient Greece. Beginning in the waning years of the Ottoman Empire, explorers and archaeologists began to dig through layers and layers of rubble and found shards of materials even older than the two-thousand-year-old stones of the Roman-era ruins. Digging even deeper, the archaeologists found pillars and pottery, seals and coins, walls and roads, and tablets with names and dates inscribed, which scientists were able to date to what historians call the Bronze and Iron Ages—the time the Bible refers to as the reigns of Kings David and Solomon.

What the archaeologists found among those stones are the remnants of the City of David, physical, tangible, proof that the Jewish people have been indigenous to the land for more than thirty-eight hundred years.

In *When the Stones Speak*, those stones will finally tell their stories.

More than three thousand years ago, a king named David, a thirty-year-old man of short stature, with red hair and bright eyes, was anointed king of the tribe of Judah. He conquered a small hilltop not far from what is known today as the "Old City" of Jerusalem. David managed to reunite the other eleven tribes of Israel into a single nation and govern them from his hilltop capital, known as the City of David.

King David's heirs wrestled both with foreign rulers and each other over this hilltop city. Despite these challenges, David's descendants managed to forge a dynasty that lasted the better part of a thousand years, until their final defeat and dispersal by the legions of Rome in the year 70 CE.

Successive rulers—including Romans, Persians, Muslims, and Crusaders—established a city at the top of a neighboring hill just to the north of the City of David, which came to be known as the Old City of Jerusalem—but the walls they built around this city actually excluded David's original site. The City of David eventually fell into disrepair and was abandoned and covered by the sands of time until it was forgotten.

So, while the site known today as the Old City of Jerusalem is thousands of years old, it actually excludes the oldest part of Jerusalem from the Bible, the City of David.

Being forgotten was perhaps what saved the City of David, for over the next two thousand years while the Old City of Jerusalem was frequently the site of war and was ransacked countless times by marauders searching for treasures from the Bible, the City of David and its biblical treasures lay buried, protected, and largely undisturbed.

During those centuries while the City of David lay buried, the Jewish people were forced to wander from land to land, going from exile to exile, suffering persecution, finding new homes, attaining wealth and success, only to be expelled again and again. Since the founding of the State of Israel in 1948, the Jewish people have faced nine different wars[1] against multiple enemies, most recently fighting enemies on seven fronts.

But a war more dangerous than these physical wars has been

waged against Israel and the Jewish people, a war fought on a deeper ideological level, one created with cunning by certain Arab leaders, and echoed wittingly or unwittingly by international institutions such as the United Nations. This more-dangerous attack seeks to erase the ancestral connection of the Jewish people to the Land of Israel, severing the Jewish people's ancient tie to the land, casting them as outsiders, imposters, colonialists, and "settlers."

In many ways, one of the only things standing in the way of this campaign in recent years is the rediscovery of the ancient City of David and the excavations unearthing the stunning evidence that clearly proves the indigenous connection of the Jewish people to the Holy Land.

The archaeological evidence from the City of David threatens to deal a fatal blow to the propaganda and historical revisionism that has tried—and unfortunately been largely successful in—convincing many people around the world that Jews and Israelis are foreign outsiders, with no connection to the land itself.

Every shovel of dirt from the City of David shows that while many people may claim to be indigenous to Jerusalem, the Jewish people are more indigenous to the Land of Israel than are perhaps any other people living anywhere in the world.

Today, the City of David has become Israel's largest excavation site and one of the most active excavations in the world. The uniqueness of these excavations is that the guidebook to the dig and the discoveries is none other than the Bible itself. The names found inscribed on tablets discovered in recent years do not need to be looked up in an encyclopedia. They almost jump off the pages of the Bible, as if delighted to be rediscovered.

This book tells the story of the dramatic uncovering of the City of David excavations and the courage of those who continued with this task while confronted by some of the world's most powerful agencies and organizations, all seemingly determined to prevent these discoveries from coming to light. These international organizations have been aided and abetted by terror groups that use all means at their disposal, including intimidation, libel, and ultimately violence.

The City of David story also foreshadows the events that unfolded in 2023 with Hamas's attack on Israel on October 7.

On October 8, the day after the Hamas massacre, I was in military uniform, standing on the southern border with Gaza, on an empty highway near the Israeli city of Sderot. Silence hung heavily in the air. The road was a graveyard of hundreds of abandoned vehicles—overturned, smashed into light poles, burned-out metal frames left as the grim remnants of chaos. The ground was littered with what remained of disrupted lives: backpacks, baby bottles, scattered belongings left behind in panic.

I stood by one of the wrecked cars with a fellow soldier who had driven south with me. The bodies had already been removed by the first responders, but the driver's ID lay untouched on the seat—a silent testament to the lives that had been taken there. Holding that ID in my hands, the weight of what had happened pressed down on me, piercing the silence. Innocent civilians—men, women, and children—had been slaughtered. And we, the soldiers of Israel, had not been able to shield them.

My companion pointed to a pile of white zip ties discarded near the car door. I stared at them, not understanding. "They used these to bind the hands of the hostages," he said, his voice flat, "before dragging them into Gaza." The words hit me like a punch to the gut. I stepped back, disturbed, yet unable to look away. The quiet of the scene, the lifeless cars—the horror of what had happened struck me. What had happened there was not just murder; it was something darker, driven by a hatred I could hardly comprehend.

Before October 7, I was immersed in writing this book. But after being called up to serve, witnessing the reality on the ground, and enduring ninety-six days of continuous duty, I was profoundly changed. The subject of this book—the deliberate attempt to erase Jewish history and sever the bond between the Jewish people and their land—had come to life in the most brutal, undeniable way, tied now to the massacre of more than twelve hundred innocent lives.

This book, initially a recounting of archaeological discoveries in the City of David and the efforts of Israel's adversaries to bury this truth, now holds a deeper meaning in light of what I saw. The evidence of the Jewish people's historical presence in this land is not just history—it is the front line in a battle that Israel will be fighting for the foreseeable future, to ensure that the truth cannot be erased.

The campaign to erase Jewish ancestry in Israel can be found in the ideology of the Hamas terrorists who massacred so many innocents, but sadly it can also be found in the worldview of many of those who took to the streets with chants of Jewish annihilation like "From the river to the sea, Palestine will be free."

I worked as vice president of the City of David for more than two decades. During that time, I was privileged to witness, firsthand, the transformation of a neglected hilltop outside the Old City walls into the archaeological wonder of the City of David.

Over the years, as the site rose to prominence, I took hundreds of people—including donors, diplomats, professors, and politicians—deep into the City of David's tunnels. The list of people I accompanied included entertainment figures such as Jerry Seinfeld, Helen Mirren, and Demi Lovato, and politicians and diplomats such as Secretary of State Mike Pompeo, Secretary of Defense Pete Hegseth, Ambassador Nikki Haley, and Governors Gretchen Whitmer, Ron DeSantis, and Gavin Newsom. While often holding vastly different political views, after seeing the evidence of thirty-eight hundred years of Jewish history unearthed, these visitors seemed to agree on one thing: that the story of the City of David must be told to a wider audience.

This is not an academic account by a historian or a Middle East history professor. I am neither. It is a personal account, based on my own experiences. Where I have relied on research done by historians and archaeologists, references are provided so the reader can explore further.

Given that the connection between the Jews and their land is once again being challenged, understanding the objective proof of this connection—along with understanding the importance and centrality of this bond to so many Jews and non-Jews—is more important than ever.

When the Stones Speak is a sweeping story of history, one that becomes more relevant every day. As each brush sweeps away the dust, and with every fresh find uncovered, two shockwaves are sent off: The first is the veracity of the historical connection of the Jewish people to their homeland; the second is the doctrine of denialism that seeks to eliminate this connection.

You are about to read a story that spans more than three thousand years. However, its end is not yet known. Perhaps those of you reading this story will play a role in how it unfolds. Perhaps you will witness its unfolding.

Before you do, I ask you to let the stones speak.

Introduction

The City of David and the Indigenous Jews

One month before the Hamas massacre on October 7, 2023, Palestinian Authority President Mahmoud Abbas gave a speech to his Fatah revolutionary council that shocked much of the Western world. Aired on Palestinian television, he declared:

> They say Hitler killed the Jews for being Jews, and that Europe hated the Jews because they were Jews. Not true! It was clearly explained that they fought the Jews because of their social role, not their religion. He fought the Jews because they were dealing with money lending...In his view they were engaged in sabotage and that is why he hated them.[1]

Abbas claimed that the Holocaust couldn't be about anti-Semitism because "European Jews are not Semites." Instead, he quoted a disproven historical theory claiming that European Jews are not descendants of ancient Israel. Rather, this theory asserts, Ashkenazi Jews are instead descended from a now extinct "ninth-century Tatar kingdom that converted to Judaism." This theory has no basis in reality. Genetic and linguistic studies have not linked the Ashkenazi Jews of Western Europe to these Tatar or Khazar roots. Genetically, Ashkenazi Jews are linked to Sephardic Jews or Jews from Iran, Iraq, or Syria.

Nevertheless, this denialist claim persists among Palestinian and Arab academics and has spread to Europe and America.

Although Abbas's remarks were quickly condemned in America and in European capitals, even a cursory look at Abbas's history shows these remarks were in keeping with anti-Semitic ideas he has held and expressed his entire life. To understand his true bias, one need only look at his doctoral thesis, written in 1984, titled, "The Secret Relations Between Nazism and the Leadership of the Zionist Movement."[2] In this PhD thesis, he went even further, blaming Zionist Jews for bringing on the Holocaust as a means of gaining world sympathy for a Jewish state:

> The Zionist movement led a broad campaign of incitement against the Jews living under Nazi rule to arouse the government's hatred of them, to fuel vengeance against them and to expand the mass extermination.[3]

Little more than two months after his remarks and one month after Hamas's attack, Mahmoud Abbas was being touted by both the United States and European countries as the top contender to run the postwar Gaza Strip, as if this was a different man from the one that had spoken only two months before.[4]

One might ask, isn't there a better person to represent the Palestinian people, one without such hatred of Jews?

But Mahmoud Abbas is not alone in his denial of the Holocaust and the indigenous rights of the Jewish people. In the Hamas charter, originally written in 1988 and held sacred by many in Gaza, Jews are cast as similar to Nazis. Article 20 reads, "In their Nazi treatment, the Jews make no exception for women or children. Their policy of striking fear in the heart is meant for all. They attack people where their breadwinning is concerned, extorting their money and threatening their honor."[5] Other articles in the charter are similarly filled with hatred, not only of Israelis but of Jews worldwide.

If the story ended there, it would be enough to fill the pages of a book in its own right.

However, the story only *begins* there.

The dehumanization of the Jews is just one small part of a carefully constructed ecosystem of falsehoods that Arabs have been taught to believe about the Jewish people.

Building on the narrative of Holocaust denial, a narrative of illegitimacy has been constructed, one that has sparked the ire of Palestinians not only toward Israelis but toward Jews worldwide. To construct this narrative, there could not be two competing legitimate claims for the same piece of land: One would have to be delegitimized. Any indigenous rights of the Jews to the land had to be eliminated and erased from history.

First the Jewish people and the State of Israel were depicted with words like *colonialist* and *occupier* and *Apartheid*. A false picture of the diverse population of Israel as white and European had to be created—despite that more than 50 percent of the Israeli population comes from North Africa and the Middle East.[6]

The Palestinian leadership embarked on a systematic campaign to eliminate any and all Jewish claims to the land by eliminating the 3,800-year history of the Jewish people in the Land of Israel. They did this despite historical and archaeological evidence to the contrary, despite hundreds of biblical references, despite numerous passages in ancient Jewish, Christian, and Islamic texts, and despite common sense. They attempted to convince the world that the Israelis are nothing more than "settler colonialists," that the State of Israel was unjustly given to white European Jews after World War II by guilt-ridden white European Christians who had no right to give it to them in the first place, and that the Palestinians are the only true indigenous people in the region.

The world had long understood that Jerusalem was the city of King David, the Jewish king, and that the Temple Mount, upon which now stands the Al-Aqsa Mosque and the Dome of the Rock, which sits above the Western Wall, was originally the holiest Jewish site of Solomon's and Herod's temples. Therefore, a narrative had to be created to reverse that understanding and to reposition Jerusalem as a purely Muslim city.

This was not easy to do: Centuries of Islamic scholarship and liturgy clearly stated that Al Aqsa was the site of the first two temples of the Jews, the "people of the Book," as the Koran refers to Jews. Nevertheless, influential Palestinians like Sheikh Ikrima Sabri, the Mufti of the Temple Mount in Jerusalem and one of the founders of Al Quds University, began to make statements denying that the Temple ever existed or that the Jews had any connection to Jerusalem: "There is not the smallest indication of the existence of a Jewish temple on this place in the past," he claimed to a reporter. "In the whole city, there is not even a single stone indicating Jewish history...It is the art of the Jews to deceive the world."[7]

Another influential Palestinian scholar, Walid Awad, in charge of publications for the Palestinian Ministry of Information, said: "The fact of the matter is that almost thirty years of excavations did not reveal anything Jewish....Jerusalem is not a Jewish city, despite the biblical myth implanted in some minds."[8]

And Yasser Arafat, the head of the Palestine Liberation Organization and founder of its current rendition, the "Palestinian Authority," himself nearly derailed the Camp David Accords, when shortly after signing them, according to US Ambassador Dennis Ross, Arafat declared that the Western Wall was a "Muslim shrine" and that a Jewish temple in Jerusalem had never even existed. President Bill

Clinton, who had been hoping that the Camp David Accords would be remembered as one of his greatest achievements, threatened to get up and leave the table unless Arafat retracted his words.[9] Only recently, on May 15, 2023, during a speech to the United Nations, the "moderate" Palestinian leader Mahmoud Abbas claimed that there was no proof whatsoever of Jewish ties to the area of the al-Aqsa compound. He stated that Israel "dug under al-Aqsa. They dug everywhere and they could not find anything."[10]

The ultimate result of this campaign was the horrors of the Hamas massacre on October 7, followed by the cries that shocked so many, when hundreds of thousands of people, marching in cities throughout the Western world called out, "From the river to the sea, Palestine will be free."

The goal was clear: *Deny the Holocaust, deny Jewish history, dismantle the State of Israel, and eradicate the Jewish people.*

One thing, however, stands in the way of the denialists: the more than three thousand years of history that can be witnessed at the City of David.

The Jewish people of today have had three different names throughout the millennia: Hebrews, Israelites, and most recently, Jews. Each of these names reflects a stage in the development of the People.

Our Hebrew ancestry begins with the patriarch Abraham, who lived in approximately 1850 BCE. According to the Bible in Genesis, Abraham was born in the Mesopotamian city of Ur, located in modern-day Iraq. The term *Hebrew*, or *Ivri*, as it is pronounced in the Hebrew language, likely means "one who came across," a reference to Abraham, who literally had to cross over the Euphrates and Tigris Rivers on his journey from Ur, through the Fertile

Crescent, and into the land that today is called Israel and was then called Canaan. To the local Canaanite population, Abraham was a foreigner, and thus, his descendants were called the Hebrews, as in "those who crossed over."

These are the earliest roots of the Jewish people. Looking to fortify the Hebrews' connection to the land, the Bible goes into great detail in describing how Abraham purchased the area of Hebron, known today as the Tomb of the Patriarchs, from Efron the Hittite for the vast sum at the time of 400 shekels of silver. This process would be followed by Abraham's grandson, the patriarch Jacob, who purchased Shechem (modern day Nablus) from the Canaanites, and hundreds of years later, by King David, who purchased the Temple Mount in Jerusalem from Arunah the Jebusite.

The patriarch Jacob, also known as Israel in the Bible, had twelve sons. These twelve sons became known as the Twelve Tribes of Israel. They established themselves in the Land, and over the centuries, their descendants took the name Israelites. While the name Hebrews didn't disappear altogether, the term *Israelites* lasted for close to 1,300 years and was recorded throughout history, both in the Bible and in numerous extra-biblical sources, cuneiform tablets, and writings. During Jacob's lifetime, a harsh famine struck the land of Canaan, forcing Jacob and his family to move to Egypt, where Jacob's second youngest son, Joseph, became viceroy to Pharoah.

In a paradigm that would follow the Jewish people throughout their history, the freedom first experienced by Jacob's children was eventually seen as a threat by the Egyptians, and the Israelites were ultimately enslaved. It was from just after the Israelites had been freed from slavery during the thirteenth century BCE that the earliest reference to the word *Israel* was found written on an inscription by Pharaoh Merneptah, who ruled Egypt from 1213 to 1203 BCE.[11] Merneptah was the thirteenth son of Pharaoh Ramses II,[12] often considered to be the Pharaoh of the exodus story.

In approximately the thirteenth century BCE, the Israelites, led by Moses, were liberated from slavery and left Egypt. They began the forty-year trek through the Sinai Desert back to the land of their forefathers. Moses and the original generation of Israelites died in the desert; however, the next generation was led into the Land of Canaan by Moses's loyal student Joshua. Joshua led the Israelites on a fourteen-year military campaign, which was only partially successful. Large pockets of Canaanites and other tribes remained in the land. The next two hundred years or so were characterized by a lack of Israelite leadership. The Israelites fell into subjugation by enemy tribes and then regained partial independence.

In approximately the year 1000 BCE, King David, of the tribe of Judah, succeeded in unifying the twelve tribes and established Jerusalem as the capital of the Israelite people. During this time, Jerusalem was referred to in the Bible as the City of David.

In approximately 960 BCE, David's son, King Solomon, built the Temple on the Temple Mount in Jerusalem and brought the Ark of the Covenant to rest inside of it. The Temple became a pilgrimage site for both Israelites and non-Israelites, who were drawn to the unique Israelite theology, known today as monotheism, that there was one central God of all of humankind.

In the year 722 BCE, approximately 240 years after Solomon's Temple was built, the Assyrians conquered ten of the twelve tribes who were living in the north of the country, and dispersed them across the vast Assyrian Empire. This left the large tribe Judah dominant in the land, along with a smaller tribe, Benjamin, which eventually was absorbed into Judah.

The remaining two tribes, along with refugees that had escaped from the other ten tribes, established a vast and wealthy kingdom in the land, centered around Jerusalem as the nation's capital and Solomon's Temple, which remained standing throughout this entire period. In 586 BCE, however, the Babylonians destroyed Jerusalem and exiled the leadership of the tribe of Judah to Babylon, located in modern-day Iraq.

In total, King Soloman's Temple stood for close to four hundred years, from 960 BCE until its destruction in 586 BCE. This period is called the First Temple Period.

Then, seventy-one years after the Babylonian exile, in 515 BCE, the kingdom of Persia conquered Babylon and allowed the Jews to return to their ancestral land and rebuild the kingdom of Judea.

It was at that point in time that the Israelites, having been reduced to the tribe of Judah, or Yehuda, became known as Yehudim—or Jews. The name of the Land of Israel was also changed; from this point forward it was referred to as Judea, the land of Judah. Persia issued coinage to identify this region. The coins, thousands of which survive to this day, bear the three-letter insignia which spells *Yahad*, or "Judea," the land of the Jew. When the Jews returned to Judea, they once again repaired the Temple, which had fallen into ruins, and once again they rebuilt a thriving kingdom in antiquity. This began what is known as the Second Temple Period.

During this time, the kingdom of Judea was rocked by various tumultuous events such as the Greek invasion. This resulted in the Maccabean revolt and the victory of the Jews commemorated in the holiday of Hanukkah.

Throughout, the Temple remained standing.

In the year 70 CE, the Roman Emperor Vespasian conquered Judea, destroyed the Second Temple, and exiled large segments of the Jewish people throughout the Roman Empire. The destruction ended the Second Temple Period, which had lasted 585 years.

One final attempt to regain Jewish independence in the land happened sixty-two years after the destruction of the Temple. In the year 132 CE, the Jews still living in the land rose once again against their Roman oppressors. It took the Romans three years to suppress the revolt, but in the end they succeeded. Hadrian, the Roman emperor of the time, destroyed whatever was left of Jerusalem and forbade Jews to visit the city. According to the Roman historian Cassius Dio, Hadrian destroyed 985 villages and killed 580,000 people.[13]

It is hard to imagine such a large number of Jews killed in the ancient world. All these killings were done face-to-face by the hands of the soldiers. Hadrian did not stop there, however, and in a final act to ensure the Jews would never return to the land, he changed the name of the land from Judea to Syria Palestina, a term first employed by the ancient historian Herodotus that is a reference to the Philistines, a nation of people who had been wiped out by the Babylonians 700 years earlier and who had been a great enemy to the Israelites. This was Hadrian's attempt to sever the connection between now dispersed members of the tribe of Judah and the land that bore its name.[14]

It was Hadrian who ensured that the name Palestine became associated with this land. For the next two thousand years, the area of land called Palestine was a backwater province inhabited by numerous warring nations. The people living there were subjects of the nations who conquered the land, such as the Romans, the Byzantines, the Fatimids, the Crusaders, the Mamluks, and the Ottomans. They identified themselves by the names of the conquering nations.

Throughout this entire time, there never was an independent government or country of Palestine, nor an independent Palestinian people.

As this book will show, archaeological evidence and DNA evidence, along with the continued use of the Hebrew language, the Jewish religion, and Jewish traditions attest to the Jewish people of today being part of one of the longest running civilizations still in existence in the world.

There are no other people on the face of the planet who can so carefully trace their history back to a land that bore their name. Even while the majority of the Jewish people were in exile over the past two thousand years, that land always had at least a remnant of Jews who lived there. One of numerous reminders of the connection between the Jews and Jerusalem is that, throughout the two-thousand-year exile of the Jews, every synagogue, wherever it was built in the world, always faced the direction of Jerusalem.

Given that the evidence speaks so clearly, it is then beyond surprising—in fact, it is ludicrous—that there are probably no other people on earth who have been as vilified for returning to their land, or whose historical connection to their land has been challenged as much as the Jews of today.

The legacy of the Roman conquerors of the Jews, who tried to sever this connection by exiling the people and changing the name of the land from Judah to Palestine, seems to have been passed down to our day.

Indeed, it has certainly taken root again.

We need only look to the crowds of protestors, including students and even Ivy League professors, who marched through campuses around the world following Hamas's massacre of Israelis on October 7, 2023, chanting "From the river to the sea, Palestine will be free."

If the "river" is the Jordan River and the "sea" is the Mediterranean, where is Israel on that map? Nowhere.

The chant is a call for the extinction of the Israeli people and the extinction of the land known today as Israel, just as Hadrian tried to do two thousand years ago.

For more than twenty years, I arrived at work each morning greeted by the soft, steady sounds of pickaxes as archaeologists carefully pried through the earth in search of the buried City of David. For many of those years, it was nearly impossible to imagine—let alone convince anyone—that King David's ancient city lay hidden beneath a hilltop of decrepit homes and a single ailing street, just south of the Temple Mount and outside the Old City of Jerusalem.

But as the days and years passed, puzzle piece after puzzle piece emerged, revealing the site that was once the cradle of Jewish civilization. From the moment King David made Jerusalem his capital to the final hours of the Second Temple's destruction by the Romans more than a thousand years later, the ancient city slowly rose from the ground, reclaiming its place in history. Today, it is one of the most active archaeological excavations on earth, a national park on land originally purchased by Baron Edmund de Rothschild under both the Ottoman Empire and the British Mandate in the early 1900s, well before the founding of the State of Israel.

After Jordan illegally occupied Jerusalem between 1948 and 1967, the land had to be repurchased for the second time in less than a few decades.

This book will set the record straight about what was found in the archaeological excavations at the City of David. We will see those that unearthed these treasures, as well as those that tried almost any means to stop the excavations from happening, and to prevent the discoveries from coming to light.

Given that the connection between the Jews and their land is once again being challenged, understanding the objective proof of this connection, along with the importance and centrality of this bond to so many Jews and non-Jews, is more important than ever.

This is what I hope the following pages will do.

The story of the rediscovery of King David's ancient city in the modern era begins, most appropriately, with a queen.

Part One

VICTORIAN EXPLORERS AND THE SEARCH FOR JERUSALEM

Chapter 1

Charles Warren and
the Diamond-Shaped Stones

It is 1867. Queen Victoria is celebrating the thirtieth year of her reign. In addition to granting royal assent to the British North America Act, and turning Canada into a federal dominion, she has sponsored the newly created Palestine Exploration Fund, and they have recruited Second Lieutenant Charles Warren of the British Royal Engineers to conduct their first archaeological expedition to the Holy Land.

Given the recent and temporary alliance between Britain and the Ottoman Empire, permission is given to Warren to unearth biblical-era antiquities, concentrating on those of King David and King Solomon. Warren will be allowed to bring some of those treasures back to the British Museum.

Warren is given unprecedented access with one caveat:
The Temple Mount is to remain off-limits.

Upon arriving in the Holy Land, Charles Warren bribed his way through the ranks of the Ottoman bureaucracy and launched his expedition as close to the Temple Mount as he could. He knew that the Mount, upon which today stands the Dome of the Rock, was a Muslim holy site, upon which once stood the first and second Jewish Temples.

When his team began excavating, the initial results were disappointing: pottery and coins but nothing that reached the time of the Bible.

Had Warren's adventures ended there, his name would likely have been one more in a list of treasure hunters who came before and after him. But Warren went on to uncover something extraordinary, something that neither he nor the queen—nor anyone else, for that matter—thought had been lost: Warren discovered the original site of Jerusalem, known in the Bible as the City of David, a discovery that changed the way we understand history.

One day Warren decided to leave the safety and security of the Old City walls and explore the mostly barren, rolling hills outside the Old City. He walked through some vegetable fields, down a mountainside to the valley floor, where he happened upon an arched entrance into a cave, leading to a flight of stone stairs that descended beneath the mountain. At the bottom of the stairs, Warren found a spring of water flowing softly. When his eyes adjusted to the dark of the cave, he realized that the water was flowing not into the valley, but rather through a stone tunnel bored into the heart of the mountain itself.

Warren gathered his team, and they followed the waters of the spring through the bedrock of the mountain. After a few dozen feet they noticed, over their heads, a man-made shaft leading up into the mountain. They built scaffolds and began digging. As they examined the pottery shards coming out of the shaft, they were stunned. The pottery was thousands of years older than what they had found in what everyone at the time considered to be the "Old City" of Jerusalem inside the walls.

There was something older than the Old City.

Warren and his team spent the next few months digging out the entire shaft until they burst out of the ground into a vegetable field on the surface of the mountain above.

They realized that they had discovered a secret passageway that had once connected an ancient people living on the top of the mountain down to the spring of water on the valley floor.

But what was the purpose of this passageway?

Warren was an aficionado of the Bible and knew the story of King David word for word. As he thought about the shaft, little knowing that one day it would bear his own name and be called "Warren's Shaft," he remembered a cryptic line from the Bible in which King David himself describes how he captured Jerusalem from an enemy people called the Jebusites, three thousand years earlier: "And David said on that day, he who conquers the Jebusites, will capture the water channel."

In all the explorations inside the Old City walls of Jerusalem, such a water source had never been found. The "water channel" referred to by King David had always remained a mystery.

Warren understood that he had found a water channel flowing beneath the mountain, along with a shaft that would have been used by people during the time of the Bible to secretly reach the source.

But how could King David use this water channel to capture Jerusalem if the hill he was standing on was outside the Old City Walls?

Unless...

Warren looked up from the hill he was standing on, and gazed toward the Old City walls in the distance and had a thought: *What if the actual site of Jerusalem from the time of King David was not inside what everyone thinks are the Old City walls? What if, instead, it lay beneath the small hilltop on which I now stand?*

Over the next three years, Warren dug where he was allowed to—and sometimes where he was not allowed to—sometimes through a hundred feet of rubble or tunnels—locating sources of water leading to and from the Gihon Spring and the Pool of Siloam along with a broad section of an ancient wall that would be identified years later by Kathleen Kenyon, a British archaeologist, as King

Solomon's Wall, predating the medieval walls that surround the Old City today by more than 2,500 years.

It became clear that outside what is today referred to as the Old City of Jerusalem there is a much older city, the site of Jerusalem from biblical times.

Charles Warren had discovered what would later be identified as the City of David.

At one point during the excavations, an artist, part of the team sent by Queen Victoria, drew a picture showing Warren's assistant, Corporal Henry Birtles, dangling on a rope and holding a candle, climbing down the rope between two massive, diamond-shaped stone blocks suspended at the top of a tunnel.[1]

The drawing raises many questions: Researchers would debate whether the drawing was based on a real event, and if so, where did it take place? What are the two large stones in the drawing, and why are they suspended in the roof of a tunnel?

This thought-provoking drawing survives to this day in an archive in Greenwich, England, along with the other antiquities that Warren and his team discovered.

Charles Warren's discoveries changed our very understanding of what and where Ancient Jerusalem was.

The story of the City of David is also a personal one for me. Over the past twenty-one years, I have had the privilege of working closely with the modern-day founder of the City of David National Park, David Beeri, known in Israel simply as "Davidleh" ("Little David"), along with Yehuda Maly, cofounder of the project, and a small group of people who have dedicated their lives to transforming the site from a neglected hilltop village into one of the most important archaeological heritage sites in the world.

One of the many digs Davidlch took us on was an early-morning journey to the past. In 2010, a digger on the evening crew made one of those discoveries that changes everything.

He was using his pickaxe to clear away the archaeological fill that had accumulated at the upper section of an ancient water tunnel, built during the Second Temple period and likely commissioned by King Herod, when suddenly, the top two feet of a wall gave way, exposing a long, dark tunnel. This was a very unusual experience, the kind of thing that only happens in Indiana Jones movies. Climbing closer to get a better look, he peered inside the tunnel with his flashlight. The tunnel extended far into blackness. He crawled in with the flashlight for around twenty feet before having the good judgment to crawl back out again.

The crew immediately called archaeologist Eli Shukron of the Israel Antiquities Authority, who spearheaded the excavations at the site. The tunnel was part of an ancient underground water system, only parts of which had been explored. Shukron worked his way up and into the narrow shaft and crawled a dozen meters or so. The tunnel continued into the distance. Realizing it wasn't prudent to continue alone and without necessary supplies, Shukron crawled out. He needed a small team of people willing to head into the narrow tunnel without knowing exactly how long they would be crawling, people who would be able to keep their wits about them.

At around ten p.m. that evening, he contacted Davidleh, who immediately agreed to join him. Shortly afterward, Davidleh called me, recognizing the immense significance of the moment. He understood that as the one responsible for representing the site to the world, I needed to experience this moment firsthand. Without hesitation, I agreed, fully aware of the significance of what was about to unfold.

I brought with me a new colleague of mine, Eli Alony, who would go on to play an instrumental role in raising the finances needed to grow the City of David in the future. Cofounder Yehuda Maly was in, and since he was always conscious of the historical significance of the work we were doing, he recruited Gil Mezuman, a videographer, to document the crawl.

We were to meet at five a.m. the next morning, before even the day shift arrived at the site.

The tunnel was called Herod's Water Channel, and excavators had been digging it for six years straight. King Herod was both a madman and an architectural genius, and he was both feared and respected by his Jewish subjects. The achievement he is most known for was his reconstruction of the Second Temple.

Following the return of the Jewish people from the Babylonian exile in 515 BCE, they built the Second Temple, using whatever materials they could scrounge together from what remained of the destroyed First Temple. The result was a Second Temple patchwork of stones that lacked the beauty and grandeur of the original First Temple structure.

Herod decided to transform the Second Temple structure into an edifice that would rival anything in the Roman world at the time. He created an architectural masterpiece. Although the Temple itself was subsequently destroyed by the Romans, the platform upon which he built the Temple, called the Temple Mount, stands to this day. It has a surface area large enough for twenty football fields. Today, the Dome of the Rock and the Mosque of Omar, two Muslim holy sites, stand on top of the original Temple Mount.

The western supporting wall that holds up this massive structure is the Western Wall holy site.

King Herod's Tunnel is one of the most important discoveries made in the City of David. It ran the entire length of the City of

David from top to bottom. The theory was that Herod's teams built the tunnel, which was more than half a mile long, as a drainage system for rainwater that fell in the area of the massive Temple Mount, which was located to the north of the City of David and at higher elevation. The water would drain through culverts or drains in the ground around the Temple Mount and follow gravity through the tunnel, all the way past the City of David to the valley floor, into a pool at the far end.

In 2005, the entrance to the southern section of Herod's Tunnel was discovered at the bottom of the City of David, next to a pool we were excavating. This section of the tunnel is called the Lower Tunnel, and inside it we found the site where the last Jews of Jerusalem had been hiding until the Romans found and killed them.

Since then, archaeologists had been inching along, heading away from the pool, all the way north toward the area of the Temple Mount, removing bags of dirt for years. Now the crews had made it to the upper half of Herod's Tunnel, known as the Upper Tunnel. There was still another three hundred feet left to go to see if the tunnel reached the area of the Temple Mount and the Western Wall.

No one could know for sure where the tunnel actually ended up until the dig was completed.

We gathered in the early dawn, and Shukron laid out the rules: We would crawl single file, head to tail. We would go for as long as we could, until we hit the end of the tunnel or decided we couldn't continue any farther physically.

If we couldn't find a place to turn around before heading back, we would have to crawl in reverse all the way out of the tunnel.

He estimated that we would be able to keep up the crawl for around two hours.

"This is game time," he told us, "and if anyone wants out, now is the time."

We set off into the narrow opening with Shukron in the lead, followed by Davidleh, me, Yehuda Maly, Eli Alony, and finally in the rear videographer Gil Mezuman.

One after the other we squeezed into the small opening. The roof of the tunnel rubbed against my back, forcing me to inch my way along, my face down, crawling like a dog.

Driven at first by our adrenaline, the beginning was okay. But after around ten minutes, Yehuda Maly called out to all of us to stop. He said that Gil, the videographer, was only getting video of our rear ends. Gil needed to be in front, between Davidleh and Eli Shukron, so he could document what was happening. We ruled out heading backward out of the tunnel both because of the time it would take and the exertion.

Yehuda said that we should all lie down flat and Gil would crawl over us.

I could hear both Eli Alony and Yehuda behind me grunting as Gil slithered over them. He was using his boots to get traction on their bodies and push himself forward in the narrow space. Then it was my turn.

I tried not to suffocate as he went over me and made a mental note to myself: *Always let the video guy go in front.*

We continued forward in silence, each one of us with his own thoughts. I tried not to think about how I was basically locked underground, with no place to go either forward or backward. I hadn't forgotten the claustrophobia I had felt when we had first uncovered this tunnel, years before, hundreds of meters to the south. I felt the sensation creep up on me, and paused at a certain point to calm my heart, which I could feel beating loudly in my chest.

With nowhere to go, the panic passed, and thankfully it didn't return.

After around forty minutes, Shukron paused and called back to us that the tunnel veered sharply to the left. That was a new development. For the entire length of the tunnel up until that point, it had been on a straight course from the Siloam Pool directly up toward the Temple Mount. I saw Shukron disappear around the sharp corner followed by the cameraman and Davidleh. When I rounded the corner, I could see the three of them propped up, sitting against the walls of the tunnel.

The roof of the tunnel in this section was much higher, shaped like a dome over their heads, and it was at least a foot wider. I breathed a sigh of relief. They were smiling. We all knew at least one thing for sure: We wouldn't have to back out in reverse on the way back! We had more than enough room to turn.

Shukron was examining the sharp angle the tunnel had made, mumbling something to himself, like a mathematician trying to figure out a formula.

He then looked at us and told us what was on his mind.

"The only reason that I can think this tunnel suddenly breaks to the left is because something is on the other side of this wall that the tunnelers wanted to avoid."

He looked back at us and continued. "I think that the foundations of the Temple Mount are right on the other side of this wall, and that we are now skirting the southern edge of the Temple Mount toward the west."

We all stared at him open eyed. The foundation stones of the Temple Mount!

Pointing to the domed roof over our heads, he continued, "This also explains why the roof here is domed, as opposed to the rest of the tunnel. The structure of the Temple Mount is massive, and it must put an enormous stress on the ground and anything built around it. As the original tunnelers neared the area of the Temple Mount itself, they constructed an arched ceiling with a much stronger weight-bearing capacity than the rest of the tunnel, which is simply a flat roof." He pointed up to the keystone in the middle of the tunnel that held the arched dome in place.

I looked at the gray limestone wall next to me. Just a few feet on the other side of that wall lay the holiest site in all of Judaism, the place our ancestors had been praying to for thousands of years. And now, deep inside the earth, the six of us were crawling along the very foundation stones upon which it had been built.

We sat there for a few minutes reflecting, until Davidleh turned to Shukron and said that we should probably continue if we were going to go any farther that day.

Shukron led the way again and we continued crawling. After around fifty feet, the tunnel turned sharply back to the right again, which was the original trajectory we had been following. We were once again heading north, and realized that we were now probably crawling along the edge of the Western Wall of the Temple Mount. After a few feet, the tunnel led to a small opening approximately a foot and a half high. Shukron tried to squeeze his head through, but he got wedged in.

Davidleh pulled him back out.

Davidleh was smaller, and he thought he could make it through. He squeezed in through the opening and dropped in on the other side. After a few seconds, his voice echoed back to us. He said he was in some kind of round chamber. He told Shukron to put his arms first and head through. Davidleh pulled him and Shukron made it in. The next was Gil. He lowered his camera gear and was then pulled through. By the time I came through, the area had already been a bit dug out by the pulling. I put my arms first and felt two big hands of Davidleh and Shukron take me and pull me through. After a few minutes we were all in.

We were crouched down on a pile of dirt that filled a circular room carved into the bedrock of the mountain.

Shukron said it looked like a cistern that had been filled with dirt. On the wall opposite us, we could see another small opening, which led out of the cistern and continued north. Shukron crawled over and looked with his flashlight. He said that he could see the drainage channel continuing on the other side and a few big rocks hanging down from the roof of the tunnel.

Over our heads, in the roof of the cistern, a hole had been carved out heading upward. Shukron called us to take a look. At the top of the shaft, around twenty feet above us, a ray of sunlight was shining down on us from above. After crawling underground through the belly of the earth for so long, the sight of the sun was exceptionally beautiful.

Shukron thought that likely in Temple times, people had dropped their buckets into the cistern through the shaft above to draw water before heading up to the Temple. We were elated and started asking Shukron questions in loud voices when he abruptly hushed us all.

We could hear the faint sound of voices coming from the top of the shaft. I moved closer to listen, and I thought I could hear someone speaking English. I discerned a male voice. He was speaking loudly, explaining something to a group of people. As my ears adjusted, I could make out his words.

"Here we are, standing next to the southern section of the Western Wall. If you look closely above our heads, you can see a row of stones jutting out—those are the remains of Robinson's Arch, one of the original entrances to the Temple." The voice was that of a tour guide giving an early-morning tour to a group at the southwestern corner of the Temple Mount.

Unknown to him—but because of him—the six of us underground now knew where we were! We had gone all the way from the Siloam Pool and continued under the Old City wall, and we had now reached the original gate to the Temple, known as Robinson's Arch, located at the southern end of the Western Wall.

Davidleh's vision—that one day we would make it to the area of the Western Wall—had finally come true. We had made it from the City of David to the Western Wall of the Temple Mount—and in one morning and in one crawl.

Gil Mezuman recorded the moment when we spontaneously burst into cheers and gave each other high fives.

It dawned on me while we were cheering that it was imperative that the group above would not hear us. I hushed the group.

Where we were located carried significant implications. We were underground, next to one of the most important and sensitive structures in the entire world. We knew we were not under the Temple Mount itself. However, if rumors began to circulate that there was an excavation taking place beneath the ground, this close to the Temple Mount, it could easily be construed that we were underneath the Temple Mount itself.

Those who were constantly inciting that the Temple Mount was in danger would see this as a ripe opportunity to inflame the Arab world into fiery protests—or worse. In fact, in 1996, when a tunnel had been opened leading from the Western Wall into the Arab Quarter, such a claim had been made, and while not true, it had ignited a massive clash between Israelis and rioting Palestinians. The clashes lasted four days and left seventeen innocent Israelis killed along with fifty-nine Palestinian rioters and militants. Now that we had connected the City of David to the Western Wall of the Temple Mount, we had entered the realm of geopolitics. We would have to be incredibly careful to make sure that our momentous discovery did not cause the same reaction. We all agreed that until further notice, no one was to breathe a word of our adventure that day, or of how far the excavation reached.

Before crawling back to the Givati Parking Lot, we still had one more area to explore.

We formed back into our crawling order and exited on the

northern side of the ancient cistern into the continuation of the drainage channel. After a few paces, we came to an extraordinary sight: There, cracked right through the roof of the tunnel, two massive stones were poking through, like diamonds that had fallen from high above, wedged into the roof of the tunnel. Each looked like it weighed a few tons.

Shukron thought that they had been carved to be used in the construction of the Temple, and perhaps, during the construction, had fallen from above and gotten wedged down here. Then he reached down and pulled something out of the ground. It looked like the remains of an old kerosene lamp and some metal chisels. We all looked at this discovery confused. It looked like someone had been here before us.

Shukron ran his hands along one of the diamond-shaped stones and told us that they were the same stones used by Herod's men to build the Temple Mount and the Western Wall.

Shukron kept staring at the diamond-shaped stones.

"I've seen these stones before," he said.

We looked at him in confusion. It wasn't possible that Shukron had been here before, unless he was two thousand years old.

"I think Charles Warren was here," he blurted.

"What I mean," he said, "is that I have seen a drawing of these stones before. There is a drawing of Warren's assistant Corporal Henry Birtles, dangling on a rope between two diamond-shaped stones.

"The stones we are looking at are the stones in the drawing."

It was a hot summer day in 1880, ten years after Charles Warren returned to England.

Jacob Eliyahu, a fifteen-year-old boy from a Turkish-Jewish

family, was shepherding his flock of sheep in the Kidron Valley, which borders the area of the City of David on its eastern side. In the blistering heat of summer, the temperatures in Jerusalem can often exceed 100 degrees Fahrenheit. Thirsty for water, Jacob grazed his flock over a small hill and made his way to a stone staircase that led down to a freshwater pool that was known to the local shepherds in the area. Jacob bent down and drank from the cool waters, while his flock crammed in for space around the pool and dipped their heads in and drank.

While the sheep drank, Jacob carefully lowered himself into the pool. He waded through the knee-high water toward a cleft in the mountain rock, from which the water flowed to fill the pool.

He poked his head into the cleft of the rock and saw a dark tunnel heading beneath the mountain. The water was flowing past him to the pool behind, from some unknown source lost in the darkness ahead of him. He came out, took a wooden torch from his bag, lit it, and went back in to explore. The tunnel was filled with shallow water and continued into the distance. As he walked inside, he ran his fingers along the chisel marks of whoever had carved the tunnel out of the limestone mountain long ago.

We know from Jacob's account that after around twenty yards in the darkness he slipped on a stone and fell into the shallow waters. As he pulled himself back up out of the water, he felt something protruding from the wall. He relit his torch and looked closely. The protrusion was a rectangular stone tablet that had letters carved along its surface. The letters resembled Hebrew, but with an odd shape, including many letters he had never seen before.

Jacob Eliyahu ran out of the tunnel, excited to report his discovery. As the story of the inscription circulated through the narrow streets of Jerusalem's Old City, some villagers from Silwan eventually removed the tablet, probably hoping to broker a deal with a European museum. As they removed the sign, it broke into six or seven pieces. The Turkish governor of Jerusalem apprehended the villagers and sent the sign to the Istanbul Archaeology Museum in Turkey where it remains to this day. Several linguistic experts examined the sign, first in its original location in the tunnel and later at the museum, in an effort to decipher the writing.

They were stunned. The sign was written in the ancient Hebrew of the Israelites, dating back to the Biblical First Temple Period, around the eighth century BCE. The linguistic experts concluded that it was the oldest biblical inscription ever discovered.[2] They also noticed something remarkable: The event described on the inscription closely matched an event in the Bible attributed to King Hezekiah, a descendant of King David who lived in the eighth century BCE.

The "Siloam Inscription," as it came to be called, describes the construction of the water tunnel Jacob Eliyahu had waded through, a tunnel that stretched more than half a kilometer in length. The inscription told the story of the workers who dug the tunnel and managed to meet from two opposite ends in the belly of the earth in what we recognize as the year 702 BCE.

What most astounded the scholars is that the tunnel—and the time period of writing on the inscription—matches the biblical description of a tunnel that was dug out under the orders of King Hezekiah, who ruled Jerusalem in 702 BCE. Hezekiah was besieged by the leader of the Assyrian Empire, King Sennacherib, who had at the time the largest army in antiquity. The Bible describes how Hezekiah, desperate to secure the city's water supply, ordered the waters of the Gihon Spring to be diverted inside the mountain.

In the Second Book of Chronicles, chapter 32, it reads:[3]

When Hezekiah saw that Sennacherib had come, intent on making war against Jerusalem, he consulted with his officers and warriors about stopping the flow of the springs outside the city, and they supported him. A large force was assembled to stop up all the springs and the wadi that flowed through the land, for otherwise, they thought, the king of Assyria would come and find water in abundance.

The gamble paid off and, in the end, Sennacherib's army never reached the water source. The Bible praises Hezekiah for this historic move:

It was Hezekiah who stopped up the spring of water of Upper Gihon, leading it downward west of the City of David; Hezekiah prospered in all that he did.

The story is recorded both in the Book of Kings and the Book of Chronicles in great detail, making the Siloam Inscription one of the most important pieces of evidence ever found that corroborates the biblical text with archaeological evidence.

Adding to its importance, a rare nonbiblical reference to the same event was uncovered by explorers excavating Sennacherib's palace in Iraq. They discovered a hexagonal prism, known as Taylor's Prism, which recounts Sennacherib's attack on Jerusalem from his perspective. Today, the prism is on display in the British Museum.

In July 2007, we were notified that the then mayor of Jerusalem, Uri Lupolianski, had made an official request to the Turkish ambassador to Israel to return the Siloam Inscription to the State of Israel as a sign of goodwill between the two countries. The Turkish president agreed in principle.[4]

However, a few months into the diplomatic efforts, the Hamas terror organization made their violent takeover of the Gaza Strip, ousting the Palestinian Authority and killing many of the Palestinian leaders. In response, Israel blockaded the area from the sea and a diplomatic crisis developed between Israel and Turkey. A flotilla, named the Mavi Marmara, was launched from Turkey with 590 passengers in an attempt to break the Gaza blockade. Israeli Navy warnings to stop approaching the blockade and to change course were ignored. When Israeli special forces attempted to board the ship, they were confronted by forty men armed with iron bars and knives. In the fighting that ensued, nine of the Turkish combatants were killed.

The diplomatic crisis that developed between Israel and Turkey put any chance of recovering the Siloam Inscription on hold for well over a decade.

Little did Jacob Eliyahu know, on that hot summer day in 1880 when he slipped in the darkness as he quenched his thirst and the thirst of his sheep, that the inscription he had uncovered was one of the most important biblical inscriptions ever found in Israel, or anywhere else in the world, for that matter. Three independent sources—the Bible, the Siloam Inscription, and Taylor's Prism—all verify a historical event dating back to biblical times, and recognized by Muslim scholars in nineteenth-century Istanbul.

Twenty-three excavations over the past one hundred years have confirmed that Captain Charles Warren was right: Over the course of thousands of years, the inhabitants of Jerusalem had moved only a few hundred yards away from the City of David, the original location of Jerusalem from the Bible, to safer ground at the top of the mountain. Jerusalem was a city often at war, and conqueror after conqueror would build a new set of walls around the upper city to protect its new inhabitants. Over the centuries, the City of David at the bottom of the hill was buried, and the actual site of ancient Jerusalem—this tiny stretch of land, only 2 percent the size of New York's Central Park—was forgotten, covered by the sands of time and the rubble of conquests.

Only 450 years ago the Turkish ruler Suleiman the Magnificent captured Jerusalem and built the picturesque walls we see today that surround what is commonly referred to as the Old City. To contemporary people, 450 years seems like a long time ago, but when we consider that many events in the Bible, verified by archaeological discoveries, took place 2,500 years ago, Suleiman the Magnificent's reign seems more like modern history, especially in terms of the history of Jerusalem.

While today the validity of the Jewish connection to Jerusalem is often a topic of heated debate on university campuses, in government parliaments and criminal tribunals, and of course in the media, already by the late 1800s the initial excavations in the City of David proved without a doubt the historical connection between the Jewish people and Jerusalem, one that precedes the advents of Christianity and Islam by thousands of years.

However, the political upheavals of two world wars, and the subsequent wars fought over the State of Israel, put the City of David excavations and the proof of the Jewish connection to Jerusalem in jeopardy once again.

Chapter 2

Baron Rothschild and the Tombs of King David

It was 1909, and Baron Edmund de Rothschild was not at all pleased.

For twenty-seven years, Baron Rothschild had been legally purchasing land from local Arab families and the Ottoman authorities in Turkey who had ruled the area for over four hundred years.

As early as 1880, Baron Rothschild had assisted Jews from Russia to escape the frequent pogroms which had made life untenable. Between 1880 and 1895 he financed more than thirty groups of Jewish refugees. He helped them cultivate farmlands for growing citrus and avocados and helped create industrial enterprises for silk and wine production. His land purchases were always scrupulously conducted and dutifully recorded, as the baron was very concerned with keeping good relationships with the Ottoman officials and Arab residents.

Like most educated men of his generation, Lord Rothschild was interested in archaeology, but his top priority was always the purchasing of land and creating a better life for his less-well-off Jewish brethren. Unless the land was owned legally, he strongly maintained, there could be no basis for Jewish immigration. So, he set out to purchase as much land as he could, and by 1918, one-twentieth of Palestine's fertile lands belonged to Rothschild; every one of those purchases was recorded in Ottoman records.

However, in 1909, a British aristocrat, Montagu Parker, the 5th Earl of Morley, launched an expedition to Jerusalem that threatened the delicate peace the baron had maintained for the previous twenty-seven years. Parker had been persuaded by a Finnish scholar named Valter Henrik Juvelius that by digging under the shaft and tunnels Charles Warren had found, they could uncover treasures like Solomon's crown and Moses's staff. Juvelius claimed to have decoded numeric ciphers in the Bible that would lead them to the remains of Solomon's Temple beneath the Temple Mount as well. Parker was of a like mind, having claimed to have attended a séance at which, in perfect English, King Solomon told him where to look for the treasures.

To appear more legitimate to the archaeological communities in England and France, they enlisted the help of Father Louis-Hughes Vincent, a French archaeologist and Dominican friar. He had been studying at the École Biblique in Jerusalem since 1891, and he was respected in Europe and Palestine. Father Vincent's later writing and detailed maps provided documentation for what Parker actually found.

Parker and Juvelius thought Hezekiah's Tunnel would lead from Warren's City of David site to a tunnel underneath the Temple Mount that contained the secret treasures, perhaps even the Ark of the Covenant itself. At first, the Arab locals cautiously welcomed their efforts. They provided hundreds of jobs, and by clearing out the channels in the Siloam Tunnel, they caused water to flow more easily to the village of Silwan. They made significant finds, including walls and rooms that were used in the Canaanite and Israelite periods, and pottery that dated back to 1800 BCE and that validated Warren's identification of the site as the City of David.

However, despite the discoveries they had made, after almost two years, they had found none of the treasures Juvelius's ciphers had promised, and King Solomon's spirit never returned to give Parker any further guidance. With little to show in the way of obvious treasures, enthusiasm for the dig began to falter, and when Juvelius contracted malaria and had to return home, Parker was forced to continue alone.

Desperate, Parker bribed the caretaker of the Dome of the Rock, Sheikh Khalil al-Zanaf, to let them dig under the forbidden Temple Mount. Underground, they reached the area directly beneath the Foundation Stone, upon which the Jewish Temple's Holy of Holies was thought to have stood.

What happened next was truly like a scene from an Indiana Jones movie.

One of the Temple Mount night guards, who, according to various accounts was either there by accident or had not been sufficiently bribed, discovered Parker's team defiling the sacred space. He let out an alarm and an angry mob assembled. Riots ensued, and a chase followed. Parker and his men were able to escape only by fleeing to Parker's yacht in the port of Jaffa, where the Ottoman authorities were persuaded that no treasures had been stolen and allowed the men to return to Europe.

Sheikh Khalil was arrested, the Ottoman governor lost his job, and the events, to Rothschild's dismay, only increased the mistrust among the Arab locals for archaeological processes. The events were captured on the front page of the *New York Times* dated May 7, 1911, headlined, "A MYSTERIOUS EXPEDITION, APPARENTLY NOT COMPOSED OF ARCHEOLOGISTS, HUNTS STRANGE TREASURE UNDER MOSQUE OF OMAR, SETS MOSLEMS IN A FERMENT, AND MAY CAUSE DIPLOMATIC INCIDENT."

While neither Parker nor Juvelius was Jewish, their adventures kindled a nascent distrust among the Arab population for foreigners in general and Jews in particular. There were protests in Jerusalem over the defiling of the Temple Mount, and hearings were conducted in the parliament in Constantinople, at which an Arab delegation protested that the Ottoman officials in Jerusalem had been too lax in allowing foreigners to take ancient relics. The villains, as depicted by the Arab delegation, were not only the archaeologists, but also the Jews.

The Baron could see that it was not enough to dig on land that belonged to other people—owning the land under which the dig was conducted was essential. And any purchases for archaeological purposes had to be as scrupulous as his purchases for agriculture, perhaps even more so.

Rothschild also began to realize that whatever would be found at the site of the City of David would be instrumental in laying the historical foundation for a future Jewish state. No other archaeological site had the possibility of proving so definitively that the Jewish people were indigenous to the land. Rothschild began to understand that the land over and around the City of David would be the most important land he would purchase.

And so, the baron looked and found several available parcels surrounding the edges of Charles Warren's excavation site. One was owned by a Sephardic Jewish family that had come to Jerusalem in 1510.

The Meyuhas family traced their ancestry to the expulsion of the Jews from Spain in 1492. In 1873, shortly after Warren's expedition, Rabbi Rahamim Nathan Meyuhas, a butcher from within the city walls, purchased a plot of land at the southern tip of the hill, across the Kidron riverbed from the thinly populated Arab settlement in Silwan. Meyuhas grew vegetables and slaughtered animals for his butcher shop, and the family lived in peace with their Arab neighbors, where they shared water from the Siloam Spring.

In 1913 Albert Antebi, a representative of the Rothschilds, went to the Meyuhas family and offered to buy their entire property.

With additional purchases on the southern end of the City of David and a large tract of land on the eastern slope, the baron enlisted a French-Jewish archaeologist named Raymond Weill, who had experience with Ottoman authorities and Arab residents from his excavations in Egypt and the Sinai. Raymond Weill became the first Jewish archaeologist to excavate in the Holy Land.

Just above the Meyuhas property, Weill made one of his most notable discoveries: a limestone dedication plaque, inscribed in Greek from the Second Temple period. The inscription read, in part, "Theodotus, the priest and synagogue leader, son of a synagogue leader and grandson of a synagogue leader, built this synagogue for the reading of the Torah and studying of the commandments." It was the first solid evidence of a synagogue built in Jerusalem during the end of the first century BCE or the early part of the first century CE, as Judaism was evolving from temple worship to synagogue prayer. It was concrete, physical proof of the continuing presence of Jewish people in the area surrounding Jerusalem.

The outbreak of World War I interrupted Weill's expedition, and the City of David once again fell silent.

But as the Great War descended, Warren, Rothschild, Weill—and even Parker, Juvelius, and Father Vincent—had proven to the world that Jews had been living in the area around Jerusalem for more than three thousand years.

In 1536, when the Ottoman emperor Suleiman the Magnificent conquered the Mamluks, he encouraged Jews who had been expelled from Spain and Portugal to settle in Jerusalem. He even granted tracts of land for Jewish settlement in the city of Tiberius.[1]

Suleiman's treatment of minorities, including the Jews, was unique and unfortunately would not last. Ottoman governors in Jerusalem over the years vacillated in their tolerance, and the Jews were often subject to the heavy "non-Muslim" tax and even imprisoned and tortured for failure to pay. Nevertheless, the Jewish presence in the Old City of Jerusalem continued to grow, and by 1863, the British consulate in Jerusalem estimated that of the city's 15,000 residents, 8,000 were Jewish. They also estimated there were 4,500 Muslims and 2,500 Christians.[2] This was more than eighty years before the establishment of the State of Israel.

Sultan Suleiman is best known for the renovations he made to the Old City of Jerusalem, including the construction of the Old City walls that we see today. Suleiman also ordered the consecration of a 1,300-square-foot prayer plaza for the Jews in front of the Western Wall and declared that Jews would have the right to pray there "for all times."

That declaration was short-lived.

Over the next few centuries, the muddy plaza was littered with trash and animal droppings by Arabs passing through with donkey carts. The plaza was finally paved in the mid-1850s. In 1866, Sir Moses Montefiore, a British financier who was beginning to help Jews settle in Palestine, made inquiries about purchasing the plaza.

Montefiore's offer was rejected by Ottoman authorities.

In 1887 Lord Rothschild made a second bid—this time, one million French francs—to purchase not just the plaza but the entire cramped Mughrabi Quarter, which had been constructed in front of the Western Wall. Rothschild promised to relocate the Mughrabi inhabitants to "better accommodations" elsewhere and to rebuild the plaza.

According to some accounts, the Ottoman authorities gave their approval, as did secular and religious authorities in Jerusalem, but the plan floundered when the chief rabbinical authority of the Sephardic community expressed a fear that a massacre of the local Jews would ensue if the purchase were to take place.

That fear was indeed prophetic.

Observing all of these events was a well-spoken Russian immigrant to England named Chaim Weizmann, a biochemist who was to go on to become the face of the Zionist movement and the first president of the State of Israel. Cultured and educated, a scientist who dressed as a gentleman, he was at ease with British officials and aristocrats. For years he had been in close contact with the highest levels of British society, urging them to see how a Jewish homeland in the Holy Land was also in the best interests of the British Empire. Weizmann also understood the double game the British were playing by supporting Jewish and Arab interests.

When the First World War broke out, the British set about wooing Arab leaders across the Middle East, hoping to persuade the Arabs to revolt against the Ottomans and unite with Britain and France against Germany and Turkey. Weizmann met with Lord Rothschild in 1914, and Rothschild instilled in Weizmann his belief that only by owning property in Palestine could the Jews ever hope to have a homeland. The impression he made on Weizmann would have an important impact on the site in the years to come.

In 1916, the Arab Revolt against the Ottoman Empire began. In 1917, the fighting moved into Palestine. In November and December of that year, Jerusalem was the site of an epic battle in which British forces allied with Arab legions eager to end the centuries of Ottoman rule fought side by side with smaller regiments of Jewish fighters who were hoping to establish a Jewish homeland.

When the Ottomans and Germans were defeated, the British Mandate took charge, and the British continued to promise everything to everyone.

Lord Balfour, the British foreign secretary, issued his famous declaration to Lord Rothschild, declaring that "His Majesty's government view with favour the establishment in Palestine of a national home for the Jewish people." The Arab world was enraged, and following the declaration, riots broke out.

Rothschild immediately resumed purchasing additional land in various areas of Palestine, including around the City of David. Weizmann recruited Eliezer Ben-Yehuda, the founder of the modern Hebrew language, and the two worked together with the baron on land purchases in the City of David and launching additional excavations. Ben-Yehuda volunteered to become the deputy director of the Jewish Palestine Exploration Society.[3]

One of the plots Rothschild purchased was owned by a local Arab named Mohammed Gozlan. Rothschild hired Gozlan as caretaker to watch over that property, the Meyuhas house, and Rothschild's other properties around the City of David. This would be a fateful decision.

Rothschild was now fully focused on the City of David. He brought Raymond Weill back to continue the excavations at the site. The Meyuhas house became the headquarters for Weill's second expedition.

It was during this second expedition that Weill excavated the southern part of the City of David, including its eastern fortifications. Based upon his understanding of the exact location of the graves of David and Solomon as described in the biblical books of Nehemiah and Kings, Weill had his team, consisting now of two hundred workers and thirty donkeys, clear the area down to the bedrock. What he found were the remains of monumental tombs carved into the bedrock of the mountain, above an ancient pool, precisely as described. The tombs had been damaged when the Romans quarried the area to rebuild Jerusalem as the pagan city of Aelia Capitolina, and remove any vestige of indigenous Jews, but two of the most prominent tombs remained, and Weill identified them as the tombs of King David and King Solomon.

Weill's excavations at the City of David ended in 1924. When Lord Rothschild died ten years later, the Rothschild properties were transferred to the Jewish National Fund.

On August 24, 1929, fabricated rumors spread in the biblical city of Hebron that Jews in Jerusalem were planning to seize control of the Temple Mount, and sixty-nine Jews were killed in cold blood. As the killing spread to Jerusalem, thousands of Jews fled the neighborhoods outside of the Old City walls. The City of David area was no longer deemed safe for additional excavations. When another series of riots erupted between 1936 and 1939, any remaining Jews in the area fled, or were forcibly removed by the British authorities, not to return for decades.

The excavations in the City of David went silent, and any Jewish life in the city, and in the village of Silwan across the valley, began to fade.

With the excavations now dormant, Mohammad Gozlan, whom Rothschild had hired as a caretaker, stayed on, gradually taking more and more control over the properties.

When the British withdrew from Palestine in 1948, they left chaos behind them.

In September 1947, the British announced that their mandate would expire on May 14 the following year. Two months later, the United Nations voted on a partition plan to divide the mandate area into a Jewish state and an Arab state. Jerusalem, which still maintained a clear Jewish majority, was to be internationalized. The Jewish leadership accepted the plan, but the Arab League met and vowed to respond to partition with military opposition.

At midnight on May 15, 1948, the mandate expired, and David Ben-Gurion announced the independence of the State of Israel.

During the war that followed, thousands of Israeli soldiers and civilians died. Many thousands more were seriously injured. By the end of the war, the small Jewish nation of 600,000 people had lost more than 6,000 people.

The battle over Jerusalem was one of the fiercest of the War of Independence. Outnumbered Israelis fought the Arab Legion, desperate to keep access to the Jewish Quarter in the Old City.

On May 28, 1948, the Jewish Quarter was forced to surrender: 340 Jews were taken captive, and 1,500 Jewish residents were expelled from the Jewish Quarter by Jordanian forces. An armistice agreement was signed between Israel and Jordan on April 3, 1949, that guaranteed Israeli "free access to the Holy Places and cultural institutions and use of the cemetery on the Mount of Olives."

Jordan never honored the agreement and the United Nations failed to enforce it.

Over the next nineteen years of Jordanian occupation, no Jewish person was allowed to visit the Jewish Quarter of the Old City, the Western Wall, or the City of David.

Chapter 3

The Plot to Destroy Jewish Jerusalem

History records that Jerusalem was attacked fifty-two times, captured or recaptured forty-four times, and destroyed twice: once by the Babylonians in 586 BCE and once by the Romans in 70 CE.[1] While separated by six hundred years, the Babylonians and the Romans shared the same goal: not only to destroy Jewish Jerusalem but also to eradicate the very memory of the Jewish people from the land.

What many people do not know is that one does not need to investigate ancient history to find attempts to destroy Jerusalem and more specifically to erase the very remnants that prove the indigenous connection of the Jewish people. Two such attempts were made in more recent years: The first was the destruction of the Jewish Quarter by the Jordanian Arab Legion after the 1948 war.

Between 1948 and 1967, Jordanian forces occupied eastern Jerusalem, including the area of the City of David; and on April 24, 1950, Jordan formally annexed the West Bank. Although that annexation was considered "illegal and void" according to international law, no action against Jordan was ever taken by the United Nations.

The Jordanians ransacked the Mount of Olives and desecrated the graves. Arab residents were allowed to uproot the tombstones and plow the cemetery land. A two-lane road was built directly over the graves.

In 1954, Israel protested to the United Nations about the desecration of the Mount of Olives, but the United Nations remained predictably silent.

Overall, some 38,000 tombstones were smashed and used as building material for an Arab Legion military camp, including the floors of latrines, on which the names from the tombstones could still be seen.

The Jewish Quarter of the Old City was completely destroyed. The Jordanians desecrated numerous Jewish religious sites, including fifty-eight synagogues, many of them hundreds of years old. Some Jewish religious sites were turned into animal stalls.

The Hurva synagogue was blown up by Arab Legionnaires, and a jubilant Arab crowd proceeded to systematically pillage and raze the Jewish Quarter.[2]

Colonel Abdullah el Tell of the Jordanian Arab Legion, who commanded the attack, described the destruction of the Jewish Quarter in his memoirs, which were published in Cairo in 1959:

> I knew that the Jewish Quarter was densely populated with Jews....I embarked, therefore, on the shelling of the Quarter with mortars, creating harassment and destruction....Only four days after our entry into Jerusalem the Jewish Quarter had become their graveyard. Death and destruction reigned over it....As the dawn of Friday, May 28, 1948, was about to break, the Jewish Quarter emerged convulsed in a black cloud—a cloud of death and agony.[3]

He added that "the systematic demolition inflicted merciless terror in the hearts of the Jews, killing both fighters and civilians."

In a chilling statement, he was reported to have told his Jordanian superiors: "For the first time in one thousand years, not a single Jew remains in the Jewish Quarter. Not a single building remains intact. This makes the Jews' return here impossible."

During these nineteen years, the excavations in the City of David became buried once again, this time under sewage and garbage. Despite the area having been declared a protected archaeological site by the British, the Jordanians, interested in solidifying their hold over Jerusalem, encouraged Arab families to build hundreds of homes in the area. A number of these homes were built on property that was sold by a local Arab who claimed to be the owner of large tracts of land. His name was Muhammed Gozlan.

The second attempt to destroy Jewish Jerusalem took place in 1999, when the area had long been under Israeli sovereignty. This attempt struck at the very heart of Jewish history, and at the holiest site in the Jewish religion, the Temple Mount.

In 1996, the Waqf, an Islamic organization responsible for managing Islamic religious sites in Jerusalem, disregarded the status quo on the Temple Mount and converted two ancient underground Second Temple Period structures into what became the largest mosque in Israel, with room to accommodate ten thousand worshippers. The area, located in the southeastern corner of the Temple Mount, was called "Solomon's Stables," a name given to the site by medieval Crusaders of the knightly Order of Solomon's Temple, who used the site in the twelfth century and believed it was the location where King Solomon had stabled his horses.

Despite the unauthorized construction, in 1999 the Israeli Police urged the Waqf to create an emergency exit for the Muslim worshippers in the new mosque. The agreement stipulated that the construction of the exit be done with Israeli archaeological supervision to prevent damage to the numerous antiquities buried underneath the Temple Mount.

Despite the agreement, without an archaeologist on site, and with none of the necessary permits, the Waqf used heavy machinery and tractors to bulldoze out a massive crater, 18,000 square feet in size and 36 feet deep, directly into the Temple Mount itself.[4] Tens of thousands of tons of ancient fill was removed from the site over three days and nights. One-third of the fill was dumped into a Jerusalem garbage dump, mixed with other garbage and lost forever. Two-thirds, however, were dumped along the Kidron Valley in Jerusalem. The haphazard bulldozing and destruction of such a sensitive and ancient site weakened the structural stability of the Temple Mount. As a result, the Southern Wall of the Temple Mount, which had stood intact for nearly two thousand years, began to bulge outward.[5]

Israeli archaeologist Eilat Mazar was the first to observe that the Temple Mount on the southern side was bulging outward in a bubble-shaped form. She described it as taking a box full of sand and placing an enormous amount of weight on top of the box. If you then removed half of the sand from the box and kept applying the pressure, the box would begin to bulge outward.

Eilat Mazar pointed out that the bulge was a threat not only to the Southern wall, but also to the Temple Mount, the Dome of the Rock, and the Al Aqsa Mosque. Mazar's discovery caused a public outcry that spread across Israel. One of the broadest petitions ever signed in Israel, covering all sides of the political spectrum, condemned the act. The State of Israel issued a moratorium on any material leaving the Temple Mount, keeping everything frozen in place, as it is to this very day. Pillars and priceless artifacts can be seen to this day on the Temple Mount, strewn in piles.

I have seen these with my own eyes.

Prime Minister Ehud Barak, under whose watch the destruction had occurred, agreed to allow the Jordanian Waqf to repair the bulge. An ugly white patch of new stone can still be seen on the ancient wall today.

After Eilat Mazar uncovered what was happening, in February 2001, the City of David sent an undercover crew to the Temple Mount to assess the damage. Photographs revealed that the destruction was ongoing: They provided evidence showing that beautiful ancient Roman columns, clearly recovered from the Second Temple period, were being cut up with large masonry saws to make paving stones for the Temple Mount.

Given that Israel had issued a moratorium on any material leaving the Temple Mount, this was a clever attempt by the Waqf to repurpose the ancient stones and permanently erase their historical significance. We released the pictures to the authorities and the work was immediately halted.

The persistent destruction of Jewish remnants on the Temple Mount was clearly intentional on the part of the Jordanian officials who appointed the members of the Waqf, the Palestinian Authority, and the Grand Mufti of Jerusalem. The move was calculated not only to reinforce Islamic claims over the Temple Mount, but also to remove archaeological evidence that a Jewish temple had ever stood there.

While today the destruction of the Temple Mount has been publicized, few people realize that this was possibly the largest archaeological destruction in world history. When the Islamic State destroyed Nineveh and other historic sites in Iraq, UNESCO called it a "war crime." But when the Palestinian Authority destroyed fifteen thousand tons of treasures from the First and Second Temples in Jerusalem, the world organizations were all silent.

Despite the colossal destruction, there was one silver lining:

There had never before been an archaeological excavation or survey conducted on the Temple Mount itself. The Waqf, in its hasty decision to save money and speed up the operation, had ordered two-thirds of the archaeological material to be dumped in trash piles in the Kidron Valley.

Ironically, the archaeological material tossed away as trash subsequently provided the basis for the first archaeological study of the Temple Mount.

By the time I joined the City of David in 2002, the true extent of the archaeological destruction of the Temple Mount just a few years earlier was becoming clear.

Soon after I started working, I met Dr. Gabi Barkay and Zachi Dvira. Gabi Barkay was the one of the most senior archaeologists in the State of Israel, and Zachi Dvira was a student of his at Bar-Ilan University. One day in 1999, while walking through the Kidron Valley, Zachi discovered the piles of archaeological refuse that had been dumped there by the Waqf. When he began going through them and uncovering bits of ancient pottery, he announced his find publicly. Ironically, he was arrested by the Israeli police for disturbing antiquities. While Zachi was soon after released, this was probably the best thing that could have happened. An enormous amount of public attention was drawn to the piles of trash the Waqf had left there.

Barkay and Dvira began a project called the Temple Mount Sifting Project, enlisting hundreds—ultimately thousands—of volunteers to comb through the dirt and extract the archaeological artifacts.

A collaboration was formed between the National Parks Authority, the City of David, and the two of them. With proper funding and archaeological supervision, we turned it into a site where hundreds of thousands of volunteers over the years were able to come and dig for a day and help us to separate out the medieval, early Muslim, Byzantine, Roman, and biblical antiquities.

Among the ten thousand tons of fill that remained from the Waqf destruction, numerous archaeological treasures were found, including seals and other artifacts, not only from Herod's Second Temple but reaching even further back to the era of King Solomon's First Temple. The statistical mapping of the finds showed the archaeological fill of the Temple Mount to extend over three thousand years. Thirty-three percent of the items were from the First and Second Temple Jewish periods. Twenty percent came from the Early Roman and Byzantine periods and fifteen percent dated to the Muslim period.

The extent to which the Waqf had gone to dispose of the archaeological remnants from the Temple Mount—mixing them with garbage, dumping them in the Kidron Valley, trying to crush them into small pieces—showed the determination of the Waqf and the Palestinian Authority to purposely destroy archaeology and erase the Jewish narrative.

What we came to understand about the Temple Mount strengthened our mission regarding the City of David. There was a clock ticking: If we could get to a site and establish ownership and archaeological excavation over the property, that property would be safe and we could preserve it for the general public.

However, if we were not vigilant and if there was an opportunity to erase any element of Jewish history, the Palestinian Authority, the Waqf, the Jordanian authorities, and Hamas would do whatever they could to destroy that archaeology and that site.

Part Two

WHEN THE STONES SPEAK

Chapter 4

My Journey to the City of David

At the age of eighteen, before starting my undergraduate degree, I took my first trip to Israel.

I joined a tour called "Masada" with six hundred American teenagers. Over the course of a month, we saw Israel from top to bottom—hiking in the mountains, floating on the Dead Sea, experiencing history, religion, and beautiful beaches.

One experience had a surprisingly profound effect on me: During a night out on the town, in a popular bar in the middle of Jerusalem called the Underground, I was walking across the dance floor to get something to drink and bumped into a pile of around twenty-five M-16 rifles that had been stacked neatly in a pyramid by a table full of soldiers. There was a mammoth rattling and shaking, and I looked down and saw that I had knocked over all the guns. The soldiers, much to my relief, thought it was extremely funny, and when they came over to pick up the guns and re-stack them, they smiled at me and clapped me on the back.

The story I brought back to the States about that incident reflected how different my life was from those of the Israelis: They were eighteen years old, just like me, but I was living a nice, safe life in the United States—going from high school to college to law school and from there, presumably, to a safe job in a nice safe law firm—while they were training to fight for their country's survival, never knowing when the next war would start or when the next terrorist bomb would go off in a café or at bus stop.

Despite the ever-present threat under which they lived, those soldiers' lives seemed to have so much more meaning than mine. They were Jews, just as I was, but by accident of a few turns in history, my family had come to America and theirs had come to Israel.

That simple, obvious truth obsessed me: Why them and not me? And why *not* me?

Over the next four years, I visited Israel three more times, once with a rabbi for two weeks, another time for a full year, doing volunteer work on the United Jewish Federation Otzma fellowship, and the third time learning Jewish texts and history in the Pardes Institute in Jerusalem. By the time I enrolled in law school at the University of Southern California, all of my waking thoughts were on Israel, the people I'd met there, the friends I'd made there, and the soldiers I had come to know who were serving in the army.

All of my family, whom I loved deeply, were living in the United States, and the thought of leaving them was just too difficult. So, I wandered my way through the first few months of law school in a daze, completing assignments and even somehow managing to pass a Socratic exchange with my contracts professor in front of three hundred people.

But I couldn't shake off the thought of moving to Israel and joining the army. I was approaching the age of twenty-six, which would probably be my last chance to join the Israeli army. The average entry age is eighteen or nineteen. My older brother, Jeffrey, saw how unhappy I was in law school, and he remembered how alive I had seemed when I came back from my travels to Israel.

He called me on November 1, 1999, and gave me one of those talks that change your life: "You've got to stop living other people's dreams," he said. "If you want to go live in Israel, go live in Israel! Follow your own dreams—but stop living Mom and Dad's."

That was the push that I'd needed. I made *aliyah*, the first step toward Israeli citizenship on January 10, 2000. In Hebrew, the words literally mean "going up"—and that is exactly what it felt like for me: I was rising in my life to a higher place.

I went through months of intensive Hebrew-language study and joined the army in September 2000. As history would have it, four days after I went into the army, Israel began to face one of the bloodiest events in its history, the Second Intifada. During that period, the army quickly needed people to represent the country. I was fast-tracked and made an officer and an IDF spokesman to the international media, something that probably wouldn't have happened if we were not in war mode.

But something else life-changing happened to me as I was about to join the army. I was on a bus, on my way to a wedding, when a woman with long, brown hair and deep almond eyes walked onto the bus. There was only one seat free, next to my friend who was sitting next to me. I quickly swapped with him, and she sat down next to me.

We arranged to meet the next evening and spent the night walking around the Old City of Jerusalem, talking and sharing stories about our lives, families, and dreams, from eleven o'clock until five in the morning.

Two years later, Sarah and I got married, and today we are blessed with six beautiful children.

At the end of my army service, I took a job as a business consultant in the high-tech sector, which was burgeoning in Israel at the time. The intifada was still raging and I spent my time like other

Israelis, going between work and my reserve army service. After a particularly intense reserve duty at the Church of the Nativity in Bethlehem, which Hamas had taken over, I felt something nagging at me. One Saturday, while taking a shabbat stroll through the quiet Katamon neighborhood of Jerusalem, I told Sarah that I felt like there was something bigger I needed to connect to. I didn't know who to turn to.

"You pray three times a day," Sarah told me. "Ask for help from above."

Later that evening after sundown, Sarah and I were on the phone, making save-the-date calls to people we were inviting to our upcoming wedding. One of the people I called was a tour guide named Moshe, who had guided my family when they came to visit me in Israel. My parents had enjoyed Moshe's tour, and I thought it would be nice for them to sit with someone they knew.

After congratulating me on the wedding, Moshe said, "I've been meaning to call you. Have you ever heard of the City of David?"

A week later, Moshe introduced me to Davidleh, the founder of the City of David, and Yehuda Maly, the first person to join him there. Davidleh quickly sized me up and said, "Come visit me in the City of David—and bring your fiancée, too."

In early 2002 Sarah and I were given a tour of the City of David—which at the time consisted of only Warren's Shaft, the original site dug by Captain Charles Warren and his team 150 years earlier, which led to a small excavation near the Gihon Spring—and of Davidleh's home, which was built into a cave in the side of the mountain.

One of the workers brought us to the cave, and when the door—about the size of a Hobbit hole—opened, Davidleh was smiling at us with his bright, shiny, deep brown eyes.

It is impossible not to smile back at Davidleh.

Ducking our heads, Sarah and I entered the cave. Just above us was wooden scaffolding. At the top of the cave, Davidleh had made a loft, where his six children slept. Davidleh and his wife, Michal, slept in a small room in the back of the cave.

Davidleh sat us down next to the window on some soft cushions and began to tell us the story of how he came to the City of David.

Davidleh had led one of Israel's most important military units, called Duvdevan, which conducted undercover missions to apprehend terrorists who were hiding inside densely populated Arab villages. During one of these missions, he found out from one of his Arab informants that there had been Jewish archaeological work done at a site in what was then known as the Arab village of Silwan. Davidleh did the research and realized his informants were talking about the City of David property that had once been owned by Baron Rothschild before the Jordanian occupation.

He did some more research, about Rothschild and Charles Warren, and discovered that Rothschild had bought some of the land from a local Arab man named Gozlan and that the baron had then hired Gozlan as caretaker.

Davidleh also found out that Baron Rothschild, Chaim Weizmann, and Eliezer Ben-Yehuda were all involved together in those early excavations. They all considered the City of David to be one of the most important archaeological sites in the Holy Land.

But all Jewish efforts had ceased when Jordan illegally occupied the area in 1948. Throughout the nineteen years of the Jordanian occupation, the City of David became filled with Arab homes—the Jordanian authorities had steadily been moving Arab families into East Jerusalem, wanting to establish a strong Arab presence around the Old City.

By 1967, all of Charles Warren's excavation sites were covered over, either with hastily built homes or with garbage.

While Davidleh was doing this research, he was also trying to decide if he should leave the army. He went to his former military commander, Ariel Sharon, who would later become the prime minister of the State of Israel, and asked him, "Should I stay in the army, or should I go try to rebuild the City of David?"

Ariel Sharon told him, "If you leave the army, somebody else will fill your place. But if you don't go to the City of David and try returning the Rothschild land to Jewish ownership, no one will fill your place." With that, Davidleh made up his mind.

Pausing his story, Davidleh took a group of pictures off the mantelpiece and brought them down to show us the first home that he bought. "This is the Meyuhas home," he told us. "It was the home of the first Jewish family to move outside the Old City walls in 1873. They left the Old City walls because they were shepherds and tanners, and they needed an area to let their animals run freely and also to tan animal hides, which produced a very harsh smell. Back then, there were only two Arab families on the hill, and the Meyuhas family was the third family there. They lived in this home, which was eventually purchased by Baron Rothschild, until they were forced to leave by the Arab riots in 1938."

Knowing that Baron Rothschild had owned the home, Davidleh searched around the neighborhood for the current owner, or for someone who could give him an idea of who had taken possession of the home.

"It turns out," Davidleh continued, "that the current owner was none other than the Gozlan family, the family Baron Rothschild had bought the land from in the first place, the man Rothschild had hired to guard his land."

Forged documents revealed that, after the illegal occupation of Jerusalem by Jordan in 1948, the Gozlan family had rewritten their names on the Rothschild deeds and presented themselves as the rightful owners of a number of parcels of property in the area.

Davidleh found Gozlan and confronted him with the forged deeds. Gozlan did not deny the charges, and told Davidleh that for a fee, he would give up any claim of possession. He also told Davidleh that he had never actually lived in the house himself, because, he said, "The house is cursed."

Gozlan took Davidleh to the Meyuhas house. Taking out a set of old iron keys, he opened the door and pointed to the lintel, where there was a hole carved out with a mezuzah inside.

Gozlan said, "It is inside this hole that Rabbi Meyuhas placed the curse, and that's why I, and no one in this neighborhood, have ever lived here. In fact, we changed the name from Bayt Meyuhas to Bayt Manhus, the House of the Curse."

Even though Gozlan was not the legitimate owner of the home, Davidleh raised the money to purchase the house from him, just so that Gozlan would relinquish any type of possession he had over the property. That way, ownership could legitimately revert back to its original owners, the Rothschilds, who had deeded their properties to the Jewish National Fund.

As Davidleh finished his story, Sarah and I were fascinated—and inspired.

"Our goal is twofold," he said. "First, we want to excavate the City of David. We want to bring David's city back to life. The entire world knows the name Jerusalem—they may not know the name Israel, but they know the name Jerusalem—and billions of people around the world are going to want to come here and explore with the Bible and see the archaeology of the site."

He paused before going on, and just as he did, his four-year-old son, Barkai, his youngest, came running out of the shower, dripping wet, and jumped on his father's lap. Davidleh didn't even seem to notice, gently stroking Barkai's back as he told us his dream.

"The second mission is to have Jewish people live here. This was land that Baron Rothschild bought so that Jews could live in

Jerusalem. The fact that there are Arabs living here as well is fine, as long as they're not living on property that they stole. We can live together in peace, and millions of tourists will one day come to the site."

He explained that the site needed to raise money for all their activities. Nissan Khakshouri, an Israeli businessman, and Roland Arnall, a courageous donor and a United States ambassador, were among the first to support the site and had spearheaded the funding up until then. However, if the site was to achieve its goals, other donors would need to get involved. He wanted to know if I would partner with him and help him to raise the funds and grow the site.

After that meeting, Sarah and I looked at each other, and she said to me, "You need this man and these people in your life."

A few days later, I left my job in Tel Aviv and joined the City of David.

Chapter 5

Minimalists, Denialists, and King David's Palace

Two years after I joined the project, the plans for building a visitors' center at the top of the City of David site were approved. We had met a donor named Eugene Shvidler, who had committed the funds to build the project. Before construction could begin, there would have to be a mandatory archaeological survey of the land.

Archaeologist Dr. Eilat Mazar, the first person to have noticed the Temple Mount wall "bulge" after the Waqf destruction, approached us. Eilat's grandfather, Dr. Benjamin Mazar, one of Israel's best-known archaeologists, had excavated much of the Old City of Jerusalem following the Six Day War. Eilat herself, a widowed mother of four with reddish blond hair, was known as a bold firebrand of an archaeologist, who was fully dedicated to continuing her grandfather's work.

She refused to take cues from the often politically motivated archaeological "fraternity" that characterized much of the profession in Israel. The main point of contention between the two factions surrounded the question, "Can the Bible be relied upon as a valuable historical reference?"

Over the past few decades, a new cadre of archaeologists had arisen in Israel known as the minimalists, Israeli academics who built their careers by minimizing the Bible as a reliable text—or outright denouncing it. A charismatic archaeology professor from Tel Aviv University named Israel Finkelstein was often considered the figurehead of this movement.[1] Finkelstein and his cohorts were so entrenched in their thinking that Finkelstein himself described archaeologists who were willing to use the Bible as a reference as saying "primitive things," and that when he saw them presenting their views on stage, he wanted to "die from embarrassment."[2]

Eilat Mazar, on the other hand, was an independent thinker, not swayed by academic trends she considered to be fleeting. She believed that—in numerous instances—there was extensive evidence that archaeology did in fact correlate with the Bible and that one should at the very least take it into account. Whenever challenged by the minimalists, Dr. Eilat Mazar had a straightforward and compelling response: "Let the stones speak for themselves." She firmly believed that the stones, when uncovered, would reveal the undeniable truth. In tribute to her relentless pursuit of truth and her unwavering commitment to honest inquiry, I chose to name this book *When the Stones Speak*, drawing inspiration from her oft-repeated adage. We all knew her background and reputation when Eilat met us in what was then our small, temporary, two-room wooden office.

Eilat took out a picture of a large stone carved capital—the upper part of a column—that had once adorned the top of an ornate pillar and laid it on our desk.

We had all seen the picture before. The capital had been found in the City of David in 1963 while the area was under Jordanian occupation, and it was now in the Israel Museum. A British archaeologist named Kathleen Kenyon had discovered it and identified it as a "proto-ionic" capital, meaning that it contained the characteristic elements of Phoenician-era royal architecture, dating to the tenth century BCE, the time of King David and King Solomon.

Although Kathleen Kenyon correctly dated the structure and concluded it was royal, she was reluctant to identify it as part of

King David's palace. Her reluctance sparked controversy, with some suggesting she believed the site lay outside the Biblical City of David, while others point to her known anti-Zionist views. Kenyon frequently downplayed Israelite culture, arguing that "there is little in the record…to suggest that much progress towards civilization was made during David's reign," while crediting Phoenician influences for Israel's development. Her reference to West Jerusalem as "Israeli-occupied" further reflects her political bias, which may have influenced her hesitation to link the discovery to King David.[3]

Nevertheless, the capital in Eilat's photograph was remarkable. Other similar capitals had been found in excavations at other sites throughout Israel, but the one Kathleen Kenyon found in the City of David was far larger—and far grander—than any of the others that had been discovered.

Eilat told us that before her grandfather died, she had spoken to him about Kathleen Kenyon's discovery. They both believed that the capital was likely made by the Phoenicians, a seafaring people based in the city of Tyre, located in Lebanon of today, because the Phoenicians were then considered the great artisans of the ancient world.

She told us that she often eavesdropped on our tour guides at our site as they were describing King David's capture of the City of David in the Bible. "But they stop too soon!" she said.

The most significant part of King David's capture of Jerusalem, according to Eilat Mazar, was in lines from the Book of Samuel following the description of the military victory. She took out her own, well-worn Bible and read to us: "King Hiram of Tyre sent envoys to David with cedar logs, carpenters, and stonemasons; and they built a palace for David," she said, emphasizing the last four words. "A palace for David."

She closed the Bible and went on. "After David captured the city, he called upon the greatest artisan in the ancient world, Hiram, the King of Phoenicia, to build him a palace!"

Still seeing blank looks on our faces, she impatiently tapped the picture lying on the table with her finger. "This stone capital is Phoenician in origin. It was carved by King Hiram's workers for the palace King David had built for himself, right here at the top of this mountain. Kathleen Kenyon discovered it just *down* the mountain, a few dozen yards from where we are sitting right now, where it rolled after the palace was destroyed."

She let the silence hang in the air.

Davidleh broke the silence, and asked what was on everyone's mind. "Where exactly are you saying King David's palace is located, Eilat?"

Eilat smiled with a twinkle in her eye—the same smile that would appear in every newspaper in the world six months later.

"Right here," she said, tapping her foot on the floor of our ramshackle, temporary City of David office.

"Right here beneath our feet."

Eilat told us that her wish was to be the archaeologist in charge of conducting the survey of the land beneath the visitors' center to see if her theory was correct. The Israel Antiquities Authority could grant permission to another archaeologist from a university if they so chose.

Eilat was sure that she could make a good case and get the Antiquities Authority to agree to let her conduct the excavation, but she wanted to be sure that we had no objections.

In theory, we would have been delighted to have someone like Eilat Mazar dig the site, but there were two problems with what she was proposing: The first was that private excavations, such as what she envisioned, did not have access to the kind of government funds that the Israel Antiquities Authority, as a government agency, would receive. Second, and more important, the IAA worked all year round, while university excavations typically worked only seasonally for a few months.

We could get bogged down for years waiting for her to finish the dig.

Eilat was prepared to answer our dilemma.

She told us she had a donor who had already pledged to fund the excavation. His name was Roger Hertog, a philanthropist and retired investment banker who had been president of Sanford C. Bernstein & Company in New York. He and Eilat had sat together and studied the chapters of the Bible that supported her theory about the location of the palace. Roger thought it was a good bet and committed half a million dollars to the excavation, enough money to employ year-round workers and archaeologists.

Another advantage was that the Shalem Center, a prominent think tank chaired by Roger Hertog, had agreed to publish her work.

If Eilat was as thorough an archaeologist as she was thorough in preparing for our meeting, we felt we were in good hands. If she could get the support of the Israel Antiquities Authority, we were on board.

A short time later Eilat and her excavation crew broke ground right next to our office at the site and began digging down in square shafts heading toward the bedrock. Before long, a tic-tac-toe-like pattern appeared in the ground outside our front door. While the excavation had been cordoned off with a tarp-covered fence, visitors stood in lines to peep through holes in the tarp and watch the workers digging through the ground and then passing buckets from hand to hand, until the fill reached the examination station.

It took only two weeks until the eureka moment came:

Approximately ten feet beneath our office, Eilat hit the surface of a stone structure. Peering over from on top of the trenches, we could see workers clearing away dirt and revealing a long wall of large stones built directly on the bedrock below. As the excavation went on, it became clear that the wall stretched for almost one hundred feet to the cliff edge, where there was a valley hundreds of feet below. The section of the wall that ran along the edge of the cliff was twenty feet thick, the largest of its kind found anywhere in Israel, and it was likely built to protect whoever had been inside from attack.

As the pieces came together, it became clear that Eilat had found a major structure. In fact, she had found the largest of its kind from the period, built for someone important enough to need serious protection.

Pottery samples found beneath the structure, which predated its construction, matched pottery common to the Jebusites in the eleventh century BCE. The Jebusites, who were descendants of the Canaanites, inhabited Jerusalem during King David's conquest. However, the pottery found within the structure itself was markedly different, indicating that whoever had built it had likely captured the area from the prior civilization and erected the structure directly over its remains.

The pottery within the structure matched pottery found in other excavations in Israel, such as those in Arad in the south of Israel, which accorded with the tenth century BCE, the time of King David. Looking solely at the pottery, one could see a picture remarkably similar to the Bible's description unfolding in front of us: the remains of an early structure belonging to the Jebusites that had been conquered by King David. Then, directly over the former Jebusite structure, a new palace had been built, with columns and capitals carved by artisans from Phoenicia, sent by King Hiram of Tyre. The palace had thick walls to protect someone especially important living inside of it. Finally, and perhaps most compellingly, the structure was located just to the south of Mount Moriah, where the Bible says King David was told by God that the Temple would be built.

While digging, Eilat's team had also unearthed organic matter that could be analyzed for carbon dating, including an olive pit buried deep within the structure. The olive pit was sent to Oxford's laboratories in England. The results would take a few weeks.

Before long, word of Eilat's discovery got out, and a number of archaeologists visited the site—both from the biblical school of thought and from the minimalists.

All agreed that Eilat Mazar had found a monumental structure.

That, however, was where the agreement ended.

The biblical school of archaeologists concurred with Eilat's assessment that the building dated to the approximate time period of King David's capture of the City of David from the Jebusites. Archaeologists such as Seymour Gitin, the director of archaeology of the W. F. Albright Institute in Jerusalem, said, "This is an extremely impressive find, and the first of its kind which can be associated with the tenth century."[4]

In the *New York Times*, Dr. Gabriel Barkay said, "This is one of the first greetings we have from the Jerusalem of David and Solomon, a period which has played a kind of hide-and-seek with archaeologists for the last century."[5]

Those in the minimalist camp, however, were loath to say that this was King David's palace, and in fact they criticized Eilat for doing so. The *New Yorker* magazine reported that Israel Finkelstein responded to Eilat's claim to have discovered a "majestic building from the tenth century, and that it's the palace of King David" by saying, "Not one word in that sentence is true."[6]

Other minimalists echoed Finkelstein's unequivocal rejection of the King David Palace theory as well. They all deemed the structure to be anything besides being something connected to King David. It was perhaps, they said, a Jebusite building from *before* David—or a building from two hundred years *after* David.

Some even dated the lower supporting structure to the Hellenistic Greek period—more than seven hundred years after David.

The fervent opposition from the minimalists was based both on a scientific disagreement and for some, as many would later come to believe, an ideological one.

On the scientific front, the minimalists came to believe in what they termed "low chronology," meaning that they considered pottery samples to be dated two hundred years later than the standard timeline that Eilat and many other archaeologists used. In other words, if Eilat thought that a piece of pottery was indicative of the year 1000 BCE, the minimalists automatically placed it at 800 BCE.

Yet the more serious opposition came on the ideological front: The minimalists had built their careers over the last two decades on denying King David and denying what is known as the "United Monarchy"—when King David united the Twelve Tribes of Israel around Jerusalem as his capital. Just four years earlier, Finkelstein himself, along with another archaeologist, Neil Silberman, published a bestselling book in which they claimed that "Not only was any sign of monumental architecture missing but so were even simple pottery shards."

If David and Solomon existed at all, the minimalists maintained, they were no more than "hill-country chieftains."[7]

Now that Eilat had identified a monumental structure that she claimed to be King David's palace, those absolute statements left no room for the minimalists to reevaluate new discoveries. If any one of the minimalists had acknowledged that Eilat had discovered a major structure relating to King David, it would have been a career-ending move.

But as the debate raged around the pottery found at the site, the carbon-14 dating results from Oxford University arrived. To the minimalists' dismay, the olive pit was dated to 1000 BCE, smack dab in the middle of the period of King David.

And for a while, it seemed as if an ancient olive pit had settled the debate.

It was no small coincidence that the dramatic rise of "Minimalism" took place in the mid-1990s during the period of the Oslo Accords.

Israeli leaders such as Shimon Peres and Ehud Barak were pursuing a peace agreement with Yasser Arafat, premised on Israel ceding territories to the Palestinians that were located in the Biblical heartland of Israel—the West Bank, as the Palestinians called it, or Judea and Samaria, as it was referred to by Israelis. On the chopping block were biblical cities such as Hebron, Bethlehem, Shechem (Nablus), and Shilo, among others. East Jerusalem was slated to become the capital of a future Palestinian state, and it was the biggest hurdle to be crossed for any agreement to be made, as it was the location of the City of David along with every other archaeological biblical site in Jerusalem.

As desperate as the Israeli public was for a peace deal in the 1990s and early 2000s, news of these discoveries that were found in areas slated to be given away to the Palestinians was seen by some as fueling nationalist and religious feelings, and thereby strengthened the already-existing opposition to such a deal. The minimalist school of thought, originating in Tel Aviv University, the epicenter of the Oslo Accords, offered a convenient alternative: Dozens of books and articles were published that undermined the biblical connection between the Jewish people and the Land of Israel. These ideas flourished and found fertile ground, both within the Israel media such as the left-wing *Haaretz* newspaper, and in numerous European publications where anti-Semitism, anti-Zionism, and anti-Israelism were on the rise.

In the beginning, the minimalists posited that King David was a mythic legend akin to King Arthur and the Knights of the Roundtable.[8] This theory, however, only lasted a few years—until 1993, when the Tel Dan Inscription was uncovered in northern Israel. The inscription, which refers specifically to the "House of David," is from the ninth century BCE, barely one century after King David and King Solomon reigned, proving conclusively that both were real living figures. Furthermore, "House" in this context implies "dynasty," indicating that by that time, the descendants of David and Solomon had already created a flourishing dynasty.

At that point, the minimalists reframed their argument and admitted that while King David most likely existed, they now began using the phrase "hill-country chieftain" rather than calling him "king"—and in doing so, reducing the significance of the City of David to something that, in the words of Professor Israel Finkelstein, "was no more than a poor village at the time."[9]

It has taken decades for the minimalists to slowly reconsider some of their original assumptions. A number of recent excavations and discoveries, such as the Elah Fortress, discovered in Khirbet Qeiyafa, an ancient fortress city to the southeast of Jerusalem, along with roads linking it to other tenth-century BCE cities, such as Beit Shemesh Stratum IV and Lachish Stratum V, have provided increasing support for the theory that King David ruled over a well-developed kingdom, with roads connecting cities.[10]

However, as the arguments of the minimalists began to lose their grip on the Israeli public, another, more insidious controversy began to spread.

Taking advantage of the debate over King David's palace in newspapers throughout the world, the Palestinians saw an opportunity to place another nail in the coffin of what they deemed "the Zionist Lie."

One Palestinian archaeologist, Hani Nur el-Din, a professor of archaeology at Al-Quds University, outright dismissed Eilat Mazar's findings, stating, "She doesn't give any archaeological context to her findings other than dating pottery shards," and adding, "The Bible should be put aside. It's not a history book."[11]

This was part of the broader, long-standing trend of denying Jewish history in Jerusalem that had persisted for decades. These persistent denials played a significant role in motivating me to pursue a more meaningful career. Ultimately, they led me to the City of David, where my goal became to uncover and preserve the true historical legacy of Jerusalem's Jewish past.

As these Palestinian claims of Jewish erasure gained momentum, I received a call one day from a reporter from the prominent German newspaper *Der Spiegel*. She asked me if I had any information on Eilat Mazar's dig in the City of David, to which I responded that as soon as Eilat finalized her research conclusions, she would open the site to the press.

The reporter then told me she had spoken to some Palestinians who claimed that the structure that Dr. Mazar had found was from the Roman or Byzantine Period, more than one thousand years after King David, and that, in their words, "any claims that it was connected in any way to the Bible were a Zionist plot to seize the land in the village of Silwan."

I told her that the pottery at the site clearly proved that their claims were groundless, as did carbon-14 dating. I finished the call but not before quoting Eilat's line, "Let the stones speak, they will reveal the truth."

After hanging up the phone I began to consider what could

happen next: The Palestinians would continue to make unequivocal statements that there was absolutely no proof that we had found
anything connected to the Bible, and that what we were doing was
just another "Israeli land grab." Although statements like that would
be unverifiable, the international press would freely quote their
viewpoint.

Meanwhile, Israeli archaeologists couldn't even agree with each
other.

The world would soon be enraptured by the Palestinians and
their groundless claims of conspiracy, while we Israelis would bore
them to sleep with arguments over the provenance of pottery shards
and olive pits.

It was precisely at that critical crossroads, on a Thursday evening
in the summer of 2005, that Eilat Mazar called and told us she had
some news she wanted to share with us face to face.

We met inside the same wooden office where Eilat had convinced
us to give her a chance. Now the office was perched on the edge of
a precipice leading down to the palace she had discovered below.
Eilat took out a small square box and set it on the table alongside a
magnifying glass. She opened the box and we saw a small, roughly
circular piece of clay on a white background.

The day before, Yoav Farhi, one of her top excavators and a bud-
ding archaeologist himself, had spotted the miniscule object while
digging. Eilat had been studying it all night long.

"This is a clay seal," she told us. "It was a technique used only
by the highest-level officials, attendants to the king, or by the king
himself, to seal written documents of importance. The document,
usually written on papyrus, was rolled up and bound with string.
Then the official would stamp his signet ring on a small piece of clay

over the folds of paper, sealing the document. The only way to read the document would be to break the seal."

It was, we gathered, the ancient precursor to the wax seals that are still used to seal official deeds in our day.

Yoav had pulled the seal out of a thick layer of dark ash, indicating that it was from a time when a major conflagration had taken place. Due to the fire, the clay seal had been baked like a ceramic in a kiln and hardened.

"If it wasn't for the fire," Eilat explained, "the seal would have disintegrated long ago. The chances of all these factors coming together—including Yoav's keen eyesight to pick this out of the ash—are very rare."

She passed around the magnifying glass and the small box, and one after the other we examined the tiny object. It was rough around the edges, and across its narrow surface, I could see faint, raised letters poking out, though I couldn't make out the type of script.

Knowing we were trying to read the inscription, Eilat said, "The letters are written in paleo-Hebrew, an older version than the Hebrew used today. This type of script dates back to the biblical period…"

We all looked up at her.

"It took me many hours before I could make out what is written here," she said. And then she smiled, the same coy smile, with the glint in her eye, for which she is known. And she picked up her same worn Bible and opened it to the Book of Jeremiah.

She proceeded to tell us a story.

The Prophet Jeremiah lived in the sixth century BCE, during the period leading up to the destruction of the First Temple. King Zedekiah, a descendant of King David, ruled over Jerusalem at the time, but unlike his great forebear, Zedekiah was weak and sought favor from the city's elites, allowing corruption to flourish throughout the kingdom. While the wealthy lived in comfort, the orphans and widows begged for bread in the streets. Jeremiah rebuked the king, warning that although Zedekiah may have been deaf to their cries, God, who had granted him his power, was not. If the injustice continued, Jeremiah foretold, God would send an enemy from the north to destroy the kingdom.

Four years later, Jeremiah's prophecy was fulfilled. The largest army in world history, the Babylonians, descended upon Jerusalem from the north, surrounding the city on all sides. As fear spread, the people gathered around Jeremiah, desperate for guidance. Jeremiah told them their only chance was to surrender. If they allowed the Babylonians to enter the city, they would be taken captive as punishment for their sins, but Jerusalem would one day be restored to Jewish independence.

Among the crowd listening to Jeremiah were four of the king's officers, including his most trusted, Yehuchal, the son of Shelemiah.

Eilat paused and repeated the name, ensuring we remembered it: "Yehuchal, the son of Shelemiah."

Yehuchal and the other officers rushed to the king, reporting Jeremiah's words. They warned that not only had the soldiers heard the prophecy, but the people were already fleeing the city in fear. The four men devised a plan.

"Let us kill the prophet," they urged the king, "for he demoralizes the soldiers and the people still in the city." The king, paralyzed with fear, gave them permission to act as they saw fit.

Yehuchal and the others seized Jeremiah, dragged him to a deep cistern in the prison courtyard, and threw him in, leaving him to starve as he sank into the muddy waters below.

This might have been the end of Jeremiah's story if not for the courage of one of the king's advisers, described in the Bible only as "the king's official from Cush"—modern-day Ethiopia. This official begged the king for permission to save the prophet. The king, still gripped by fear, did not give a firm response but did not prevent the rescue, either.

It took thirty men to haul Jeremiah out of the mud at the bottom of the cistern. But against all odds, the prophet was freed.

On the ninth day of the month of Av, approximately mid-August, in the year 586 BCE, Babylonian forces stormed the city and destroyed Jerusalem.

Before being blinded and taken away in chains, King Zedekiah watched while his family was killed. The city was burned, including the king's palace and the temple of King Solomon. The people of the city were taken into exile, and Jeremiah elected to go with them. Along the way, he gave them a prophecy of hope that future generations would one day rebuild the city.

Seventy years later, the Persian Empire captured Babylon, and the Jewish people were allowed to return to Jerusalem.

Eilat pointed to the words in her Bible where the name of the man that had tried to kill Jeremiah was printed, and repeated his name: "Yehuchal, the son of Shelemiah."

Then she pointed to the open box on the table. "That is the name that appears on this seal."

Later that week, the discovery of King David's palace and the royal seal of Yehuchal appeared on the front page of the *New York Times*.[12] The usual critics made their voices known, but the importance of the discovery superseded any other coverage.

More than that, it touched the hearts of millions of people around the world.

Within Israel the impact was even greater. Israelis are a proud and dedicated people, who put their lives on the line to protect the only country the Jewish people have had for two thousand years. We have faced and continue to face physical enemies that have tried to destroy us and ideological enemies that have tried to strip us of our history.

First Eilat Mazar predicted where King David's palace was located. Then she found a massive structure dating back to King David's time. Now she had a seal, unearthed from the excavation, that matched exactly with the name in the Bible. This was solid proof that the Bible was not just a book of fairy tales or myths, but that it reflected real people and real history.

It also provided definitive archaeological evidence that the Jewish people have roots in Jerusalem going back more than three thousand years.

King David's palace became a beacon calling people home. Israelis began to flock to the site, whether from secular or religious backgrounds, whether from the military or the yeshivas. Ashkenazi, Sephardi, Mizrahi—men and women of all ages began to visit the City of David to see the story the stones tell, the bedrock from which our ancestors have come, a story that continues in the State of Israel today.

If I look back over the years of a graph showing the growth of the City of David as a line heading from left to right, and I look for hot spots where the line slants upward at a steep angle, there is no question that this was one of the defining moments.

It was around this time that Holocaust survivor and Nobel Prize Laureate Elie Wiesel visited the site on the Ninth of Av, the date of the destruction of the Temple.

In the morning, he visited Yad Vashem, the Holocaust memorial. In the afternoon, he came to the City of David. At the end of the tour, Elie Weisel was deeply moved. He told us that Yad Vashem and the City of David were two chapters of the same story: "The

Holocaust," he said, "was the closing of one chapter of Jewish history, of the horrors and death Jews experienced in the long exile. The City of David," he continued, "is the beginning of a new chapter of Jewish history, one in which Jewish life returned to the State of Israel."

He said on video that day, "Whatever you discover in the City of David has significance to the entire world's culture. The City of David is a center of meaning. You dig deep down—not into the ground but into thousands of years of history—and it comes back to life."

Elie Weisel became one of the closest friends and staunchest supporters of the City of David over the years. Despite the controversy that would grip the site, he never faltered in his support.

He became the first Chairman of the Public Council of the City of David, a position he held until his passing in 2016.

On May 25, 2021, Dr. Eilat Mazar died at the age of 64 after battling a long illness. With her passing, Israel lost one of its most preeminent archaeologists and a fierce fighter for the archaeological truth. Dr. Mazar's discoveries at the City of David shifted the entire academic discussion in Israel away from decades of denialism by the minimalists, into a more intellectually honest pursuit in which the clear discoveries that coordinated with the historical events in the Bible were brought to light.

Following her example of courage, other archaeologists began new excavation sites that were thought to be biblical and old excavations were renewed. And then in April of 2024, archaeologists from Tel Aviv university, the very home of the minimalist movement, along with researchers from the Scientific Archaeology Unit of the Weizmann Institute in Rehovot, and along with archaeologists from the Israel Antiquities Authority, published a report in the *National Academy of Sciences Journal* on new the findings they had made in the Givati Parking Lot and in other locations in the City of David.[13]

Using newly developed advanced carbon-14 dating techniques on more than one hundred samples—mostly charred seeds cross-referenced with calendar-dated tree rings—researchers concluded that ancient Jerusalem during the tenth to the twelfth centuries BCE, which includes the time of King David and King Solomon, was much larger than previously thought. Notably, more than 20 percent of the carbon-dated material at the site was from this period.

Professor Yuval Gadot, head of Tel Aviv University's Department of Archaeology and coauthor of the new study, has shown a notable display of scientific integrity by revisiting his earlier stance. He once claimed that all findings from King David's era could fit "into a shoebox," but now acknowledges that while the evidence doesn't directly point to King David or Solomon, it strongly suggests that Jerusalem during their time "was more developed than we thought." He added, "If my pendulum has to move somewhere, it now goes more in the direction of the city than the village because of these results."[14]

Israel Finkelstein, the most well-known critic of Eilat Mazar's dating of the City of David to the time of King David, based on a disagreement over pottery samples, conceded that the new dating techniques were a breakthrough and that they could help to clarify the dates of pottery samples at other sites. *Haaretz* newspaper, which had previously been the bullhorn of the minimalists, announced, "First large-scale radiocarbon study of Jerusalem casts doubt on the paradigm that David's capital was a small village. It already extended over a vast area more than 3,000 years ago."[15]

Three years after she died, when the stones at the City of David spoke, Eilat Mazar was vindicated.

Following Eilat's discovery in 2005, the City of David was now on the map, and the number of visitors skyrocketed, doubling in just a few months. With the increase in visitors, projects at the site also expanded. We were now beginning to build the first part of the visitors' center to the north of the palace and planning the second phase of the palace excavation to the west.

In addition to all this, more and more schools around the country wanted to bring their students to see the digs and learn about their history. This had been our original goal for the City of David and we provided subsidies for many of them, especially schools located on the periphery.

To cope with all of this we would need a lot more money. We needed to expand our donor base.

On one of my tours, I met a person named Raanan who was a hedge-fund manager. He was enthralled by the site, and he asked me if I would come to New York to explain what we were doing to his friends in Manhattan. He thought that if we could tap into the philanthropic wealth of New York City, we could make a big impact on moving the site forward.

A few weeks later I was in his living room in front of around twenty Manhattan families from the Upper East and Upper West sides. I knew that all these people were used to hearing speeches and fundraising pitches from numerous organizations, everything ranging from emergency rescue to educational initiatives, and for funding scholarships for IDF soldiers once they finished the army.

They were inundated with requests. Why would giving to an archaeological site four thousand miles away impact them, sitting comfortably here in Manhattan? The story was interesting for sure, and they would certainly want to visit, but what could I say that would cause them to sit on the edge of their seats and give real money to what we were doing? It would have to be something that affected them directly.

I had prepared a presentation about the City of David with a PowerPoint showing the stages of the excavation and the discoveries.

At the last minute, before the presentation started, I turned off the projector and stood in front of them.

I bent down toward the floor and picked up an imaginary stone.

"What would you say," I asked the unexpectant crowd, "if I were to tell you that not a single stone in Jerusalem refers to Jewish history?"

They looked at me in confusion. *Good*, I thought.

"What would you say if I said there is not a shred of proof that the Jewish people had ever been there?"

I could see that people were shocked. "And what would you say if I said that the Jewish claim to Jerusalem is the 'art of the Jews to deceive the world.'"[16]

I let the silence settle in until it became uncomfortable.

I then told them, "These are not my words. They belong to Ikrima Sabri and others from the Palestinian Authority, including Arafat himself. They belong to Hamas. These words are not just reaching the Arab world; they are reaching people all around the world, including the growing anti-Israel movements on the college campuses where your kids are studying."

A few people were nodding.

"These people are convinced about what they are saying. The question is, do we know how to answer them? What will we say to our children when they come home from high school, from university, or from listening to the news and hearing this?"

Over the next half hour, I told them that I would explain to them how we at the City of David are providing the answers.

I asked them if they knew why we were called Jews. No one had an answer.

The word *Jew*, I explained, means "from Judea" the same way *American* means "from America." The name was given to us because we were originally from a province in the Land of Israel named Judea after the tribe of Judah, one of Jacob's twelve sons.

The capital of Judea was Jerusalem, built by King David and known in the Bible as the City of David. For centuries before the advent of Christianity and Islam, our Judean ancestors were living, praying in, and defending that city, until they were exiled by the Romans.

The key to understanding the Jewish connection to the Land of Israel, I concluded, is to understand our Jewish roots in Jerusalem.

Finally, I turned on the presentation and showed them artifact after artifact that we had uncovered in the City of David, each one helping to prove Jewish history in Jerusalem. I read the story of the Prophet Jeremiah right from the Bible I was holding—just as Eilat Mazar had done with us that day in our offices. I then showed them the seal with the name Yehuchal, son of Shelemiah, the same name that appeared in the Book of Jeremiah.

"The Bible is not just some book that we received as a bar or bat mitzvah gift. It's not just a book sitting on some dusty shelf. It is our living history. It is who we are, the People of the Book."

When the PowerPoint was over, I could see that some people were in shock, others teary eyed. Many lined up, eager to hear more and to find out how to get a behind-the-scenes tour at the site. The presentation drew the same reaction in living rooms and conference rooms across New York, Boston, Los Angeles, San Francisco, and in Florida.

Other meetings began to spring up. Back in Israel, Yehuda Mali, Davidleh, and I began to host dozens of people who had heard about the City of David and were now coming to Israel to see the site firsthand.

We were inundated with requests for tours, too many for our existing staff to handle. We recruited and trained a fleet of VIP tour guides to meet the demand.

Many of those who visited became committed donors to the project. Our existing donors were delighted that they no longer single-handedly had to support the project. To encourage others to get involved, they made matching commitments toward the projects, which attracted even larger donors who were inclined to make higher level commitments once they knew their funds would be matched.

Around this time, our marketing team came up with the slogan for which the City of David would be known henceforth: "The Place Where It All Began."

Chapter 6

The Pool of Siloam
and the Pilgrimage Road

On a summer day in June 2004, Eilat Mazar and her team were digging at the top of the site, still searching for the seal. However, down at the bottom of the site, all work had come to a halt. The day before, a sewage leak had erupted, spraying rancid sewage water into the orchard at the bottom of the excavation site. The old sewage main, dating back to the 1920s British Mandate era, had probably been developing a crack for years, and it had finally erupted. The municipality sent someone to clear the area around the drain so the repair crew could come and fix it.

We thought it would be a quiet day.

But then a call came into the office from Eli Shukron, the Israel Antiquities Authority archaeologist at the City of David. I could hear Davidleh on the phone, his voice raised, saying, "What? What are you talking about?"

As I walked over to see what was going on, Davidleh grabbed his keys from his drawer—and his gun—and said, "Come with me to the site. Shukron found something, but I can't understand what he's saying. There was too much noise in the background."

We went to the very southern tip of the City of David, where according to archaeologists, the ancient city would have ended before extending into what was the wilderness. What existed in this area now was a spring of water that filled the ruins of a pool built by the Byzantines in the fifth century CE. The Byzantines had named it the "Pool of Siloam," but scholars had long determined that it was not the original "Pool of Siloam" mentioned in the Bible, which would have been built close to a thousand years before the Byzantines.

But that original Pool of Siloam had long gone missing.

On a whim, Eli had decided to go and see how things were progressing with the sewage leak when he saw a yellow JCB tractor trying to break a large stone into pieces so that it could be cleared out of the way. After unsuccessfully trying to convince the driver to stop digging, Eli finally leaped down into the ditch in front of the JCB and called Davidleh on his cell phone. With the bucket of the tractor frozen over his head in midair, Eli looked down and saw that the driver was about to smash what looked to be a long limestone stair, not a single stone.

Eli did not know what a staircase would be doing under an orchard, but he was not going to let it be destroyed.

When we got to the site, we found an angry Eli Shukron, arms folded, standing in a ditch, in an apparent standoff with a tractor. When the driver saw Davidleh and me, he realized the argument was over and went to smoke a cigarette. Eli told us to come down into the ditch, and when we got there he showed us where the driver, digging through the ground, had begun to break apart the stone.

We could see this was no ordinary stone. Eli reached over, moving aside some of the dirt. What we saw was a glistening, white expanse of limestone, perfectly cut, inside the dirt.

"Look at this," Eli said excitedly, bending down to brush aside more of the dirt the JCB had dug up. We could see that the stone stretched four feet before ending in dirt on all sides.

Eli told us, "This is a staircase—and I think it's much longer than what we see."

Eli climbed out of the trench and took us to see another trench also made by the JCB, before this one. There he showed us another section of a ninety-degree cut limestone reflecting in the bright sun. He said, "I believe this is an extension of the same stair—which means it is at least twenty feet wide, possibly much wider."

This stair, however, was broken in two. Eli pointed at the crane. "I think the culprit was that driver. It was sheer luck that I got here when I did."

"You know what this means?" Eli asked us. "We're going to have to dig."

Eli Shukron organized a team of archaeologists and diggers, including Arab and Jewish residents from the area, who excavated by hand, carefully following the surface of the stairs. Within a matter of days, what had started as a sewage leak turned into a massive flight of stairs descending beneath the ground.

As the excavation went on, the stairs grew in width until they reached an astounding 180 feet wide, with sixteen large steps heading down in batches of four deep beneath the fruit orchard that was at the bottom of the City of David. Archaeologists wondered where such monumental stairs were leading.

The excavation continued for the next six months. When word got out, people came from all over to see what we had found. Local Arab and Jewish families, archaeology students, tourists, and Israeli leaders all came to watch, as the staircase hiding beneath the fruit orchard was slowly uncovered.

Some of the people joined the efforts and volunteered with the excavation under Israel Antiquities Agency supervision. One in particular was Malcolm Honlein, the head of the Conference of Presidents, the overall umbrella organization of Jewish organizations in North America. Malcolm and his family joined the crews and worked for days as we uncovered the sixteenth stair, the final stair of this stage of the excavation.

Few things are more powerful than being a part of the uncovering of the excavation itself, and to this very day Malcolm, who has represented the interests of American Jewry to world leaders over the past forty years, says that despite everything he has seen and done in life, one of the things that impacted him the most was digging the sixteenth stair of the Pool of Siloam.

Over the years Malcolm became a close friend of the project. His support of what we were doing opened doors for us into the Jewish community abroad and helped to make the City of David a project of the Jewish people both in Israel and the Diaspora.

Based on evidence unearthed by Eli Shukron and another archaeologist, Zvi Greenhut, the pool was in use as early as the eighth century BCE—thirteen hundred years earlier than the Byzantine Pool that had borne the name until this real pool was found.

Two thousand years after the Romans destroyed Jerusalem, we had at last uncovered the actual Pool of Siloam from Temple times.

When taking into account the dimensions of the staircase that had been uncovered and the boundaries of the orchard on the other three sides, it was estimated that the Pool of Siloam was larger than an Olympic-sized pool.

It would have been a true phenomenon in the ancient world and would become one of the most important and impressive discoveries ever made in Jerusalem.

After five months of digging, it was now December, and the rainy season was about to descend on Jerusalem. Professor Ronny Reich, one of the chief archaeologists of the State of Israel and Eli Shukron's senior colleague on the excavation, asked Davidleh, Yehuda Maly, and me to meet Eli Shukron and him at the Siloam stairs.

He began by stating the question that had plagued all of us for months: "Constructing a pool of this size in the ancient era would have been a feat of great engineering. If it was simply for drinking water, why would they have gone to so much trouble?"

The answer to this question would forever change how people viewed ancient Jerusalem.

Ronny had spent weeks in his Haifa apartment, poring over ancient maps and studying the notes of early explorers, including Charles Warren. He was confident he was onto something.

He gestured toward the steps we had uncovered just a few feet from where we stood, gleaming in the afternoon light. "Strange, isn't it?" he asked. "You wouldn't design stairs like that for a second floor. Someone could easily trip and get hurt."

As I looked at the stairs, I understood what he meant. The staircase was made of sections of four uniform steps, each leading to a wide platform about four feet across, followed by another set of four stairs, and so on. The design was not convenient for walking; it seemed rather uncomfortable.

Ronny explained that there was only one other place in Jerusalem where he had seen such a unique staircase—at a mikvah, a ritual bath, south of the Hulda Gates entrance to the Temple. Pilgrims would use the platforms to quickly undress before immersing in the water.

With a smile, he continued. "What we are looking at here is not just another ritual bath. This staircase solves a mystery that archaeologists have grappled with for years."

He went on to explain that ancient Jewish sources describe huge crowds, both Jews and non-Jews, flocking to the Temple, especially during holidays like Passover. Estimates ranged from tens of thousands to millions of pilgrims. According to Jewish law, every Jewish man or woman had to purify themselves in a mikvah before entering the Temple precinct.

But there was a problem—mikvahs were typically small, far too small to handle the massive crowds that visited the Temple. Over the years, several small ritual baths had been found near the Temple Mount, but they couldn't have accommodated the multitudes.

So where did these people purify themselves?

Ronny pointed to the orchard that partially covered the excavation site, like a rectangular cake with a wedge removed, exposing the stairs beneath. He explained that when fully excavated, the site would reveal a pool large enough to accommodate thousands of pilgrims every hour, enabling them to immerse before continuing in a state of purity toward the Temple.

The ancient Pool of Siloam, it seemed, was the mother of all mikvahs, built to serve the masses on their journey to the Temple.

Davidleh chimed in. "So, Ronny, you're saying the pilgrimage to the Temple actually began here, at this pool, where people purified themselves before ascending to the Temple?"

Ronny nodded. He and Eli Shukron had almost hit a home run. Only one thing was missing from their theory.

It was Yehuda Maly who raised the issue. A biblical scholar with immense knowledge, Yehuda pointed out a critical detail in Jewish law: If a purified person came into contact with someone impure before entering the Temple, they would need to purify themselves again.

"How could people purify themselves here at the pool," Yehuda asked, "and then traverse the crowded City of David—seven hundred yards—without touching someone impure?"

Ronny smiled. It was an excellent question, one he had been pondering for weeks.

He motioned for us to follow him and led us to an area at the top of the staircase, where sandbags covered the ground. He and Eli removed a few bags, revealing what looked like a paved road made of large limestone slabs, laid side by side.

The road continued for about twenty feet before disappearing under a mountain of dirt, compacted over thousands of years and towering more than forty feet above us. This thick layer of fill covered most of the ancient City of David, like a blanket of densely packed earth.

Pointing to the road, Ronny said, "I believe that if we dig further, we'll uncover a road that leads all the way to the Temple."

"A road for the pure," Yehuda said quietly. "This would have been the very path the throngs of people took in a state of purity, walking from the Pool of Siloam directly to the Temple."

The possibility was exhilarating. But one daunting question remained: How could we excavate an ancient road beneath an entire neighborhood filled with modern homes, both Jewish and Arab? Undertaking such a dig was no small feat. Excavators had done something similar in Rome near the Colosseum subway station, but there were few other attempts that had been made anywhere in the world.

In addition to the fact that we didn't actually have proof that this little piece of a sidewalk extended north toward the Temple, the cost of that kind of work would be prohibitively expensive. Just the cost of the structural supports would run into the millions of dollars.

The answer came two months later, in February 2005 when Eugene Shvidler, the donor who had funded the visitors' center, came back to visit.

Eugene was born in the USSR in the 1960s during the harsh Soviet years, and he grew up standing in lines for basic necessities. Like all the other Jews in the former Soviet Union, he had lived under constant government-mandated anti-Semitism. Despite harsh quotas that limited the number of Jews in universities, Eugene was exceptionally smart and determined and he managed to study applied mathematics at the National University of Oil and Gas in Moscow. Managing to get an exit visa to the United States, he went on to earn an MBA at Fordham University in New York before returning to the Soviet Union to join the then-ailing government-owned Sibneft Oil Company, along with a man named Roman Abramovich, who had bought a controlling interest in the company. Together with Roman and their team, Eugene helped transform Sibneft into one of the most successful petrochemical companies in the world.

Eugene never forgot how he and other Jews had suffered under the intense Soviet pressure to give up their Judaism. One of the first things he and Roman did with their wealth was support Jewish communities in Russia. They also generously funded a wide range of non-Jewish causes, from university scholarships and sports camps for underprivileged youth to groundbreaking cancer research. The State of Israel, where Jews could live freely and with dignity, held a special place in their hearts, the City of David in particular.

Davidleh and I sat with Eugene on a second-floor overlook at the top of the City of David from which we could see the Temple Mount and Hulda Gates a few hundred yards to the north and went over the plans for the visitors' center. We would build a grand entrance to the site with a bronze harp of King David, an entrance garden for events, a ticket office, and a gathering area for groups who wanted to see King David's Palace. We would also transform the overlook into a 3D-movie and scenic viewpoint. We told him that we hoped to grow the site to 250,000 visitors annually within three years, a phenomenal increase of more than triple the number of visitors we previously had on an annual basis. Eugene was fine with everything, and we finished up in the evening in great spirits.

We then told him that the next morning, we would meet up again and take him to see the exciting new excavations around the Pool of Siloam.

When we met the next morning at the excavation site, the evening winter rains had given the Jerusalem stone, which lined all the walkways, a deep golden tone of freshly washed limestone. We were greeted by a very excited Eli Shukron, who told us that he had just discovered something that he was bursting to show us—but first he wanted Eugene to see the pool.

Eli walked us around the stone stairs he had recently discovered and explained Ronny Reich's theory about it being an ancient mikvah. He then walked us up to the platform where they had found the beginning of the paved road heading to the Temple Mount—the Pilgrimage Road.

Eugene was blown away, and he looked at us with a knowing smile. "You guys are way off," he said. "You are selling yourselves short if you plan for only 250,000 visitors. What you are doing here at the site is amazing, and everyone is going to want to walk on the Pilgrimage Road journey. You need to be planning for at least a million people."

A million visitors were beyond our dreams.

We studied the mountain of fill blocking the continuation of the Pilgrimage Road, and I explained that to continue the excavation we would have to shore up the entire neighborhood with building supports, something that hadn't been done before on this scale anywhere in Israel.

Eugene understood exactly what I was saying: It was going to cost a lot of money.

There was another problem, I explained: Even if we were able to start the dig, we couldn't be sure that the Pilgrimage Road continued on the other side of the fill. We had found a map made by McCalister and Duncan, two British archaeologists who had dug in the area more than a hundred years before, and they had seen something that looked like a road a bit farther up the mountain—but it wasn't a lot to go on.

I felt we needed to be completely clear about the speculative nature of the dig.

"Eugene, it's possible that we will go to all the effort and find that there is nothing else to—"

Eli cut me off. "Actually," he said, "I may have found something this morning that will shed some light on that."

He motioned for us to follow him to a section of the road that had been covered with dirt when I last visited the dig. The workers had clearly made progress as the section now had a layer of sandbags covering it. Eli hauled off the sandbags, casting them to the side.

There was a hole in the ground between two of the paving slabs.

We crowded around to have a better look. Eli took a flashlight from his pocket and shined it inside. The hole led into a short tunnel around two and a half feet deep. At the bottom was a soggy mass of black water that had probably collected with the recent rains. Reeds and plants could be seen poking out of it.

Davidleh took the flashlight and poked his head all the way down inside the hole. When he got up, he asked Eli if he was right in thinking the tunnel was headed north toward the Temple Mount.

Eli nodded his head and said, "I believe it was a drainage channel built beneath the Pilgrimage Road in Temple times. It may have been built in order to direct rainwater from the area of the Temple Mount down to the pool, where it could be collected, or into the valley beyond the pool to irrigate fields."

Eli pointed to the mountain of fill blocking the road.

"If this tunnel goes beneath the Pilgrimage Road, then maybe we can crawl through it, under the road. It will be like crawling through a sewer beneath a road. If we see the flagstones of the road continuing over our heads, then we will know the road continues. That should be proof enough for us to start to dig."

Eugene asked Eli, "When will you know?"

"I'm planning to try and crawl through the tunnel later this week," Eli said. "It's mostly an issue of wearing clothes that one doesn't mind ruining—and finding a few workers who will agree to crawl with me through the tunnel. It isn't a good idea to go by oneself."

Davidleh turned to look at Eugene and me, and then turned back to Eli.

"And what if we were willing to ruin the clothes we are wearing right now?" Davidleh asked. "Could we go today?"

"Well," Eli answered, taken by surprise, "we would need to make sure everyone has knee pads and headlamps."

Davidleh turned to us and smiled.

"But," Eli added, "you're going to ruin your clothes."

Davidleh's brown eyes were shining in the clear winter sun, and he put his hand on Eugene's shoulder. "Eugene, you're about to have an experience you will remember forever."

It was impossible to say no to Davidleh. Eugene looked down at what he was wearing and then at the dark hole in the ground with all that schmutz and said hesitantly, "Let's go ruin our clothes."

Two hours later, we were wearing headlamps and knee gear, but we were still wearing the same clothes. Eli had gathered a few workers who opened up the entrance to the small sewage drain. It was filled with the winter rains, and it was icy cold. In addition, there was a thick layer of mud along the bottom.

Eli lowered himself into the tunnel first, followed by Davidleh. Eugene went next, swearing when his knees splashed into the cold mud below. I followed at the rear.

I turned on my headlamp before dropping into the tunnel. The last thing I saw before going in was a couple of the diggers watching us with curiosity, a bit of envy—and a little bit of fear that we would not make it out alive.

The water was icy cold and murky. Eli called back to see if we were all there. After hearing that we were, he started to crawl forward, sloshing through the water. As we followed, our headlamps lit up the narrow walls of the channel. The underside of the Pilgrimage Road was right above our heads, but the space was narrow—very narrow. My shoulders brushed against dirt and weeds that had collected along the sides of the channel for who knew how long. There were roots sticking out of the mud that immediately began poking at me as we crawled north. But I was not about to complain.

Like hunched over mules, we inched our way forward.

After a few minutes, Eli called back saying that the roof of the tunnel was getting a bit lower. Then we heard him grunt as he pushed through. His voice echoed back that it was tight but he was fine.

Davidleh went next, without so much as a peep, and then it was Eugene's turn. I watched him struggling to get through, unable to help him. Finally, he managed to grasp hold of something and pull himself through.

Much swearing followed.

I had a few seconds to wonder if it had been a good idea to do this with our newest and largest donor to date. But before I could dwell on the question for too long, it was my turn.

At first, I tried to see if I could bend down far enough to slide through the opening without having to lower myself any deeper into the disgusting water.

I couldn't fit.

I put my head through the hole and I could see Eugene's headlamp cast a glow in the distance. It looked like the tunnel evened out after this and became easier.

after countless Jews had been slain by the Romans in Jerusalem, there still remained a small group that had survived in hiding. Josephus writes of their hope that "after the whole city would be destroyed, and the Romans gone away, they might come out again, and escape."

Unfortunately, the survivors were wrong, and the Romans continued their search. At some point realizing it was only a matter of time until they were discovered, the Jews took to the tunnels that ran beneath the city, which they hoped would lead them to the desert. From there, they would have fled most likely to Masada, a desert fortress where some of their brethren were still holding out against the Romans.

Not sure how long they would remain in hiding, the last survivors brought some meager belongings along with some food in clay jars.

Josephus records that before they managed to escape through the tunnels, the Romans discovered them: "And when they found where they were, they broke up the ground and slew all they met with. There were also found slain there above two thousand persons, partly by their own hands, and partly by one another, but chiefly destroyed by the famine."

Eli looked at us and said, "This was one of the underground channels of the city, and I believe that these pots were left behind by the last Jews as they tried to escape to their freedom two thousand years ago. This tunnel was the place where they perished."

We sat there in the semi-darkness beneath the stone staircase in the tunnel, chilled by what we had found. We were the first to return in two thousand years to where our brethren had died, simply for being Jewish and defending Jerusalem.

When we exited the tunnel after being underground for so long, the light was blinding. As my eyes adjusted, I could see that the workers were staring at us, buckets and shovels paused in midair. I looked at the other three and knew I must look the same. We were covered with a greenish slime over all our clothing. Our hair was covered with twigs and dust, and we were soaking wet.

We looked down at the hole in the ground and felt that we had emerged from the last moments of the destruction of Jerusalem. We had been a part of something historic, and we knew it.

I walked Eugene out of the excavation in our dripping clothes. Before getting into the car that was waiting for him, he turned to me and said, "Whatever it will take to get this excavation going, I am behind you."

And with that, he got into his car and drove off.

After Eugene left, I went back into the excavation and updated Davidleh on the incredible news that Eugene had said he would back us. The reality that we could begin digging the Pilgrimage Road began to set in.

Davidleh asked me to follow him, and he walked us over to the northernmost edge of the excavation. We could see the Old City walls rising beyond the northern tip of the City of David in the distance. We had not only found the water tunnel, but more importantly, we had seen the stairs of the Pilgrimage Road over our heads—proof that the Pilgrimage Road continued toward the Temple Mount.

He pointed up at the Old City and said to me, "We now know that the Pilgrimage Road continues north all the way from here, from the Pool of Siloam, most likely all the way up to the area of the Temple Mount and the Western Wall. Archaeologists are going to dig the Pilgrimage Road all the way up to the Western Wall, and millions of people are going to take the Pilgrimage Journey just like our ancestors did two thousand years ago."

I turned from him and looked toward the walls. They seemed impossibly far. Not to mention, an entire neighborhood of homes and streets lay between us and them. Even if we managed to traverse the whole neighborhood underground, the Old City wall stood blocking the City of David from the Old City.

What Israeli prime minister would have the courage to greenlight the Israeli Antiquities Authority to do such an excavation?

I told Davidleh the list of reasons I couldn't see it happening.

He didn't answer me directly. He just spoke in the same faraway soft voice as before. "We will find a way. Don't worry, we will find a way."

Many years later, when Davidleh received the Israel Prize for Life Achievement, the country's highest civilian honor, he was asked what he would like to share with the public. He answered that when he began in the City of David, people thought he was crazy, even his own family. "Now that the City of David is a great success," he said, "they call me a visionary. In order to accomplish a dream, something big, that is going to cause a shift in the way people understand things, maybe you have to be a bit crazy."

Davidleh has always been able to see something no one else could imagine. If asked about the challenges that lie ahead, Davidleh can always list them better than anyone else. He knows the playing field, the opposition, the risks, and the supporters. However, in order to dream, he silences the worries of how it can be done and rises above them. In doing so, he is able to draw upon enormous strength and purpose to envision what seems to be impossible.

In the coming years, every bit of that strength would be needed to make the excavation happen.

What we did not know then was that the Pilgrimage Road

excavation was so mighty in scale and in importance that we had begun to catch the attention of those who would do almost anything to stop it from being dug.

The excavation of the Pilgrimage Road, probably like no other anywhere in the world, would require courage among many people. These would include government officials, donors, international figures such as Elie Weisel, and the excavators themselves.

For thousands of years, King David and his dynasty had been waiting for us to return to our land.

The time had arrived.

A few weeks later, we started working with the Israel Antiquities Authority and groups of structural engineers to try and figure a way to continue the excavation of the swath of road through the forty feet of fill that covered it.

The fill had collected over the past two thousand years, burying the ancient City of David. During the British Mandate Period, new requests to build in the area had been denied on the grounds that the area was an archaeological site. However, during the Jordanian Period this had no longer been the case. In fact, it was the opposite. In a rush to put "facts on the ground," the Jordanians encouraged homes and roads to be built as quickly as possible. Aerial maps of the site show a stark difference between the mostly barren City of David in the pre-Jordanian conquest era, and the post-1967 era, with dozens of homes dotting the mountain. The homes that were constructed during this nineteen-year period were not only built indiscriminately over an archaeological site; they were also built without structural supports.

Making the situation even more precarious was that Jerusalem has a heavy rainy season every year, and the rain mixes with the fill underneath the ground, causing the dirt to shift. Given the lack of solid foundations to these homes and the shifting fill, the homes had constant cracks in their walls and were not structurally sound.

The challenge was how to safely dig under the fill, reveal the Pilgrimage Road, and keep the ground level secure.

The engineers came up with a plan: They designed a system whereby arched metal supports, like those used to hold up buildings, would be installed every meter along the Pilgrimage Road, going down all the way to the bedrock. This would not only keep the roof of the underground excavation intact; it would also effectively provide structural support for the homes that were located above the excavations, homes that had been originally built without any supports. Despite future bogus claims to the contrary, the homes located above the excavations—both Arab and Jewish alike—would become the most secure homes in the entire area.

We realized that this would require us to fund not only the archaeological side of the project, but also construction crews and metal supports as if we were constructing a ten-story building. The supports would cost almost double what the excavations cost. Despite being a young organization, we accepted the monumental responsibility of raising the millions upon millions of dollars that would be needed. A short time later, a team of archaeologists and engineers embarked on one of the most expensive and sensitive archaeological excavations ever conducted.

The excavation plan worked. Within six months, the Pilgrimage Road stairs were revealed.

Chapter 7

The Jewish Hajj

Finding the Pilgrimage Road, for us, was like uncovering Pompeii or Atlantis. The stones, at last, had a voice.

Imagine if Fifth Avenue was suddenly covered with dirt, and then, after thousands of years have passed, someone comes back and digs through the dirt and finds the same avenue underneath the ground, undisturbed. The only thing missing are the people who used to walk there. You can almost see houses along the road, with counters facing the road from which people would sell wares to the pilgrims as they passed by.

That's what it was like to walk the Pilgrimage Road when we first found it. We looked at it and said, "Are these stones new or old?" It was so strange. They looked perfectly new, as if the only thing missing were two-thousand-year-old people walking up the road dressed in pilgrimage outfits on their way to the Temple.

The stones were even shining. Hundreds of thousands of people had walked on the Jerusalem limestone with leather sandals, and over decades the stones had become polished.

It was on these stones of the newly discovered Pilgrimage Road that I first heard the story that had shaped Davidleh's life.

A few months into the dig I visited the site and noticed a massive crack on the right-hand side of the staircase. A part of the stairs was missing. Through the crack, I could see down into a narrow tunnel below. It took me a few seconds to realize that this was the tunnel we had crawled through a year before. From down there, I had seen the underside of the very staircase I was standing on now.

I remembered Eli Shukron telling us how the historian Josephus described the Romans breaking through the road to capture and kill the last Jews hiding in Jerusalem in that tunnel. I thought of the people hiding down there and how they must have felt: parents trying to keep their children busy with the little set of dice we had found, giving them tiny bits of food from the pots they had brought with them, which we also discovered during that crawl.

Chills went up my arms when I thought of how many times Jews had been hunted and chased into tunnels during our long exile in the Diaspora.

I was giving a tour to a lovely American couple named Sidney and Judy. They owned a well-known shoe-and-apparel company in Boston, and both were incredibly passionate about Israel. I told them that I had arranged for them to meet Davidleh, whom I described to them as a true Israeli hero and the founder of the City of David in the modern day.

When we reached the Pilgrimage Road excavation, Davidleh was waiting for us, wearing his standard blue work pants and open-toed sandals. Sidney and Judy were enthralled with how much we had achieved, and they asked Davidleh if he would share with them how he came to dedicate his life to the project.

Davidleh said that the answer to their question lay only a few feet away, and he motioned for us to follow him to the section of the road where the stairs had been broken by the Romans. When we got there, he pointed down at the tunnel below and said that he wanted to share with us what this tunnel made him think of.

Davidleh's father had been in the Auschwitz concentration camp during the Holocaust, and when the war ended, he had emigrated to Israel to start a new life. He never mentioned his past to the family, pointing only to the future. However, Davidleh said, before his father died, he called him to his bedside and told him a story. When his father had arrived on the train to Auschwitz, they asked him if he had a special skill. He knew that to survive, he had to say yes, and so he lied and told them he was a metal worker. They sent him to work in the factory that built the V2 Rockets, designed by the Nazis to attack Allied cities throughout Europe.

Over time he learned to work with the metal, and he began making rings from the shards that were left over. On one occasion one of the Nazi commanders saw him doing this, and took the ring. Not long after, the commander returned and asked for more rings that he wanted to give away to his friends as souvenirs.

Because of these rings, Davidleh's father managed to survive the war, protected by the Nazi commander.

Toward the end of the war, the Nazis took all the inmates on what became known as the "Death March," through snow and freezing conditions, to avoid the advancing Russian army. Of the small remnant of Jews that had managed to survive until then, many died on that final death march.

Seeing an opportunity, his father and a group of inmates tried to escape into the forest, but they were caught by the Nazis and placed in a line over a ditch. The Nazis shot them, killing all of them except for Davidleh's father, who got the bullet in his leg. When he fell in the ditch, he was covered with other bodies and could barely move.

Davidleh said his father felt like he was the last Jew alive, about to die alone. He turned his head to look up, and he could see the Nazi commander who had protected him throughout the war looking down between the bodies. Davidleh's father called out to him and, remarkably, the Nazi commander took him out of the ditch and set him free.

Davidleh looked at us and said, "When I look at this tunnel where Jews died two thousand years ago at the hands of the Romans, I remember my father and how he escaped from Auschwitz. If God had worked so hard to save my father and bring me to this world, then he must have a mission in mind for me. When I came to the City of David, I understood: This is my mission."

As we stood on those stairs, Sidney began openly weeping.

When I heard Davidleh's story that day over the broken paving stones, I gained a new layer of understanding of Eilat Mazar's words "Let the stones speak."

In Jerusalem the stones have a story to tell, a story not only about Jerusalem. Rather, it is all the stories of our people, both in the Land of Israel and in exile. It is as if the stones of Jerusalem gather the stories in our absence, catching them out of the air, storing them away safely, until a time we need to hear them, to remind us how we longed to come home.

The City of David is not just an excavation of Jerusalem; it is an experience that encapsulates Jewish history.

The stones call us home, and the home we reach when we answer that call is Jerusalem.

We were all caught up in the beauty and the historical meaning, marveling that this was the beautiful pathway our ancestors walked on, preserved like a museum piece—a ritual pathway that predated the Via Dolorosa and the Marble Road in Ephesus by hundreds and hundreds of years.

We had no idea of the furor that was about to be unleashed.

It did not take long for word of the dig to reach the ears of the leaders who had been preaching their revisionist history that Jerusalem was solely a Muslim city. The Muslim authorities immediately understood that the uncovering of the Pilgrimage Road was a challenge to their narrative unlike anything they'd ever before experienced, in terms of both scale and international respect for Jewish history.

They understood that the Pool of Siloam and the Pilgrimage Road would not only reverberate throughout the archaeological world, but also, they would create a sensation.

Not only would Israelis come to Jerusalem to walk from the Pool of Siloam to the Western Wall, but people from all over the world would want to walk on the stairs that formed the very foundation of faith for billions.

The Arab leaders sensed something about the Pilgrimage Road that we hadn't even come to fully appreciate: They realized that we had uncovered a Hajj.

What does the largest Muslim pilgrimage in the world—the Hajj—have to do with the Jews? The answer came to me in a taxicab.

In one of the best-known stories in the Jewish Bible, the patriarch Abraham is commanded to bind his son Isaac as an offering to God on Mount Moriah in Jerusalem. The place of the binding would be the site of the future Jewish Temple built by King Solomon in 960 BCE.

In the Quran, however, a story bearing similarities to the binding of Isaac is told, but with two significant changes: According to the Quran, it is Ishmael, not Isaac, his half brother who is bound by Abraham, and the binding of Ishmael takes place not in Jerusalem, but rather in Mecca at the Kaaba Stone.

While we were excavating the Pilgrimage Road, I flagged down a taxi in the center of Jerusalem and asked the driver to take me to the City of David. The driver was an elderly Arab man. As we drove, he told me that he was from Silwan, the village across the valley from the City of David.

I saw that he had a picture in his car showing the large shiny black Kaaba stone in Mecca. The Kaaba is Islam's holiest site, the culmination of the Muslim pilgrimage to Mecca, the Hajj. Every Muslim is commanded to do the pilgrimage at least once in their lives and circle the stone seven times.

I asked the driver if he had been to Mecca on the Hajj. He responded proudly, "I have been blessed to visit the site twice!" I knew this was a great honor, as most Muslims around the world are unable to do it even once in their lifetimes. He pointed to the taxi license hanging in the taxi with the prefix "Hajj" in front of his name. It is customary that when a Muslim man returns from the Hajj, he adds the prefix *Hajj* to his name.

We arrived at the City of David. While I was arranging the payment, he handed me a small pile of postcards with pictures showing hundreds of thousands of Muslims circumambulating the Kaaba stone. It was incredible to see so many people in one place worshiping together. During the peak of the Hajj season, three million people fill the area, dressed in white, all circling the stone counterclockwise.

I thought about the historian Josephus Flavius's personal account of the Israelite pilgrimage to the Temple in Jerusalem before the destruction. Josephus writes that during Passover alone, millions of Jews came from all over Israel and as far away as Babylon to appear before God at the Temple.

The pictures I was seeing of the Hajj were the closest I could imagine to what that ancient event could have looked like.

I handed the pictures back to the driver and we shook hands warmly. Just before I got out of the taxi, we acknowledged that the Arabs and Jews are cousins, descendants of Abraham, parting with the Hebrew and Arabic phrases "peace be unto you": I said "Shalom Aleichem" to him, and he said "Salam Aleikum" to me. I watched the taxi drive away into the distance feeling hopeful from the interaction.

And then it dawned on me: The Hebrew word for the Israelite pilgrimage experience as recorded in the Book of Exodus is *hag*. Although it is pronounced with a hard *g* in contemporary Hebrew, Yemenite Jews, whose dialect is considered to be the closest to early spoken Hebrew, pronounce it as a *j*, the same as Muslims do.

The words used to describe the pilgrimage in the Hebrew Bible and the Arabic Quran are virtually the same words.

This could not be a coincidence.

Once I realized the connection, additional similarities between the two pilgrimages raced through my mind: One of the five tenets of the Muslim faith is that every male is commanded to do the Hajj at least once in his life. One of the tenets of early Judaism, as stated in the Book of Exodus, is that every Israelite male is commanded to do the Hag—the Temple pilgrimage—three times a year.

Furthermore, the pinnacle of the Muslim Hajj is when the devotees rotate around the Kaaba Stone in Mecca seven times in counterclockwise direction. The pinnacle of the Israelite Hag was during the Sukkot festival, when the devotees were commanded to circle the altar in the Temple courtyard seven times in a counterclockwise direction.

The similarities continue: Jews in Temple times circled the site where they believed Abraham had bound Isaac on Mount Moriah, while Muslims still today circle the site where they believe Abraham bound Isaac's half brother, Ishmael.

I wondered why I had never noticed the similarities between the two religions before—or even heard them referenced. It seemed so obvious I was sure there had to be others who had noticed before me. But when I researched, I was able to uncover only a few scant writings here and there.

The concept was certainly not common knowledge—among Jews or Muslims.

One simple reason the link between the two pilgrimages might not have been made was that Jewish people had been exiled from the land for two thousand years, so the idea of taking the pilgrimage to Jerusalem lost its relevance to the Jewish consciousness. In our day, the term *Hag Sameach*, which Jews say on the three holiday festivals, is misunderstood as meaning "Have a nice holiday"—but, in fact, its original meaning was "Have a nice pilgrimage."

The ancient Israelites who came to Jerusalem for the Hag pilgrimage first bathed in the mikvah at the Pool of Siloam, before embarking on the ultimate ascent of the Hag festival, walking along the Pilgrimage Road all the way through the Temple Mount gates to the Temple itself.

The road we had discovered wasn't just a Pilgrimage Road; it was the Hag Pilgrimage Road used by the ancient Israelites who came to Jerusalem more than sixteen hundred years before Islam was founded.

This historical fact should have posed no challenge to Islam were it not for the Palestinian leadership. But they had been teaching an entire generation of their people the falsehood that there never was a Jewish Temple on the Temple Mount, and that the site was first sanctified by Muhammad.

It was one thing to perpetuate this falsehood with Jews praying at an old stone wall, but it would be far more difficult to spread the lie when millions of people from different faiths and backgrounds were coming to Jerusalem to take a journey, with essentially the same name, along the actual Pilgrimage Road, that predated Islam by six hundred years.

By making the Pilgrimage Road a central issue in their soon-to-be violent protests, they raised our own appreciation for what we had discovered.

But in doing so, they began to back themselves into a corner.

Chapter 8

Palestina

With the discovery of King David's Palace and the Pilgrimage Road, the City of David was transformed from a small backwater excavation into a leading archaeological site.

And with that transformation came threats of violence, against Israelis in general, against our workers, and even an attempted assassination.

Our archaeological discoveries were revealing facts on the ground that showed the Jewish people were undeniably indigenous to the area. People from Israel and around the world were beginning to pay attention.

As word got out, the City of David began to be circled on maps, and a bull's-eye was put over the site by groups who felt we had to be stopped.

It did not suffice for these groups to attack the City of David in the media or in academia. They wanted to bring their battle to the streets of the neighborhood, and they were more than willing to use the threat of violence—and violence itself—to achieve their goals.

They were just waiting for the right moment to do so.

The storm clouds arrived in the form not only of Hamas and Fatah, but also as a previously less-known movement called the Northern Islamic Movement.

Ideologically aligned with the Muslim Brotherhood, the Northern Islamic Movement was committed to an Islamic caliphate in Palestine. The ten thousand members of the organization were radicalized Israeli Arab citizens, and it was led by an Islamic cleric named Raed Salah, who had served a prison sentence a year before for having links to an Iranian spy and for channeling funds to Hamas.[1]

Having served as mayor of Umm al Fahm, a city in northern Israel, Salah was able to lead the anti-Israel movement while receiving a monthly pension from the Israeli government.

Raed Salah became known for inciting his followers to violence against Jews in Israel with the cry "Al-Aqsa is in danger"—a reference to the Al-Aqsa Mosque on the Temple Mount.[2] Salah was not the first to libel the Jews for supposedly trying to destroy the mosque. He simply resuscitated a message first used in the 1920s by the grand mufti of Jerusalem Haj Amin al-Husseini. The father of the Arab Palestinian Movement, Haj Amin was a virulent anti-Semite, a loyal supporter of the Nazis, and had personally met with Adolf Hitler in 1941, assuring him that, "The Arabs were Germany's natural friends because they had the same enemies as had Germany, namely the English, the Jews and the Communists."[3] In 1929, Haj Amin had incited thousands of Muslims into a frenzy by claiming Jews were going to bomb the mosque on the Temple Mount. Mobs of enraged Muslims stormed through the country, raping and killing hundreds of Jewish men, women, and children in Hebron, Safed, and Jerusalem.

In 2006, Salah began to see an opportunity. It was now time, he decided, for the Northern Islamic Movement to take its radical vision of an Islamic State from the villages of northern Israel to

Jerusalem, and to strike at the two foundations of the Jewish people's religious and historical connection to the Land of Israel: the Temple Mount and the City of David.

The battle for the City of David began on the morning of Sunday, January 28, 2007.

I was on my way to the site to see the excavation progress. As I drove up the central road of the City of David, there was an eerie quiet on the street. The morning hours were usually filled with people heading off to work, but that day the streets were empty. My windows were down, and I realized that I couldn't hear any of the sounds of pickaxes and excited yells from the excavations.

I saw Ismail, one of the excavators, walking down the street toward me. He and I had been friends for years, and we had sat together over many cups of Arabic coffee. I stopped the car and asked him, "Where has everybody gone?"

Not meeting my eyes, he acknowledged me with a brief nod and turned down an alleyway without a word.

At the visitor center, I found Eli Shukron, Davidleh, and members of the Antiquities Authority and National Parks Authority in the conference room. I quickly caught on to the nature of the meeting: That morning all the Muslim workers had either called in sick or simply not shown up for work.

Eli Shukron was deep in thought. He looked up and noticed me for the first time and without a word, handed me a statement made earlier that day by Raed Salah on behalf of the Northern Islamic Movement.

In the letter, Salah claimed that the City of David and the Israel Antiquities Authority were excavating "a new tunnel" that would break through the Southern Wall of the Temple Mount "into the Al

Aqsa Mosque itself." According to Salah, the tunnel was the "absolute proof" that the Israelis were out to "destroy the mosque" and "falsify history as part of the dream of building the Third Temple." He ended with a call for all Muslims and Christians to immediately mobilize to stop the excavation.[4]

I now understood why the workers had called in sick. The "tunnel" Raed Salah referred to was a clear reference to the Pilgrimage Road excavation, and there was scarcely a more loaded and dangerous charge than claiming that those involved in the excavation were out to destroy Al Aqsa.

The claims, of course, were absurd, but the truth didn't matter to those who were just waiting for an excuse to riot.

Eleven years before, in 1996, similar claims had led to bloody riots resulting in the deaths of numerous Jews and Arabs in the Old City. [5]

Eli Shukron had managed to reach a few workers on the phone that morning, and they were deathly scared of being targeted by the Northern Islamic Movement as collaborating with the Jews on the excavation. They asked him to stop the excavations for a few months, until the tensions blew over.

For more than a decade until that morning, Jews, Christians, and Muslims had been working together peacefully, side by side, on the digs at the City of David. We were proud of the cooperation and believed that the growth of the City of David would be good for Israel and all its citizens—especially for the Arab community, because they work in tourism in higher numbers than the rest of the population. Many of the Arabs in the City of David and in neighboring Silwan had begun to see it that way as well.

This ongoing cooperation between Arabs and Jews at the site flew in the face of the portrayal of the international media that solely focused on incidents that supposedly proved why Jews and Arabs could not live together in peace under Israeli sovereignty.

This was one of the key tenets repeated by those who advocated for the division of Jerusalem into two capitals, one for the Israelis and one for the Palestinians. If Israel wasn't capable of keeping the peace in Jerusalem, they always claimed, then separate Israeli and Palestinian autonomy in the city would. The impracticability of how Israel could share the city of Jerusalem, which is one-eighth the size of New York City, with either the Palestinian Authority or Hamas, both of whom oppose Israel's very existence and commit daily acts of terror against Israelis, is completely ignored.

An article would come out two weeks later in the *Economist* titled, "A Spark in a Tinderbox," belaboring this point, as would numerous other articles that amplified the claim.[6]

The slanted media coverage rested upon a series of reports that were issued on a regular basis by advocacy groups. One such group, called Ir Amim, claimed to be working "for an equitable and stable Jerusalem." On paper this sounds like an admirable cause; however a quick look at Ir Amim's financials reveals that in reality the organization is paid millions of dollars from anti-Israel European governments, in order to "monitor" and "expose" Israeli government actions in Jerusalem.[7]

I was unable to find a single mention of "monitoring" or "exposing" radical Islamic movements in Jerusalem, such as Hamas—groups that openly make death threats against Arabs in the city if they collaborate with Jews in any way, particularly selling their homes to a Jewish person. These news reports are always a one-sided bashing of the State of Israel and of Jews living in East Jerusalem.

Raed Salah's open call for violence was clearly designed to crush the cooperation between Jews and Arabs at the City of David that had built up over the years. The possibility that so much hard work to create trust in the area could end in a few days made the option to stop digging for a few months sound reasonable to the average person. To most of us in that room that day, that is what we would have chosen to do. It was only a few months, after all, we convinced ourselves.

Davidleh, however, is not an average person.

He had led the most important undercover elite units in the IDF on missions behind enemy lines and understood the psychology of terrorists. He knew the way terrorists work: They count on the terror they instill in the hearts and minds of their victims to convince them that by making minor concessions, the terror will go away. In fact, it increases. Slowly, over time, the terrorists make increasing demands, and the victims back themselves into a corner, where they live in constant fear while they fulfill all the terrorists' demands.

Davidleh was adamant that we had to do everything possible so that the same mistake wouldn't happen in the City of David. He correctly predicted that giving in to the threats would simply embolden the Northern Islamic Movement and encourage them to increase their activities and threats in the area.

Davidleh arranged a meeting with the heads of the Jerusalem police department and representatives of the Arab workers. The police said they would crack down on those responsible for the intimidation before the situation got worse, and they would put a permanent security detail at the site. Davidleh told the workers that if the security detail wasn't enough, we would add security personnel from our own budget.

The Arab workers listened respectfully. After the police left, they took us aside and shook their heads.

They told us that we were naïve.

They simply didn't believe the police could protect them against those threatening them.

It was a sad moment when we all realized that the police had lost the trust of the City's Arab residents.

The following week, two cars were found torched along the main thoroughfare in the City of David, their frames reduced to black husks of metal and the windows shattered. Both cars belonged to Arab supervisors who worked on the dig. The next morning, the residents in the neighborhood woke up to find that, during the night, flyers had been posted on telephone poles listing the names of the Muslims who worked on the dig.

The threat was clear, and most workers left that day. Out of close to one hundred employees, only fifteen agreed to stay on.

Over the years, my colleagues and I have often been visited by groups of students who come to either understand the complexities of the situation in East Jerusalem or to simply validate the "Israeli brutality" they have been taught on campuses. They usually come to us after meeting one of the anti-Israel NGOs, who feed them the narrative of the "horrors of the Israeli occupation," citing their same fallacious reports to the unsuspecting students, showing them the same media stories made by complicit reporters.

During every visit I tell the students about how our workers were threatened and forced to quit their jobs by a radical Islamic group in the winter of 2007.

"Where was the outcry by the NGO that you just met with?" I ask them. "Our Arab workers were threatened with violence by an extremist organization to quit their jobs—and none of the NGOs that claim to be protecting the rights of the Arabs living in Jerusalem spoke out. Are the Arab workers' rights any less important because it is Muslims that are threatening them? Will those same organizations that claim to be protecting the rights of the Arabs living in Jerusalem find jobs for the workers who quit?" I tell students that in some cases our former workers have turned to me for financial aid.

Not once have they been helped by the NGOs.

Just as Davidleh warned, after the workers' resignations, the situation began to spiral out of control.

Just to the north of the City of David, inside the Old City walls, Israeli workers were repairing a pedestrian bridge to the Mughrabi Gate of the Temple Mount, located next to the Western Wall. The Mughrabi Gate was the only one of twelve gates to the Temple Mount that non-Muslims were allowed to use. The pedestrian bridge that led to the gate had been seriously damaged by an earthquake two years before and needed to be repaired before it could collapse. As part of the repair work, a plan was put forward to renovate the bridge by widening it and extending the length to allow for more comfortable passage for those visiting the site of the Temple Mount.

Both the repairs and the renovations to the bridge were taking place completely outside of the Temple Mount itself, and next to the Western Wall Plaza.

Despite the fact that Muslims had another eleven gates just for themselves and that access for non-Muslims on the pedestrian bridge was limited to certain hours, for anyone looking to wreak havoc, the repair work provided the perfect opportunity.

Raed Salah led a mob of hundreds of his followers who descended from northern Israel to Jerusalem.

Along the way, they stopped in the Wadi al Joz neighborhood located next to the Old City. There, Salah made a speech to the local Jerusalem Arabs claiming that the work on the Mughrabi Gate was in reality part of a plan to "spill the blood of the Arabs and build the Temple." He riled the crowd into a frenzy saying that, "Israeli history is filthy with blood. They want to build their Temple when our blood is on their clothes, on their doors, and in their food and drink."[8]

The mob headed toward the Old City until they were stopped

at the Dung Gate by the police. According to a *New York Times* reporter covering the story, when police officers tried to stop Salah, he apparently spit in their faces and was detained for assault. [9]

Salah's arrest only served to amplify his cries that "Al Aqsa is in danger"—a message that gained momentum across the Muslim world.

Hamas claimed that Israel was committing crimes against the mosque and told all Palestinians "to awaken and focus their struggle against Israel."[10]

Palestinian Authority President Mahmoud Abbas said that "what Israel is doing at the Mughrabi Gate demonstrates its intentions and its deeds, planned in advance and entailing the destruction of the Muslim holy places."

In Damascus, claims were made that Israel had *already* demolished part of the mosque. Incendiary and racist cartoons were printed in the Syrian state-run newspaper showing a stereotypical Jew with a grenade about to blow up the Temple Mount.

Ir Amim fueled the fire by joining the growing outcry, claiming that the planned repairs and construction of the bridge were "consistent with the impression that the government of Israel is seeking, for the first time since 1967, to change the political/religious status quo on the Temple Mount/Haram al-Sharif." They alleged that this supposed change would increase non-Muslim access to the Temple Mount, particularly for Jews, who regard it as the holiest site in their religion. Ir Amim argued that the bridge renovation plans aligned with the aspirations of "Israel's most extremist national/religious elements."[11]

In an urgent attempt to calm the situation, Israel granted access to a delegation from UNESCO—followed by another delegation from Turkey—to examine the work being conducted at the Mughrabi Gate. After carefully examining the site, both delegations exonerated Israel and made public statements that the work in no way posed a risk to the mosque.

A few days later, the Israeli authorities pressed charges against Raed Salah for incitement to racism, a charge for which he would eventually be sentenced to nine months in prison.[12]

The Mughrabi Gate incident shed light on a worrying phenomenon in which radical Islamic groups have found a partner in their opposition to Israel by radical advocacy groups led by Israelis themselves. While each has different tactics, they share a common goal: to weaken the State of Israel, both internally and in the eyes of the world.

Contemporary radical Islam denies the ancient historical connection of the Jewish people to the Land of Israel. It claims the Jews are foreign, Western invaders, who have come to steal Muslim land. Radical movements such as the Muslim Brotherhood openly call for violence against the State of Israel,[13] using pressure and threats to achieve their goals.

These groups also deny the modern validity of how Israel came to possess the land within its borders. They overlook the historical reality of Israel's acceptance of the UN Partition Plan—which the Arabs opposed—and the fact that Israel obtained all the lands within its borders while defending itself from attack by enemies that surround it.

The anti-Israel foreign and local NGOs, such as B'Tselem, Ir Amim, Peace Now, and the Applied Research Institute Jerusalem (ARIJ), heavily target the State of Israel and organizations like the City of David through persistent legal campaigns, both within the Israeli court system and by filing charges with the International Criminal Court in The Hague.[14]

As part of this legal campaign, these groups make use of a dehumanizing term to refer to the men, women, and children who live in these debated areas. Unfortunately, this term—"Jewish settlers"—is now part of common nomenclature, and is often used to cover up the brutality of Palestinian acts of terror against innocent Israeli civilians.

A recent example was a CNN headline in 2023 that read, "TWO ISRAELI SETTLERS KILLED IN WEST BANK SHOOTING."[15] In reality, the two "settlers" were brothers, Yaniv and Hillel, aged nineteen and twenty-one, killed in cold blood at point-blank range in their car when they stopped at a crosswalk in the Arab village of Hawara on their way home. But by calling them "settlers," CNN risked framing the victims in a way that diminished their humanity, potentially implying that their deaths may be somehow justified.

The media story is always the same: *The Arabs are indigenous. The Jews are settlers and colonialists.*

Which begs the question: What does the word *indigenous* actually mean?

The idea of being indigenous was originally used to protect the rights of authentic peoples such as the First Nations in Canada and the Aborigines in Australia, and the term was subsequently extended to tribes in North and South America.

At that point in time, the Jewish people's deep-rooted connection to the Land of Israel was accepted as fact by people all over the world. It is only very recently on the stage of history that among certain circles the Jewish people are accused of being "settlers" and "colonialists."

To say that the Jews are *not* indigenous to the Middle East is an idea that defies history, archaeology, and common sense.

In fact, even as recently as one hundred years ago, the notion that the Jewish people had an ancient indigenous connection to the Land of Israel was formalized by the British mandate and the League of Nations. The Balfour Declaration gave way to the League of Nations' issuance of a Mandate for Palestine. The Mandate recognized the historical connection of the Jewish people with Palestine and established grounds for *reconstituting* a national home for the Jewish people in that country.

The very word *reconstitute* was used deliberately to state that the Jewish people would be *returning* to reestablish themselves in a historic homeland, a land that they once inhabited before being forcefully exiled two thousand years before.

The Office of the High Commissioner for Human Rights, the United Nations entity mandated to promote and protect all human rights for all people, has acknowledged that there is no singularly authoritative definition of "indigenous peoples" under international law and policy, therefore leaving the idea open to interpretation and abuse. The 2007 United Nations Declaration of the Rights of Indigenous Peoples again attempted to define this, but due to internal dissension and a lack of agreement on what it means to be indigenous, the declaration never became legally binding.

One point of disagreement is in regard to the term *nondominance*. As explained by Ryan Belrose, a Canadian Metis, one of the original indigenous peoples in Canada's three prairie provinces, the idea of being "nondominant" as a requirement for being indigenous meant that you had yet to realize self-determination. Therefore, if an indigenous group, such as the Jewish people or the people of Fiji, achieves self-determination, it will no longer be considered indigenous. He then further explained that the goal of all indigenous peoples is to achieve self-determination on their ancestral lands.

Therefore, the non-dominance clause is a kind of catch-22.

It is Ryan Belrose's belief—and that of other indigenous advocates— that the idea of nondomination was specifically fostered by the United Nations to deny indigeneity to the only native people who have actually achieved full self-determination on their ancestral lands: the Jewish people.

Despite the lack of an internationally accepted legal definition, there are generally three factors that may determine if a people are indigenous to a certain area.

The first is a common sense of history: There are few people in the world who have such a historical awareness of their connection to a single land. For over three thousand years, the Jewish people have always faced Jerusalem during prayer. This is in contrast to Muslims, who face Mecca, not Jerusalem.

The Passover story, which details the Israelites' exodus from Egyptian slavery and their subsequent travels through the desert until they reached the Land of Israel, is the iconic story of the Jewish religion, and is mentioned over seventy times in the Bible.

While the word *Jerusalem* never appears in the Quran, it is cited in the Jewish Bible 669 times.

Every bride and groom break a glass in memory of the destruction of the Temple in Jerusalem.

Any Jewish person that has even the most basic knowledge of Judaism cannot but help to be familiar with the central role Jerusalem and the Land of Israel play in Jewish customs, traditions, and belief.

In fact, until recently, this was an accepted fact in Islam, too. Dozens of early Muslim sources consistently reaffirm the biblical description of King David and King Solomon's connection to the Temple Mount.

In just one of many examples, Ibn Khaldun, one of the most important Islamic philosophers and historians of the Middle Ages, often quotes Jewish sources in his writings, including the Torah and the Books of the Prophets. He describes in detail God's command to the Children of Israel to build a Temple and goes on to describe how King Solomon built the First Temple in Jerusalem.[16]

Until recently, even the Islamic Waqf on the Temple Mount affirmed the Jewish connection to Jerusalem and the Temple. *The Waqf Guide to the Temple Mount*, published in 1930, states explicitly, regarding the Dome of the Rock, "Its identity with the site of Solomon's Temple is beyond dispute."

Given the Waqf's rampant denial of Jewish history in the modern era, this guide would come back to haunt them years later.

I first saw the guide in the early 2000s and added it to my lectures. The hypocrisy of the current Waqf is clear. In recent years numerous copies have been bought on eBay, causing the price of the 1930 book to go from $30 to over $800, and copies of the book have been reprinted and distributed widely.

The second factor is genealogy: As a small group of people who have often married within the group, the Jewish people form one of the most important study groups for DNA evidence today. A comprehensive DNA study published in *Nature* magazine by a group of more than twenty medical researchers from Yale, Columbia, the Albert Einstein College of Medicine, Memorial Sloan Kettering, Hebrew University, and other institutions confirmed that Ashkenazi Jews are genetically admixed with origins both in Europe and the Middle East.[17]

Genetic studies of both the Ashkenazi, Sephardi, and Mizrahi Jewish populations in the Diaspora show significant amounts of shared Middle Eastern history. In research published by the National Academy of Sciences, genetic studies showed that contemporary Jewish communities can trace their roots to a common Middle Eastern source population several thousand years ago. The study showed that this ancient source population, from which modern Jews descend, shared distinct paternal and maternal lineages.[18] Despite the wandering of the Jewish people throughout the Diaspora over the millenia, they have maintained their unique genetic lineage going back to the Middle East.

Therefore, while some Ashkenazi Jews may look less like what we think of as Middle Eastern due perhaps to centuries of mixing with European converts, they share undeniably strong DNA links to the Middle East.

The third, and perhaps most compelling factor of what a country or culture needs to be indigenous is the archaeological record: Archaeologists always attempt to eschew politics and religion, but the City of David discoveries and others that are being made in Jerusalem and throughout the entire Land of Israel every day clearly point to evidence that Jewish people were living there going back at least three thousand years.

While other people may make an indigenous claim to Israel, their archaeological record goes back no more than a few centuries at most.

The fact remains: *There are few, if any, people in the world who have maintained their religion, language, and customs over millennia and are as deeply connected to their land as the Jewish people are to the Land of Israel.*

Ironically, the indigeneity argument was initially launched in Israel during the 1990s in an attempt to establish Bedouin land ownership in the Negev. During the proceedings they claimed to have resided in the area for six hundred years. This claim is not accepted by most scholars, who view the Bedouin as the descendants of nomadic tribes located in the Arabian Peninsula, in what is today the area of Saudi Arabia, Qatar, and Bahrain.

Unlike the experience of the First Peoples of Canada and the Aborigines of Australia, there are no independent Bedouin writings or narratives that indicate their origins or that establish a historical connection to the area of Israel. The claim that they are indigenous is unsupported by evidence.[19]

But somehow the indigenous claim by the Bedouin spread into Palestinian Arab society as well, and soon it was adopted by

Palestinian leaders across the spectrum. A document published in 2007 titled, "The Future Vision of the Palestine Arabs in Israel" stated: "We are the Palestinian Arabs in Israel, the indigenous peoples, the residents of the states of Israel, an integral part of the Palestine people, and the Arab and Muslim and human nation." The document stated that the Palestinian Arabs are the only long-resident population, that they had rights over the land, and that the Jews were recent "foreign conquerors."[20]

Between the two world wars, as Ottoman influence diminished in the region, a number of new national movements began to spring up in the Middle East.

As opposed to the Zionist movement, which emerged at the end of the nineteenth century as an outgrowth of a genuine history spanning four millennia, most other movements, formed only recently from disparate tribes or previously warring familial clans, lacked a shared history. A flag and national anthem are only as good as the shared history and identity that a group of people feel and experience together.

This led to a fascinating phenomenon: Numerous peoples in the Middle East began to look back into antiquity, at the ancient nations of the world with their rich histories and lore, and to claim these as their own.

The Turks claimed the Hittite civilization, Iraqis took on the claim of being the ancient Mesopotamians, the Muslims in Egypt claimed the pharaohs of old, and the Arabs living in British Palestine reached back into the history of the Philistines, a people that had disappeared from the pages of history 2,700 years earlier.[21]

Then, following the massive Arab defeat in the Six Day War in 1967, and its parallel to the Israelite King David's victory over the Philistines in the Bible, the Palestinians changed their historical claim once again, now claiming to have descended from the ancient Canaanites.

Again, there is no historical, genealogical, or archaeological basis for this claim. The historian Bernard Lewis explains that the movement, which became known as "Canaanism," was an attempt by the Palestinians to claim a lineage that predates that of the Jews.[22]

If both the Canaanites and the Philistines disappeared from history long ago, this brings us to the question, *"What is Palestine?"*

Actually, the question should be phrased, *"What is Palestina?"*

After the destruction of the Temple in 70 CE, the Romans wanted to send a warning to anyone else in their empire who might consider rising in revolt, so they set out to sever the connection between the Jewish people and Judea. The Romans rededicated Jerusalem to their god Jupiter, crucified thousands of Jews stretching from Jerusalem for miles around, and exiled tens of thousands of Jews, selling many into slavery.

Despite these acts, the Jewish people refused to forget. Just sixty years later, in 132 CE, when the Roman emperor Hadrian forbade the Jews from circumcising their children, the Jews rose in revolt once again to reclaim their independence and to redeem Jerusalem.

In what would come to be known as the Bar Kokhba Revolt, the Jews fought hard and to the death. Rome needed to call in auxiliary legions, but in the end, they defeated the Jews a second time. Following the Bar Kokhba Revolt, Hadrian realized that wherever Jews lived, they would always seek to return home to "Judea," the region that bore their name.

Determined like many others before him to destroy this connection once and for all, Hadrian decided to erase the name "Judea" and replace it instead with "Syria Palestina"—or, simply, "Palestine," as it is known in our day—in a direct reference to the ancient Biblical enemy of the Jews, the Philistines.[23]

By the time Hadrian renamed the area "Palestina," the Philistines had already been extinct for over seven hundred years.[24]

Having originated primarily in the Aegean region, the Philistines came to the shores of Israel in approximately 1200 BCE to capture and settle the land. The story of Samson and Delilah is one of many examples where the animosity between the Israelites and the encroaching Philistines is described in detail in the Bible. Armed with superior weapons and chariots, the Philistines fought and at times subjugated the Israelites over a period of hundreds of years, until the Israelites finally rallied and defeated them in the seventh century BCE.

The remaining Philistines ultimately assimilated into the Babylonians and disappeared from recorded history.[25]

The name was brilliant revenge. By renaming the territory "Palestina," Hadrian was killing two birds with one stone: He would erase the name "Judea," severing the hope of the Jews to return to a homeland that bore their name, and at the same time he would pour salt on the wound by replacing the name with that of an enemy Israel had defeated centuries earlier.

In effect, Hadrian resurrected the memory of the Philistines from the dead and gave them a posthumous victory.

Over the past two thousand years, "Palestine" has been used as a geographic term for the land south of Syria, never signifying a government or independent nation. This held true even through the entire 900-year period of Muslim rule after they recaptured the region from the Crusaders in 1187. As the *Encyclopedia Britannica* notes:

After the Crusades the name remained in informal use as a geographic designation, but it had no official status until after World War I and the end of rule by the Ottoman Empire, when it was adopted for one of the regions mandated to Great Britain.[26]

Prior to Ottoman rule, the geographic area of Palestine had been conquered numerous times by different invading armies. One thing that all the conquering armies had in common was that none of them established an independent nation in the area of "Palestine"—nor did Jerusalem ever serve as a capital of any country, as it had under the Jews.

This was also the case with the rise of Islam in the seventh century CE.

The word *Palestine* never appears in the Quran, the central book of faith for all Muslims—not even once.

Neither does the word *Jerusalem*.

Furthermore, numerous accounts of travelers over the centuries describe the area under Muslim rule as a neglected backwater province of the Ottoman Empire, used for harvesting trees and for collecting taxes from the local residents or from pilgrims who came to visit either the Western Wall or the Dome of the Rock.

The best-known of these travelers is Samuel Clemens, known by his pen name Mark Twain. In *Innocents Abroad*, the memoir of his travels throughout the Middle East, Twain describes the Land of Israel under Ottoman Rule in 1864 as a "blistering, naked, treeless land." As he describes, "There was hardly a tree or a shrub anywhere. Even the olive and the cactus, those fast friends of the worthless soil, had almost deserted the country."[27]

Palestinians often challenge Mark Twain's words; however, he is far from alone in his description. There are dozens of descriptions of the area from the 1700s and 1800s and they all echo Twain's observations.[28] William McClure Thomson, an American Protestant missionary who worked in Ottoman Syria in the early 1800s, used these words to describe the land: "How melancholy is this utter desolation! Not a house, not a trace of its inhabitants, not even shepherds, seen everywhere else, appear to relieve the dull monotony." Fredrik Hasselquist, a Swedish doctor and naturalist, describes the land during his visit in the 1750s as "uncultivated and almost uninhabited."

Felix Bovet, a Christian theologian and professor of French literature and Hebrew, visited the Holy Land in 1858. According to him the Turks "have made a desert of it where it is scarcely possible to walk without fear. Even the Arabs who dwell there do so as temporary sojourners."

After the fall of the Ottoman Empire in World War I, the British did not want to grant citizenship to the former Ottoman subjects, and so they made them "Palestinian" citizens. At that point, the term referred to all people equally living in the province, whether they were Jewish, Christian, or Muslim.

My own mother-in-law, born in Haifa in 1941, has a Palestinian birth certificate.

At first, the Arabs strongly objected to being identified as "Palestinians." As Princeton Professor Bernard Lewis wrote, the Arabs saw the name "Palestinian" as a British imperialist device, with Zionist collusion, to slice off a part of the greater Arab homeland.[29]

At that point in time, the Arabs in Palestine envisioned being a part of "Southern Syria"—an extension of a powerful Greater Syria that would be led by King Faisal, which they believed would be established after Faisal supported the British against the Ottomans in World War I. In February 1919, the Muslim-Christian Association went so far as to declare the area to be "nothing but part of Arab Syria and it has never been separated from it at any stage."[30]

But when France deposed King Faisal in 1920, all plans for a Greater Syria ended. It was only then that some of the Arabs living in British Mandate Palestine began to adopt a new identity: "Palestinians."[31]

Many Arabs would adamantly refuse to identify with the term for decades to come, such as Awni Abd al-Hadi, who was born in Nablus in Ottoman Palestine. In 1937, al-Hadi, who was the secretary general of the Arab Higher Committee in British Mandatory Palestine, appeared before the Peel Commission and stated, "There is no such country [as Palestine]! Palestine is a term the Zionists invented! Our country was for centuries, part of Syria." [32]

Perhaps most revealing that the choice to identify as "Palestinians" was one of expedience for some Arabs, and not part of a rich Islamic tradition, is that the very word *Palestinian* is of Latin origin, the language of Emperor Hadrian, and it cannot be pronounced in Arabic, which lacks the consonant *P*.

For this reason, one often hears native Arabic speakers referring to "Palestine" as "Balestine."

While the Arab peoples have been living in the Middle East for thousands of years and have a rich heritage and history, any claim of Arab Palestinian identity before the end of the nineteenth and beginning of the twentieth centuries is pure fiction.

We have shown that Palestine existed as a geographic area, and never as a country. We have also seen that the Arabs living in the Middle East today have no direct connection to the Philistine people who became extinct 2,700 years ago. Nevertheless, there are today millions of Arabs who claim to be Palestinian refugees and claim an entitlement to the fabled country of Palestine.

Throughout the late 1800s and early 1900s Jews from around the world pooled their money to purchase tracts of land from Muslim landowners. All of these purchases were recorded in Ottoman records.

Gradually, Jewish families moved to these legally purchased lands, built homes, and established communities. In 1947 the United Nations proposed the UN Partition Plan for Palestine, which divided the land into two states, one for Arabs and one for Jews, with the areas of Jerusalem and Bethlehem to be internationalized. The Jews reluctantly accepted this plan although it provided far less than they had been promised in the 1917 Balfour Declaration and the 1920 San Remo Conference. The Arabs living in Palestine, along with the rest of the Arab world, however, flatly rejected the plan and stated that they would refuse the establishment of a Jewish state in any part of Palestine.[33]

The Arab League countries publicly announced that they would reclaim all the territory for the Arabs. The head of the Arab League, Azzam Pasha, told the British diplomat Sir Alec Seath Kirkbride, "We will sweep them [the Jews] into the sea."[34]

Seven Arab armies attacked Israel in May 1948, bent on its destruction. And when Israel survived, it expanded its borders to include parts of the captured areas. Many Arabs fled Palestine both before and during this war. While the reasons for their flight are the source of debate, many of those who fled did so convinced that the Arab countries would be victorious, and they would return to their homes.

In March 1976, Mahmoud Abbas stated in an article in *Falastin al-Thawra*, the official journal of the PLO in Beirut:

The Arab armies entered Palestine to protect the Palestinians from the Zionist tyranny, but instead they abandoned them, forced them to emigrate and to leave their homeland, imposed upon them a political and ideological blockade and threw them into prisons similar to the ghettos in which the Jews used to live in Eastern Europe.

Similar statements were made by the Syrian prime minister from 1948 to 1949, Khaled al-Azm, who wrote in his memoirs:

Since 1948, it is we who have demanded the return of the refugees, while it is we who made them leave. We brought disaster upon a million Arab refugees by inviting them and bringing pressure on them to leave. We have accustomed them to begging.... We have participated in lowering their morale and social level.... Then we exploited them in executing crimes of murder, arson and throwing stones upon men, women and children... all this in the service of political purposes."[35]

After Israel's victory, the approximately 650,000 Arabs who had fled were not allowed to return to the country as citizens.[36] Those Arabs who stayed became Israeli Arab citizens of the State of Israel, and their descendants remain citizens to this day, making up over 20 percent of Israel's population.[37]

During this time 850,000 Jews were also exiled from the Arab countries within which they had lived for hundreds and in some cases thousands of years, going back to pre-Islamic times. The countries that exiled most of their Jewish populations included but were not limited to Egypt, Jordan, Syria, Iraq, Iran, Morocco, Libya, and Tunisia. Approximately 650,000 of these Jews settled in Israel, doubling the small country's population.[38]

At the same time, not one of the twenty-two Arab countries allowed Palestinian refugees, of roughly equal numbers, to settle in their lands, effectively consigning them to becoming permanent refugees.

In 1967, once again, the Arab countries surrounding Israel told the local Arabs, along with the refugees, that this time they would attack and succeed in crushing Israel. While Arab armies massed on Israel's borders and drove tanks through their cities calling for the imminent destruction of Israel, the State of Israel did everything within its power to campaign to the international community to intervene and stop the war before it began.

The Arabs carried through with their promise: They blocked Israeli ships in the Straits of Tiran, a *casus belli* under international law; they expelled United Nations observers from the demilitarized Sinai Peninsula in contravention of the 1948 ceasefire agreement; and they proceeded to launch an all-out war on Israel.

Israel defended itself, launching a critical pre-emptive strike on Egypt's air force and battling to defend its borders, which were only nine miles wide in certain areas. On the second day of the war, believing Egyptian and Syrian lies about first-day conquests, Jordan ignored Israeli pleas and launched an attack against Israel from the West Bank of the Jordan River and from Jerusalem.

In six days, Israel fought back and not only survived but went on to defeat the Arab armies that had attacked. At the end of the six days, the area under Israeli security control had expanded significantly and now included the Golan Heights, the areas west of the Jordan River that had been under illegal Jordan occupation, and the Sinai Peninsula. Israel established itself in this territory, and although it did not grant citizenship to the local Arabs, it permitted them to stay despite their former allegiance to an attacking army.

These local Arabs from 1967, along with the refugees from the 1948 War of Independence, and their descendants, are the people who today are referred to as "Palestinian refugees."[39] Many of these people today claim refugee status despite their being the third or fourth generation since one of their relatives either fled or were displaced. Of all refugees in the world, the only group that are still considered to be refugees in the third or fourth generation are the Palestinians.[40] This classification process is inconsistent with how all other refugees in the world are classified, including the definition used by the United Nations High Commissioner for Refugees (UNHCR) and the laws concerning refugees in the United States. Younger generations would not be considered refugees if they were part of any other group.

The dealings between Jews and Muslims, the oldest of brothers, have always been complicated. But in an elliptical passage in Genesis, the Bible suggests that even Isaac and Ishmael may have reconciled after their father died. The passage reads:

> And Abraham breathed his last, dying at a good ripe age, old and contented; and he was gathered to his kin. His sons Isaac and Ishmael buried him in the cave of Machpelah...[41]

After the Mughrabi Gate incident and despite Raed Salah's arrest, tensions in the area remained high. The Arab workers never returned to the Pilgrimage Road excavations, and we had hired new crews who were making slow but steady progress. It was at this time that I had a University of Pennsylvania intern working for me named Ben. Ben was a good kid and worked hard. In return for his service, I asked Davidleh if he and his wife Michal would be kind enough to host Ben in their home for a festive Friday-night Shabbat meal in the City of David.

What I didn't know, and only found out later, was that on that very Shabbat, Davidleh had received an invitation to the wedding of one of the local Arab families living in the City of David. This wasn't as rare an experience as some would think. Behind the television cameras and the obsessive reporters looking for blood and intrigue, the City of David was a place where people lived in very close quarters. In the vast majority of instances, the Jews and Arabs are respectful acquaintances and, in many cases, friends. Given that Davidleh was known by the local Arabs as a war hero, they afforded him the respect that a person of strength receives in the Arabic world. They coined him the Jewish "*mukhtar*" (the "chosen" village leader in Arabic), and his presence at a wedding was considered an honor to the families.

In those days, Davidleh made it a point to at least drop in for a few minutes and congratulate the bride and groom.

Since Muslim weddings were often held on Friday nights in the family's home in the City of David, Davidleh would often pray his Shabbat prayers at the Western Wall and then walk to the wedding and offer his congratulations before heading to his home for Shabbat dinner.

On the Friday night of Ben's visit, Davidleh and Yehuda Mali took Ben to pray with them at the Western Wall, and the three of them stopped by the wedding on their way home. Davidleh entered the house first, followed by Yehuda and Ben, and then they went to congratulate the bride and groom along with their families.

Around this time, some of the wedding guests noticed an unfamiliar Arab man enter the home after Davidleh and slowly approach Davidleh from behind. Around three feet away from Davidleh, the man drew a twelve-inch butcher knife out of his coat and raised it, ready to stab Davidleh from behind.

Seeing what was about to happen, Wahil, one of the Arab workers who had braved the Muslim Brotherhood and still worked in the City of David, pushed Davidleh out of the way, saving his life, and wrestled the man to the ground. The guests detained the intruder and held him until the police arrived at the scene.

Meanwhile, Davidleh, Yehuda, and Ben were escorted to Davidleh's house by family members of the bride and groom, who were humiliated and furious over what had happened.

When Davidleh entered his own home, he met operatives from the Shin Bet, Israel's Internal Security Service. Along with a very nervous Michal, Davidleh's wife, they had been waiting for him for over an hour. They informed him that they had received an intelligence tip that a terrorist was planning a hit on Davidleh that evening, but they did not know the location. They had gone to search for him at the Western Wall, however, because it was Shabbat, and because Davidleh doesn't carry a phone with him, they had been unable to locate him. They had been searching the neighborhood and posted officers at his house.

Later it was learned that the terrorist had followed Davidleh from the exit of the Western Wall, but just as he was about to attack, Davidleh suddenly veered off his normal route home and headed toward the Arab home for the wedding.

That wedding invitation probably saved his life, along with the lives of Yehuda Maly and Ben.

Ben, who came for a semester to study in Israel and intern at the City of David, had gotten more than he had bargained for.

Although it was probably only because of their invitation that Davidleh was still alive, the families of the bride and groom were deeply ashamed. A fundamental standard of Islam had been broken: the requirement to guard and give sanctuary to a friend within your home. Davidleh had been invited and was therefore under their protection.

The next week, Davidleh received a formal invitation to a *sulha*, a Muslim forgiveness ceremony. Twelve elders from the local Arab community came to his home, dressed in white robes, and begged his forgiveness for failing to guarantee his safety.

Davidleh was moved by the ceremony and, of course, granted his forgiveness.

A few days later, Davidleh was told by local villagers that the house of the terrorist had been destroyed in Hebron—not by the IDF, but rather by Muslims in the city who were protecting the honor of the family.

Now I am aware that this story flies in the face of the way that the press relates to the Jewish–Arab relationships in our area. In fact, it flies so far in the face of that narrative that it may seem like the stuff of fiction.

However, it is true.

This is especially hard to fathom when we consider that just a few months before, cars had been burning in the streets of the City of David, and the workers had been forced to leave their jobs by extremists, abetted by some of the locals.

And some of those who burned the cars and intimidated the workers were the children of the same elders who asked Davidleh for forgiveness.

A few months later, the Shin Bet once again notified Davidleh that, based on intelligence, they had successfully thwarted another assassination attempt, this time originating from Gaza. In April 2007, Matsa'ab Bashir, a worker with the anti-Israel organization Doctors Without Borders, had been recruited by the Popular Front for the Liberation of Palestine, a terror group closely aligned with Hamas. Using his position as a health worker, Bashir entered Israel with the intent to target Prime Minister Ehud Olmert. After failing to get close enough to Olmert, he redirected his plan toward Davidleh, but thanks to timely intelligence, the Shin Bet apprehended him before he could reach his target in Jerusalem. Although a previous assassination attempt involving local Arabs in the City of David had led to a form of "reconciliation," this latest plot was a sobering reminder that the threats to Davidleh's life were far from over.

In so many ways, the biblical story of Isaac and Ishmael sheds insight into the complicated interactions of contemporary Arabs and Jews. The Book of Genesis relates that when Sarah saw Ishmael taunting his younger brother, Isaac, she insisted that Abraham banish Ishamel and Hagar, his mother, and Abraham begrudgingly acquiesced. That story is often used to claim that the descendants of Ishamel and the descendants of Isaac can never get along.

But then there is that elliptical passage that perhaps suggests that after many years of enmity, the two brothers reunited to bury their father, in the Tomb of the Patriarchs in Hebron.

Beneath the pride, the anger, and the emotions on both sides of the Arab-Israeli conflict, there lies an ancient and indelible familial bond. This is as true now as it was then.

Jerusalem is a complicated place, and the dealings between Jews and Muslims, the oldest of brothers, even more so.

Part Three

THE BATTLE FOR THE CITY OF DAVID GOES GLOBAL

Chapter 9

The Supreme Court, Wikileaks, and *60 Minutes*

In 2008, the opposition changed tactics, opening a new front against the City of David. A group of local Arabs who were associated with the opposition movements in the area brought a series of legal cases to the Supreme Court of the State of Israel.[1] The allegations were the same claims they had been making to the press for years, that the excavations at the City of David were damaging the foundations of their homes and causing cracks in their walls.

The difference was that now, these claims would be investigated.

Despite the lack of any clear evidence, the court placed an immediate injunction on the excavations. While it studied the veracity of the claims and the evidence to the contrary that were provided by the Israel Antiquities Authority and the National Parks Authority, the Drainage Channel that lay beneath the Pilgrimage Road and an excavation taking place under the Givati Parking Lot at the site were frozen in place.

Throughout the lengthy proceedings, the court was shown how the homes in question, like most of the homes in the City of David, were built during Jordan's occupation of Jerusalem between 1948 and 1967 following the war it had launched against Israel. Except for England, Iraq, and Pakistan, the rest of the international community of nations considered Jordan's occupation illegal.[2]

In an attempt to sway world opinion to accept that that their occupation of Jerusalem was a fait accompli and irreversible, Jordan had encouraged the construction of hundreds of homes in and around the Old City. Many of them were in the area surrounding the City of David, a sloped mountainous terrain and located only twenty miles from the largest earthquake zone in the world, the Syrian African Rift.

Scientists explained that it was only a matter of time before the hilly topography of Jerusalem, along with the frequent geological tremors of the area, caused cracks to appear in the walls of any homes with no foundations. The cracks do not discriminate if Jews or Arabs are living in the homes, and they had been a fact of life in Jerusalem for decades before our excavations began.

The litigants who brought the claims against us were now claiming that the cracks were happening *because* of the City of David excavations.

The Israel Antiquities Authority explained to the court that they had taken the foundations into account from the beginning. Engineers described the system, which used steel supports to reinforce the ground above as the archaeologists uncovered the ancient city below. The supports rested on the bedrock and could support a multi-floored building that would weigh much more than the single- or two-floor homes above.

A clear case was made that, in fact, the homes located near the excavations now had steel supports, as they should have had when they were originally constructed. The homes of the litigants and the other residents were more structurally sound than were any other homes in the area.

Once the case was brought, the National Parks Authority and the Israel Antiquities Authority promptly requested to inspect any alleged damage. They assured that if even minimal evidence showed the damage was caused by the excavation, it would be fully addressed at no cost to the residents.

The City of David and Temple Mount, circa 1910–1920 *(Library of Congress, G. Eric and Edith Matson photograph collection)*

Yemenite Jewish village in Silwan, 1900–1920 *(Library of Congress, G. Eric and Edith Matson photograph collection)*

From above: the City of David and the Temple Mount *(Copterpix, City of David archives)*

Artistic reconstruction of the ancient City of David *(City of David archives, with permission from the Yigal Shiloh Archeological Delegation; artist: Lloyd Townsend)*

The Gihon Spring: the original water source of ancient Jerusalem *(Eliyahu Yanai, City of David archives)*

Captain Charles Warren *(Carbon print portrait by Herbert Rose Barraud of London, 1890)*

Warren's Shaft, named for Captain rles Warren, who covered it in 1867 *(Max Richardson, ?05, City of David archives)*

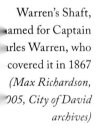

The Siloam Inscription: one of the oldest ancient Hebrew inscriptions ever discovered, detailing the biblical account of Hezekiah's tunnel construction—a remarkable engineering feat in eighth-century BCE Jerusalem *(Zev Radovan)*

The team that crawled through the upper channel: Davidleh Beeri, Doron Spielman, Eli Alony, and Yehuda Maly *(Gil Mezuman, City of David archives)*

Charles Warren's assistant, Corporal Henry Birtles, under the diamond-shaped stones that fell from the Temple Mount *(Drawing by W. Simpson, Palestine Exploration Fund, 1867)*

New York Times, 1911 cover, reports on the Parker expedition's search for the Ark of the Covenant beneath the Temple Mount *(New York Times archives)*

Field Valuation Sheet.

Urban Area : Jerus. Block No. 30125

Quarter : Silwan ? Parcel No. 54

Street : Previous Parcel No.

OPP. 3107—1000 Bks.—30-6-36 C

Name of reputed owner :	Shares	Address	T. P. R. No.	
			Vol.	Foll.
Baron De Rothschild		P. I. C. A	59	97

LAND.

Year	Description	Area Sq. M.	Value per Sq. M.	Capital Value	Net Annual Value	REMARKS
1938/9		2785	0·040	111	7	

BUILDINGS.

Year	Serial No.	Floor	Rooms	Offices	Area M2.	Capital Value								Present use and Remarks
						Building M2		Building		Land		Total		
						L.P.	mils	L.P.	mils	L.P.	mils	L.P.	mils	

	Gross Annual Value L.P.	Loss % under Section 5 (2) L.P.	Net Annual Value L.P.
Assessment Committee : (Initials of Official Members and date).			
_____ Year: 19 __			7 /
_____ Year: 19 __			
_____ Year: 19 __			
Decision on objection : (Initials of Official Members and date).			
_____ Year: 19 __			
_____ Year: 19 __			
_____ Year: 19 __			
Decision on appeal : (Initials of Official Members and date).			
_____ Year: 19 __			
_____ Year: 19 __			
_____ Year: 19			

British property registration documenting Baron Rothchild's land ownership in the City of David in 1939 *(City of David archives)*

Graves desecrated on the Mount of Olives during the Jordanian occupation of Jerusalem (1948–1967) *(Koby Herati, City of David archives)*

Illegal Waqf excavations at Solomon's Stables, destroying ancient relics and erasing Jerusalem's history from the Temple Mount *(City of David archives)*

Aerial view of King David's Palace excavation, located just steps from the City of David offices *(Skyballoon, City of David archives, courtesy of Dr. Eilat Mazar)*

Discovered by Kathleen Kenyon in the 1960s, this protoaeolic capital—once adorning a royal structure—was later used by Dr. Eilat Mazar to help identify the location of King David's Palace in the City of David *(Zeev Radovan)*

2,600-year-old clay seal of Yehuchal ben Shelemiah, discovered in the City of David, bearing the name of a royal official mentioned in the Book of Jeremiah *(City of David archives, with permission from the Institute of Archaeology, the Hebrew University, courtesy of Dr. Eilat Mazar)*

Photograph of Dr. Eilat Mazar smiling during the 2005–2008 City of David excavations *(Professor Amihai Mazar, courtesy of the estate of Dr. Eilat Mazar)*

Uncovered in 2004, the ancient steps of the Pool of Siloam, where pilgrims once ascended to the Temple in Jerusalem *(Koby Herati, City of David archives)*

Eastern section of the Pilgrimage Road, where Roman forces broke through the steps, slaughtering Jewish refugees as they fled during the destruction of Jerusalem *(Vladimir Nihun, City of David archives)*

Ceramic cooking pots used by Jewish refugees hiding in the tunnel beneath the Pilgrimage Road; inside, scientists discovered traces of food, a silent testament to their struggle for surviva. *(Vladimir Nihun, City of David archives)*

The infamous meeting between Haj Amin al-Husseini, the grand mufti of Jerusalem and a key architect of Palestinian nationalism, with Adolf Hitler in Berlin on November 28, 1941 *(Bundesarchiv [Federal Archives, Germany])*

The original cover of Abbas' book

The original cover of PA President Mahmoud Abbas's 1982 PhD dissertation, *"The Other Side: The Secret Relationship between Nazism and Zionism,"* which alleged that the Zionists and Nazis collaborated during the Holocaust *(Dar Ibn Rushd, 1984)*

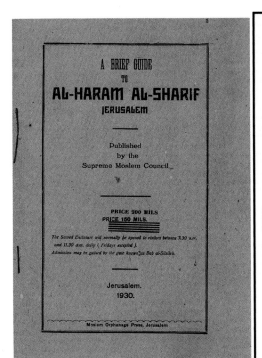

The Waqf guide to the Temple Mount from 1930 states that "its identity with the site of Solomon's Temple is beyond dispute" *(Supreme Moslem Council, Moslem Orphanage Press, Jerusalem 1930)*

The underground drainage channel beneath the Pilgrimage Road, originally used for water drainage during the Second Temple period and later as a refuge for Jewish residents fleeing the Roman destruction *(Koby Harati, City of David archives)*

Pilgrimage Road: the ancient route leading to the Temple Mount, where Jewish pilgrims once walked toward the heart of Jerusalem's holiest site *(Koby Harati, City of David archives)*

An artistic impression of the Pilgrimage Road overlaid on today's topography, illustrating t path as it once existed in ancient Jerusalem *(Shalor Kveller, City of David archives)*

Discovered during an MRI scan, the excavation beneath the Givati Parking Lot has uncovered archaeological evidence from eleven different civilizations *(Skyballoon, City of David archives)*

50 P 182

A golden bell from the High Priest's robes, discovered in the City of David's water drainage channel *(Vladimer Nihun, courtesy of Eli Shukrun)*

The cornerstone of the Temple Mount, where the Western Wall meets the Southern Wall along the bedrock of Mount Moriah *(Koby Harati, City of David archives)*

Fourth-year Prutah coin, minted in 70 CE by the last Jews fighting for the freedom of Zion during the Great Revolt against Rome *(City of David archives)*

Judea Capta coin, featuring Emperor Vespasian on the obverse and a Roman soldier standing over a weeping woman on the reverse, symbolizing the subjugation of Judea *(Classical Numismatic Group, Inc.)*

Silver Israel Liberata coin, depicting a man planting a tree on the right and a woman joyfully lifting a child on the left, symbolizing hope and resilience during the struggle for liberation from Roman rule *(Doron Spielman private collection)*

Margalit Zinati of Peqi'in village rests her hand on an eighteen-hundred-year-old limestone capital from the Roman period, inscribed with the names of the original donors to the synagogue *(Ritvo photography, courtesy of Beit Zinati)*

Davidleh Beeri, the modern-day pioneer who revitalized efforts to develop and excavate the ancient City of David *(David Ohayun, City of David archives)*

From right to left: Davidleh Beeri, Jerusalem mayor Nir Barkat, Eugene Shvidler, Yehuda Maly, and Doron Spielman *(Doron Spielman personal collection)*

Zeev Orenstein and Doron Spielman meet with Vice President Pence at the White House to present the latest discoveries from the City of David *(Official White House photo by Myles Cullen, Doron Spielman private collection)*

Not a single claimant answered this request.

In fact, none of them allowed engineers to visit their homes and examine the cracks.

They claimants were, however, eager to invite the press to see the cracks in their walls and to claim that "settlers were undermining their homes." Articles began to appear in both the Israeli press and international press with headlines such as ARCHAEOLOGICAL DIGS STOKE CONFLICT IN JERUSALEM and DIGGING TOO DEEP?[3] Additionally, the European Union and the United States State Department sent delegations of people to the area to hear their claims.

Engineers and lawyers were studying the issue as best they could without having access to the "damaged properties." It became immediately clear that a number of the homes that were supposedly damaged by the excavations were not located anywhere near the excavations at all. It was extremely unlikely that they could have been affected by work being done more than a block away.

Second, municipal records showed that a number of the claimants had appealed to the municipality to fix those cracks in their walls years before the excavation had even begun.

As soon as the case was opened in the court, any problems with any structures in the whole area were being blamed on the excavations. One case came from a UNWRA school located hundreds of feet from the excavation. UNRWA, the United Nations Relief and Works Agency, is known as a virulently anti-Israel organization that employed terrorists who were directly involved in the October 7, 2023, attack against Israel.[4] In February 2009, UNRWA claimed the excavations in the City of David caused the floor of the school to collapse underneath a classroom, causing a number of girls to fall and get hurt. Thankfully, none were seriously hurt. The school, which was nowhere near the excavations, had been built on the edge of a deep valley. Like so many of the other structures in the area, it had been built without supports, which had undoubtedly led to the floor collapse. The claim so glaringly lacked any scientific basis that at first I relegated it to the growing pile of baseless claims and PR rhetoric being pushed by the litigants and the activists supporting them.

But a week after the floor collapse at the school, I received a phone call from the United States consulate in Jerusalem asking if I would meet with one of their representatives at the City of David. In those days, the consulate was off limits to Israelis, and focused almost entirely on "Palestinian Affairs." The consulate was known to be staffed by career State Department employees who were critical of Israel's role in East Jerusalem.

After consulting with Davidleh, however, we agreed that it was better to share with them our side of the story and show them we had nothing to hide, even if we could not trust them to be objective.

A consulate employee in his mid-twenties who introduced himself as "Connor" came to visit me a few days later. At first, we engaged in small talk about the discoveries that had been made in the City of David. He told me he was a great fan and wanted to know all about the Pilgrimage Road discoveries. When I offered to take him to see it, he abruptly checked his watch and responded that he was pressed for time and hoped to come back a different day.

Minutes later, the conversation turned to why Connor had come that day. He told me the State Department was concerned because the workers of the UNWRA school claimed the floor had collapsed because of our excavations.

I took out an aerial map and spread it on the table in front of us. I pointed to where we were excavating and how the UNWRA school was nowhere in the area. There was no way the excavations could have caused the collapse of the school's floor. Connor nodded and smiled as if he understood my position. He then told me that he had heard from a number of Palestinians in the area who lived above the Pilgrimage Road excavation that their homes had been damaged by the work being done there.

Given the proximity of these homes to the dig, he asked insistently, was it not at all possible that our excavations could be affecting these homes?

I looked at Connor, who had just played his hand. He wasn't really there to hear our side of the story regarding the UNWRA school. That was just an excuse to attract the attention of his superiors for the real issue. What he and the "Palestinian Affairs" branch of the consulate were interested in was the upcoming Supreme Court decision. He was fishing for something—I just wasn't sure what yet.

Without going into any detail about the upcoming case, I offered again to show him the incredible engineering that had been developed and the great expense of creating such a solid underground structure that would not affect the area above ground.

With the same smile on his face, he told me that it was less about the engineering; rather what concerned the consulate was keeping the relations between the Palestinians and the Jews from escalating. Did I think, he asked, again pointedly, that the excavations were responsible for the tension in the area?

Looking at him, I asked him if he really wanted to improve the lives of the Palestinians in the area.

He nodded in the affirmative.

I pointed outside the window of the conference room at the Arab home next door. I asked him if he was aware what happened to any Palestinian Arab in the City of David if they wanted to sell their home to a Jew.

He reluctantly admitted that they would be pressured not to sell to Jews by Hamas or other entities.

"Pressured?" I asked him. "You mean they will be killed."

He looked at me in silence, the smile now forced. I went on. "The State Department *is* aware, I hope, that there is an official Fatwa, death warrant, issued against any Arab who sells their home to a Jew by Hamas." I reminded him that Hamas was on the United States' list of international terror organizations.

He acknowledged that he had read that in the papers, yes.

If the consulate was really interested in bettering the situation between Jews and Arabs, I told him that I thought they should start by immediately condemning what is a racist declaration and a gross violation of human rights. If Jews and Arabs can't even buy and sell homes next to each other, how are they to learn to live together in peace? Instead of addressing that, I told him, the consulate was wasting its time by listening to the baseless claims being made by UNRWA.

Connor's smile was long gone. As he got up to leave, somewhat quickly, he said that he would think about it and would get back to me.

After Connor left, I called Davidleh and updated him. I no longer had any doubt that the UNWRA school incident was just an excuse for the State Department to investigate our excavations at the City of David, and most likely they intended to stop any future excavations of the Pilgrimage Road. I told him that I was convinced that the timing of the State Department's sudden interest in what we were doing was directly connected to the upcoming Supreme Court decision on the Pilgrimage Road excavation.

If the State Department took an official position on the issue and issued a public statement, this would put pressure on the Israeli government, which could in turn influence the court's decision.

What was more important, they would have to decide: stopping an excavation or upsetting Israel's most important ally?

The official report would have to show that they had considered both sides of the issue and met with members of both sides. As an employee of Elad, the organization funding the City of David excavation, I was the member of the pro-excavation camp they would quote to put on the illusion that their conclusions were unbiased.

The opposition that had started with the Muslim Brotherhood and the radical advocacy groups now included the US State Department.

It didn't take long for our suspicions to be confirmed. Just a week later, in February 2009, I got a call from Michael Oren, who would later serve as Israel's ambassador to the United States, asking me to meet him at his office.

When we were sitting across from each other, Michael told me that Deputy Director Elliott Abrams of the State Department had contacted him regarding a series of memos written about an excavation under an UNWRA school, and about the Pilgrimage Road excavation. There were many sources quoted that opposed the excavation. I was the only source quoted in the pro-excavation camp.

Michael was informed by the deputy director that the memos had reached him for review, before they were passed on to Secretary of State Condoleezza Rice. In reading the claims, he felt that something was askew, and that it seemed to him to be one-sided and manipulative. If it were not countered, it would likely trigger a public response from the State Department.

The deputy director asked Michael to review the situation and write his version of it. Michael had called me to get the background.

I showed Michael maps of the area and pointed out where our excavations were taking place in reference to the UNWRA school. It didn't take Michael long to understand what was happening. He agreed with our assessment that the UNWRA school was just an excuse to get the State Department to condemn the excavations in a lead-up to the Supreme Court ruling.

He wrote a two-page memorandum outlining the situation,

addressing first the UNRWA claim by including the distances and the impossibility of the excavations causing damage to the school. Michael then discussed the site's historical significance to billions of people worldwide. He detailed the sensitivity of the archaeologists in excavating in an urban setting and the great investment in time and money to develop an engineering system that was providing structural support for the homes above and not weakening them. He concluded with an invitation for engineers and professionals to come and see the site firsthand.

We sent the memo to the deputy director, who sent it up the ladder to accompany the original report and over the next year, we never heard anything about the issue.

It would only be many years later, when a rogue CIA agent named Edward Snowden released classified State Department communications, that we learned the crisis that our memo had averted.

A Wikileaks report dated February 3, 2009, reported my conversation with Connor, who was simply called PolOff (Political Officer), along with other conversations he'd had in the area.

The report began with claims by unnamed residents of the area, who blamed our archaeological excavations for the UNWRA school collapse.

> In February 2 conversations with PolOff [Political Officer], residents criticized the settler organization Elad and the neighboring City of David archeological park, which they blamed for general infrastructure problems in their neighborhood. UNRWA Operations Support Officer Solange Fontana told PolOff February 2 that UNRWA is investigating.

Next, I was quoted as denying these accusations, and accusing UNRWA of being biased in favor of the Palestinians.

> Elad representative Doron Spielman told PolOff February 3 that excavations in the City of David archeological park are not being conducted near the UNRWA school and did not undermine the building. He said that Elad believes UNRWA is strongly biased in favor of the Palestinians and the results of the UNRWA investigation should be viewed in this light.

Finally, at the end of a slew of memos came the implied threat of what the Pilgrimage Road could ignite in the area. Ikrima Sabri, the radical Islamic cleric on the Temple Mount, was quoted as issuing a death threat for any Arab accused of colluding with the excavation.

> The head of the High Islamic Council in Jerusalem, Sheikh Ikrima Sabri, issued a fatwa [death threat] on September 17 calling for an end to the tunneling, which runs close to the al-Aqsa Mosque foundation. Sabri said fatwas had already been issued prohibiting Muslim families from accepting compensation for homes threatened with demolition or selling Palestinian-owned land to settlers.

It was a classic State Department "investigation" that would set the stage for an official condemnation of Israel, and to provide a basis for the State Department to demand that the Israeli government intervene to stop the excavations, lest we ignite dangerous tensions in the area.

The US condemnation never came. Looking back now, many years later, those involved agree that the memo we had sent up had apparently provided adequate evidence that these claims were unfounded, just in time to stop the condemnation before it could be announced.

We had narrowly averted what could have been a permanent blow to the excavation ever resuming.

During the same time that the State Department was weighing in on the excavations, the media, knowing that the Supreme Court decision was looming, intensified their campaign against us. During 2008 and 2009, film crews from European and American media outlets could be seen walking through the streets of the City of David on almost a daily basis. Like a movie set in which the actors did take after take, radical-advocacy group organizers and Arab activists involved in the court case posed for pictures and repeated the phrase, *"To dig a tunnel means to kill a village."*[5]

Dubious "legal experts" reinforced the narrative by using the fact that the Supreme Court was considering the case, as if that were de facto proof that there was legitimacy to the claims brought against us.

What the media never reported was that according to Israeli law, *anyone* can bring a claim to the Supreme Court for consideration.

This manipulation of the truth, aided by the media's willingness to accept it without challenge, created a David vs. Goliath narrative, in which the Arab residents were David and the City of David and its supposed collusion with the State of Israel was Goliath. As this narrative took hold, anyone following the news on Israel in the Western media saw the same story repeated time and again.

While those media crews were tromping from house to house above ground, below ground the Israel Antiquities Authority made an important clarification with the court regarding the water drainage channel, which ran beneath the Pilgrimage Road, where we had crawled, and where the last Jews of Jerusalem had tried to hide from the Romans until they were discovered. It was while crawling through that sewer that we originally saw the underside of the stairs of the road over our heads and the cooking vessels left behind from the families before they perished.

The drainage channel, they explained, had no impact on the ground above. It was buried beneath the road, similar to the way a pipe or culvert runs beneath our roads in the modern day. One could clean out the inside of the pipe without ever disturbing the ground above. Therefore, the drainage channel excavation should be allowed to proceed.

The clarification was studied by the court and accepted, and the IAA was given the green light to begin the process of cleaning out the narrow drainage channel that ran beneath the Pilgrimage Road.

With the court's approval, the excavators trudged beneath the beautiful flagstones of the Pilgrimage Road and returned to excavate the narrow and dark sewer below. Like underground workers in a fire brigade, the diggers began the arduous task of crouching single-file and passing bags of excavation dirt hand by hand till they reached the exit of the tunnel.

Eli Shukron and Ronny Reich mapped the tunnel's estimated route. It looked like an umbilical cord stretching from the Pool of Siloam at the bottom all the way up to the corner of the Temple Mount to the north. The excavation was about two thousand feet long. The tunnel did not require us to install building supports, which meant that it could move forward much faster than the road above. If we ran double shifts and came up with a faster method of removing the dirt, they thought it was possible the excavation could be completed in approximately three years.

The Pilgrimage Road, by contrast, was a complex urban-excavation project comparable to only a few others worldwide, such as the Metro C subway line excavation in Rome, which was more than twenty years behind schedule.[6] This excavation was expected to take many more years, potentially over a decade, to complete in its entirety.

We came to realize that while the tunnel would never accommodate large groups of tourists like the Road overhead, if we could finish it in three years, it could still provide something valuable.

It would prove the theory that the City of David and the Temple Mount were connected in ancient times, and it would create the irreversible facts-on-the-ground that they are connected once again, albeit through a sewer drain.

We had no idea then how vital this endeavor would be to the project.

In the years to come, when Israel would come under enormous international pressure to stop the excavations in the City of David, first by UNESCO and then by President Obama's administration, that two-thousand-year-old sewer would be the deciding factor.

In retrospect, had the coalition of radical advocacy groups *not* challenged us in the Supreme Court when it did—and had the court *not* suspended the excavation of the Pilgrimage Road and the other excavations, which resulted in our focusing on the drainage channel—it is possible that the City of David would not be connected to the Western Wall today.

There was one contingent to meeting Ronny and Eli's three-year timeline, and that was that we had to raise enough money to keep the excavation moving without stopping. After calculating the costs of funding around-the-clock IAA excavations—including all the material examination and testing they would need to do as discoveries were made along the way—it was clear that we were looking at millions of dollars. The seed funding to launch the excavation and have a window of six months to keep it going while we raised the rest of the funds was going to cost $1,040,000.

At that time the City of David had expanded tremendously and now included educational programs for soldiers and Israeli high-school pupils, the refurbishment of the ancient Jewish cemetery on the Mount of Olives, and a large tourism department, which offered tours throughout Jerusalem.

Following Eugene Shvidler's major investment in the project, other donors had joined the mix and we had grown tremendously. However, despite the growth, we did not have cash reserves to take on another project. One rule was kept in the organization by Da-vidleh: If we raised money, the money would need to be used on the project and not saved for a rainy day. As he often said to me, "The opportunity to uncover and protect Ancient Jerusalem is now. We cannot know what the future will bring."

Therefore, despite our growth, the donor funds had all been ear-marked and we were stretched to the seams.

With this in mind, Davidleh and I flew to the States in June 2008, to raise the money required to launch the excavation. When we arrived, however, we realized that news of the City of David had gotten there before us.

I had lined up a number of meetings with both existing donors, many of whom were already committed to projects, and a handful of new donors that had visited the site for the first time in recent months. From the airport, we dropped our bags at the hotel and went to our first meeting in midtown New York.

As we entered the office of a wealthy hedge-fund owner whom we had known for years, the first words out of his mouth were that he had seen us in the news a lot lately and that it didn't look good.

He wanted to know what the real story was with the Supreme Court. We explained that from all the research we had seen, the claim that the excavation was causing cracks in the homes above was not based on fact but rather was politically motivated. If we were wrong, and there was evidence to the contrary, the repairs would be made at no cost to the residents. Nevertheless, we explained, we had an immediate opportunity and needed funds to launch the new excavation of the drainage channel.

When we finished talking, he sat at his desk unmoving for a few minutes. He told us that he understood and that it made sense that this was just another attempt to stop the excavation by those who didn't want the historical proof of the Jewish people's connection to Jerusalem to come to light.

I breathed a sigh of relief. It was good to know that people were able to see through the PR assault against us. I snatched a quick look at Davidleh, and he was relieved as well.

Just then, the donor stood up and said he had to go to another meeting. As he walked us out, he said that he had committed himself to other projects that year and wasn't able to take on something new. He wished us luck.

Unfortunately, it was only downhill from there for the next series of meetings. In one meeting with a longtime donor, I asked if he would consider taking on an additional commitment. He had brought a friend to the meeting I hadn't met before. Both were finance guys on Wall Street. As I began explaining the project, the friend interrupted, turning to the donor and questioning how he could support this project. He then launched into the now-familiar tirade, accusing us of displacing Arabs and undermining their homes "to settle the entire area with Jews."

I told him that the excavation was being conducted to the highest engineering standards in the world and that it extended beneath numerous Jewish homes as well. Did he think we were trying to displace the Jews in the City of David, too?

He got up to leave but before walking out of the room, he turned to me and said, "All the problems in Israel are because of people like you."

Our donor was embarrassed by his colleague and reassured me that he believed in what we were doing. However, he said, he couldn't make an additional commitment.

Something was driving these donors to not support us, and we knew it was the controversy. From there, we split up and agreed to meet in Boston later that evening for our final meeting before heading back to Israel.

That was when I had the most unexpected meeting of all. It was with a significant donor who had supported our educational tours for school groups and new soldier recruits to learn about their roots in Jerusalem. She came to the meeting with her new philanthropy director, who had never been to the City of David before. After hearing about the excavation and our need for funding, the new philanthropy director informed me that the foundation had decided to focus on new areas and that the City of David was no longer part of the mission of the foundation. I was disappointed; however, I understood. Donors at times changed their focus, and the City of David couldn't be everything to everyone.

I asked about the area the foundation was going to focus on. The philanthropy director responded, saying the foundation had decided to focus on "Jewish identity."

I didn't understand.

I looked over at the donor, with a surprised and questioning look. I had known her for years. She and her husband had supported our educational programs precisely because they focused on Jewish identity for the young generation. What could be more connected to "Jewish identity" than the City of David? We were the ones who were literally digging up the very proof of our Jewish identity.

She finally leveled with me.

"Look Doron, we love you and we love the project; it's just that with all the great stuff that you guys do and all the archaeology that you uncover, the negative press that you are getting just makes it not worth it."

I tried to explain that there was an organized political campaign against us to try and keep the truth of the excavations from being uncovered. However, my words could not assuage their concerns.

As I left the office, I felt like someone had punched me in the stomach.

Davidleh joined me for the last meeting of our trip, with a husband and wife who owned a large adventure travel company. Alan and Harriet had visited the City of David a few months before as part of a whirlwind Israel tour. They had been raised as totally secular Jews and had virtually no knowledge of their Jewish roots. However, during their time in Israel, they were amazed at how vibrant and full of energy both the country and the people were. They did not know what the City of David was, but a mutual friend had told them if they were in Jerusalem, they should meet us.

During the tour Alan and Harriet were full of a jumpy, excited energy. They wanted to know where we were from, how Davidleh had risen through the ranks of the army to found the project, and how I had gotten there from Michigan to join him. But the archaeology didn't seem to interest them at all. They seemed to be interested only in the people. Everyone we met, every worker, the gardeners, the diggers, the security personnel—they had to know part of their life story. Before we knew it the tour was over, and they had to go. As they were heading into their car, they told us that they loved us, and that we should be in touch if we ever came to Boston. Yet, we weren't sure they would consider supporting a project they didn't seem to be interested in hearing about.

While we were in town, we reached out, and they were delighted to hear from us. Harriet was busy, but Alan invited us to meet him at a Boston dinner club where he was a member.

I tried explaining to Davidleh the concept of a "dinner club." I told him that we would likely be the only Jews there, and certainly the only people wearing yarmulkes. Additionally, I told him that the food would not be kosher, and so we agreed that we would nicely decline any food and just order a cup of coffee.

The dinner club did not disappoint. We were seated in a high-backed dark-blue leather booth. Heads of elk and other wild game hung from the walls above us. Alan came into the restaurant like a tidal wind and swooshed into our booth, saying in a loud voice, "Hey guys, you made it!" and then whispered in the ear of one of the waiters.

"We're going to have some appetizers," he said to me with a wink. I said we had just eaten and would just have coffee, but he seemed to hear only that we wanted coffee with our dinner and instructed the waiter to bring coffees as well. He asked us what brought us to Boston. Before I could answer, he interrupted me and said, "I see not everybody loves what you guys are doing."

The waiter came back with bowls of fresh pink shrimp and cock-tail sauce and set them down on the table, along with our two coffees. Shellfish is strictly forbidden for people who keep kosher. I felt bad that he had ordered so much food, but he clearly knew nothing about kosher laws.

He kept talking while eating shrimp. He had done his research, and I was beginning to sense a repeat of the other meetings. "The Muslim Brotherhood, the courts, wow," he said. "That's some serious stuff. So, what are you gonna do about these guys? They don't seem to want to let you keep digging."

Davidleh spoke for the first time. "Alan. I would like to share a story with you." Alan leaned forward to listen.

"When I was a special-forces soldier in the IDF, we were sent deep into the heart of a terrorist-filled city to carry out an operation under the cover of an entire battalion that had been sent to apprehend a senior terrorist. The battalion was just a decoy to clear out the streets, so that my three-person team and I could fulfill our mission, which to this day remains classified. The plan worked. My team did what we needed to do and radioed that we had completed our mission.

"By some miscommunication, the commander of the battalion thought we were already outside the city and ordered the battalion to withdraw immediately. That left me and my three soldiers alone in the heart of the city. As soon as the terrorists saw the soldiers withdraw, they entered the streets hooting and hollering, a sign of resistance. It didn't take long for the four of us to be noticed, and within seconds we were surrounded by hundreds of Arabs screaming at us. While we debated what to do, an Arab on the top of a building above them threw down a stone slab off the roof. I saw it just in time and moved one of my soldiers out of the way, saving his life.

"Realizing that whatever decision I made in the next few seconds would decide whether we lived or died, I told the three soldiers to do exactly as I did. I turned toward the Arabs, raised my machine gun, and while firing in the air, I ran straight into the mass of Arabs screaming at the top of my lungs. My three soldiers did the same.

"The Arab mob, collectively shocked at the response of this small group of crazy Israelis running toward them, stood aside. It was like the parting of the Red Sea."

Davidleh looked Alan in the eyes, his brown eyes lighting up his face. "Alan, today the City of David is surrounded by a mob that have all ganged up against us: the Muslim Brotherhood, the radical-advocacy groups, the media—they are trying to scare us so that we will stop the project. Not because we are breaking the law, or because we are damaging homes, but because they are afraid of what we are discovering beneath the ground: the proof that Jews have been here for thousands of years and that you cannot deny us our own land.

"They want us to succumb to fear, but, Alan, we will do the opposite. We will charge forward on our project and continue to make progress, and eventually, they will part before the City of David like the Red Sea."

Alan turned to look at me. "Doron, what are you guys looking for?"

I put my laptop on the table and showed him an aerial picture of the City of David. With the press of a button the spinelike route of the drainage channel snaked up the screen from the Pool of Siloam to the Western Wall. "The excavation is going to take around three years and will connect the City of David to the Western Wall. This is the lifeline of our project. We need $1,040,000 right now to get the team together and launch the excavation, while time is on our side."

Before I could say anything else, Alan cut me off and continued eating his shrimp.

"Okay, that's done. What else are you guys up to?"

There is a term in Yiddish called the *Pintele Yid*, which means the "Jewish spark." It is an ancient Jewish concept that buried deep inside each and every Jew, no matter how distant he or she is from their tradition, lies a spirit that can be activated on behalf of the Jewish people.

The concept of the "Jewish spark" has been brought down through the ages since the time that Moses and the Jewish people stood ready to enter the Land of Israel after forty long years of wandering in the desert. In one of his last acts before dying, Moses summoned the people and made a covenant binding them to God forever. Moses told the people that the covenant would bind not only them, but rather "all those standing with us here today, and those who are not here with us today."

From this passage, the sages derived that all Jews in every generation, every soul that would ever be born to the Jewish nation, were all standing together when Moses made that covenant. At various times, in certain circumstances, every Jew would be called, and it would be in their power to answer.

Alan answered that call. He said "done."

In October 2008, just four months after our Boston trip, global financial markets crashed. Millions of people lost their savings, including our donors, who lost millions and even billions of dollars in just a few hours. With Alan and Harriet's funds, the diggers began cleaning out the earth and ancient debris that had filled the drainage channel over the millennia.

At one point they reached stones that were roughly piled up, blocking the tunnel. As the stones were removed, they saw that on the other side of the pile, the walls were lined with a thick layer of dark gray soot. This was clear evidence of the fire the Romans had lit in the tunnel to try and asphyxiate the Jews hiding while the Temple burned in the city. In a last-minute effort, the Jewish survivors hastily erected a stone wall to try and block the smoke. In one area of the dark great soot someone had drawn vertical lines that looked like branches that led down diagonally to a base. While we cannot be sure, it looked like the branches of the menorah, the symbol of ancient Israel, possibly carved by a Jewish rebel fighter as a lasting symbol of resistance.

The job of removing the dirt and passing it back hand-to-hand over a distance of dozens of meters became strenuous and took a long time. But everything changed one day when Moishe Laor, one of the crew members with an engineering background, came up with an idea to erect a long track on the top of the tunnel with hooks attached to rollers. We could attach the bags to the hooks and send them along the track, down the tunnel to the exit.

They gave it a try, and suddenly a batch of twenty bags came careening down the tunnel to a crew at the bottom that offloaded them to be sifted. The system worked, and the excavation could now progress at a faster pace, in fact much faster than the archaeologists had originally predicted. In the early days of the rolling-bag system anyone walking up the tunnel knew that if they heard the noise of the bags rolling toward them, they had only a few seconds to duck before the bags came careening overhead.

As winter gave way to spring 2009, we were nearing the year mark since the Supreme Court had begun considering the claims against the Pilgrimage Road. They would likely hand out their verdict in the coming months.

As the date approached, Raed Salah intensified his *Al-Aqsa fi Khatar* ("al-Aqsa is in danger") campaign, which often resulted in his being arrested, charged, and then ordered not to enter Jerusalem for periods of up to thirty days. At some point he crossed a line that even the Europeans found unacceptable and insinuated that Jews were using the blood of non-Jewish children in the dough used for the Passover matza, an old anti-Semitic diatribe that had been used in medieval Europe during pogroms against Jewish communities.[7]

On September 21, 2009, the Supreme Court of Israel issued their ruling based on two petitions that had been filed against the excavations in the Givati Parking Lot and those of the Herodian Drainage Channel.[8]

Led by Justice Edna Arbel, the court outright rejected the claims made by the seven Arab families stating that they "the petitioners did not present any evidence to establish the connection between the excavations and the damage allegedly caused to their homes." The petitioners were fined the court costs for having filed what the court decreed was a baseless set of claims.

After deliberating and studying the evidence over the course of a year, the Supreme Court dealt a major blow to the groups that had paraded around with countless journalists and European and American "observers" to see what they claimed were results of the dig. Despite this, those groups would continue to push this narrative to the international community, simply obfuscating the court ruling in any interviews they gave.

While we celebrated that the court's decision verified what we already knew about the structural integrity of the excavations, the most important part of the decision came in what the court wrote about the importance of the excavations. In a rare departure from the dry language used in legal rulings, the court praised the importance of the excavations in the City of David to the Jewish people and to non-Jews as well:[9]

The hill of the City of David has been telling the history of Jerusalem for thousands of years, as we can learn more about them from the Bible and other sources. The importance of exposing the secrets of the City of David is national and international. It is not unique to the Jewish people, but it is important to anyone who wishes to trace the history of this region, which is the cradle of monotheistic religions. The importance of archaeological research is not limited only to understanding the past of the land and the possibility of examining the veracity of the details known to us from other sources about it, but rather it sheds light on the development of human culture. As such, its importance transcends nations and borders.

The court concluded its opinion by stating that the increased interest in the excavations at the site would open up the area to government investments in infrastructure that would benefit the local Arab residents as well.

The Supreme Court decision was for us like a twelfth-round knock-out by an underdog boxer.

Not only did the Supreme Court declare that the charges against the excavations of the City of David were flawed, but also it recognized that, due to the engineering methods employed, the excavations themselves actually created greater foundational support for the homes.

And the Supreme Court went further. The decision spoke to the heart of the City of David, to the heart of what we were working for, which is that the discoveries of the City of David go beyond nations and borders. It specifically spoke about the history of the Jewish people in Israel going back thousands of years, also speaking to dozens of other cultures that are represented.

As the Supreme Court said, the significance of the City of David is, in fact, universal, and affects billions of people. That these words came from an institution that is often known for its left-wing tendencies was a shock to the extreme left and a major blow to the radical left-wing NGOs and Muslim extremists who had challenged us.

The decision also heralded a new era of partnerships with the Israeli government. Government ministries, such as the Tourism Ministry, Education Ministry, and the Jerusalem Affairs Ministry, now saw the City of David as a recognized national priority for the State of Israel.

Government funding for the Israel Antiquities Authority and National Parks Authority to invest in the City of David's infrastructure began to play an important role in the growth of the site.

But the decision also brought new attention to our efforts. It wasn't long before *60 Minutes*, one of the leading news shows on CBS Television, informed us that Leslie Stahl, their top news reporter, was coming to the area to do a major feature and asked me to do an interview.[10]

By this time in my career, I knew that if *60 Minutes* was interested in the City of David, it was not interested in archaeology alone. They were hoping to uncover intrigue and be able to announce that archaeologists had dug from the City of David into the Old City. The fact that it was an excavation being carried out under the strictest archaeological standards would be of no interest to them. They would be hoping to ignite the very firestorm we were trying to avoid.

They would be hoping to stop the excavation in its tracks permanently.

The easiest thing to do was to ignore the interview request and hope the piece would die on the vine. However, while the site had grown at this time to half a million visitors, and the issue of homes being damaged had been found to be groundless in the Supreme Court, there was still a movement, fueled by European funding, that called what we were doing "settler occupation."

To keep the conflict on the burner, an "alternative visitors center" to the City of David called Wadi Hilweh was set up by a local Arab named Jawad Siam.[11]

Jawad's website claims to present "facts and history" about the area, yet it omits over three thousand years of historical context. The site completely disregards the rich history of the City of David, falsely asserting that the name "City of David" was only recently applied as part of an effort to erase the true history of the neighborhood.[12]

Most of the visitors to Wadi Hilweh were either anti-Israel activists from Israel and abroad or reporters looking for videos of locals that reinforced their narrative of Israeli occupation in Silwan.

Local Arabs in the neighborhood told us that Jawad had been approached by *60 Minutes* and agreed to do the interview. We now faced the difficult decision of going into an interview that we knew was going to be stacked against us, or letting Jawad and other radical groups completely lead in shaping their "alternative" narrative to the City of David on one of the most watched news programs in the United States.

We decided to give it our best fight.

Leslie Stahl showed up a week later. She had brought her husband with her for the first time ever on location, she explained to me. He loved archaeology, and she asked if I would be kind enough to spend half an hour showing them around before the interview. I took them to Eilat Mazar's excavation. Aware that one is never truly off the record, I was careful on the tour to stick strictly to the archaeological evidence we had found, including the different sides in the debate. When I explained about the clay seal of Yehuchal ben Shelemiah, Leslie's husband began to tear up. Leslie was deeply touched and when we came out of the palace, she thanked me profusely for how much it meant to her.

An hour later when the cameras began to roll, the smile washed off her face like a dusty window on a rainy day.

The interview was just as we expected. Leslie's questions to me were really just dressed up accusations. When she asked me about the many groups of young soldiers she had seen on tours through the site, she asked, "So, archaeology is being used as a political tool, I mean, I hate to use the word 'indoctrination' almost..."

Asking me about the archaeology at the site, "There is actually no evidence of David, right?"

Asking me about buying homes from the Arabs: "But is it Elad's goal to ease the Arabs away from where we are right now?"

When it came to Jawad on the other hand, Leslie couldn't be nicer and more helpful.

Before introducing him, while speaking with a young Jewish mother living in the City of David named Devorah, she said, "But you're like a soldier on the front line."

Devorah said, "We don't think of ourselves as soldiers at all, we see ourselves as regular people living in a very, very special place."

Leslie then introduced Jawad with the same words. She said, "Jawad Siam was born in this very, very special place and says he can trace his roots back here 930 years."

Leslie showed pictures of tear gas and clashes, and guided Jawad though his interview. He said, "Clashes are daily inside Silwan between the villagers and settlers and the gun guards for the security there."

Leslie replied, "The government pays for the gun guards?"

Jawad answered, "It's tax money, I pay, everyone who pays taxes pays."

Leslie repeated the point: "You pay taxes, and that money goes to pay for the guards to guard the settlers? So, you are helping to guard the settlers?"

Jawad made her point: "Ya. I fund the settlers and the gun guards."

Despite the bias—or maybe because of it—we deemed it a wise decision to have participated in the interview. First of all there were pictures of the City of David, and while the narration was bent against the site, the images were beautiful.

For years afterward, visitors flocked to the site asking to see the places in the *60 Minutes* episode. Leslie was so biased in her interview and so lacking subtlety that there was great pushback by both Jewish organizations[13] and Michael Oren, who was by then Israel's ambassador to the United States.

Throwing myself in the ring, I had given Leslie Stahl all the material she needed to craft a compelling story. Neither she nor her team dug deep enough—figuratively or literally—to uncover that, at the very moment of our interview, archaeologists were working through the drainage channel, on the verge of a breakthrough that would forever transform the site.

But to understand this, we need to look first underneath the parking lot at the City of David.

Chapter 10

Underneath a Parking Lot

The excavation of King Herod's drainage channel had progressed much further than anyone had realized. The Supreme Court had authorized the Israel Antiquities Authority to dig the channel two years before. Since then, the excavation teams had been working around the clock, in very tight quarters, underneath the ground. Known to only a few, by the time the Supreme Court decision was handed down to us, the excavators had almost reached the Old City Wall.

This left us with a major decision to make that would affect the trajectory of the City of David for years to come. Should we stop digging in the upper drainage tunnel and return to the Pilgrimage Road excavation at the bottom of the City of David, or continue digging the tunnel until we reach the Temple Mount? Both couldn't be done at the same time, as each required tight archaeological supervision and teams, and there weren't enough to go around.

On one hand, the Pilgrimage Road was a monumental excavation that would enable millions of people to experience Jerusalem, while the tunnel was a narrow shaft, and only small numbers could walk through it at a time. The road would take many years to complete, and the cost was now estimated at over $100 million dollars, which would require enormous government and private funding.

On the other hand, the drainage channel was close to the Old

City wall and only around 100 meters (330 feet) from the Temple Mount. If the archaeologists could finish the excavation, it would establish once and for all that the City of David was archaeologically connected to the Old City, something that could be important when justifying the Pilgrimage Road if any additional future challenges would be made to try and stop it.

There was something else as well: While the tunnel didn't have the grandeur of the Pilgrimage Road, we had discovered something incredibly poignant left behind by those last Jewish fighters as they had fled the Romans, together with their families, before getting caught and killed at the bottom of the tunnel.

Amid the rubble in the tunnel, the diggers found hundreds of small bronze coins that the Romans had apparently considered worthless, as they had simply left them on the ground. The coins, called *prutas* in Hebrew, had been hastily minted by Jewish soldiers with whatever metal they could find in the final years of the war against Rome. The coins had rough edges and the letters were often out of place, indicating that they had been minted in haste.

One side of each coin was stamped to indicate which year of the war against Rome the coin had been minted. The war lasted just over four years, from 66 to 70 CE, so a coin minted with the words "Year Four" was from the last full year of fighting, 70 CE, just before the Temple was destroyed.

On the opposite side, the words "For the Freedom of Zion" were stamped around the edges of the coin, with a wine chalice, the sign of bounty, in the middle.

I had a question about the coins and asked to meet Professor Ronny Reich, hoping to get an answer. I came to him with one of the coins from the dig in my hand.

I told him I had read Josephus's description of the war against the Romans. He describes the dire situation of the Jews and how the Jewish fighters, lacking weapons and supplies, scavenged through the war-torn city of Jerusalem for any materials that could be used for weapons.

If this was an accurate picture of the situation, then why, I asked him, were Jewish fighters using precious metal to mint coins that had no commercial value, instead of using this metal for arrowheads or daggers that could be used in their fight?

Ronny took the coin from my hand and stared at it thoughtfully. Holding it before my eyes, he said, "This is an email from two thousand years ago."

"I don't understand, Ronny," I replied somewhat suspiciously. I wasn't sure if he was joking with me or giving me an insight into a deeper meaning he hadn't yet revealed. It turned out to be the latter.

Seeing my expression, he replied, "I'm not kidding," waving the coin in front of my eyes. "The Jews who minted these coins were facing the largest army in the entire world. That army was here to destroy Jerusalem and destroy Judaism. Those Jews were not blind to what was happening; they knew they were likely to lose. So, under the harshest conditions, while being hunted by the Romans in every corner of the city, they minted these coins with the hope that maybe in a generation or two, a remnant of Jews would return to Israel and see these coins among the rubble and realize their ancestors had fought to be free in Jerusalem."

His words hung in the air before he continued. "If we were to tell them that it would take two thousand years until a nice Jewish boy from Michigan would return to Jerusalem and find these coins in the rubble of the City of David, they couldn't fathom what we would be saying. We can barely fathom it ourselves."

Ronny had an intense and serious look in his eyes. He was seeing the arc of history in his mind, the convergence between the past and the present, a trait that defines a great archaeologist. He often lived in both worlds simultaneously, unearthing clues beneath the ground based on instinct as well as science.

He smiled at me and put the coin back in my hand. "This is a message from them to you, to all of us. It took two thousand years for us to get here, but it was waiting for us when we came home."

Ronny then left and returned to supervise the excavations. I flipped the coin from one side to the other in my palm. I imagined how some Jewish fighter, possibly about my age, had held this coin in his hands and wondered if another Jew would ever see it. I felt connected to that person across the span of thousands of years, fulfilling the wishes of him and those who fought beside him, to be remembered by a fellow Jew in the future.

I felt acutely aware at that moment of where my *aliyah*, my immigration to Israel, had led me. I had left my beloved family to come to Israel and join the army. It meant leaving behind everything I had grown up with to follow a feeling that the epic of the Jewish people was being written in the Land of Israel. At that moment, I felt on the page of the epic, a part of the continuum of Jewish history, going back to Abraham and heading onward to those who would follow.

More than anything, I felt grateful to have the opportunity to be born at a time when our people had returned to our land. So many before had dreamed of this. Why we and our generation had been chosen is a question I often consider. It is the key to exploring our identity as a people, and an opportunity to connect to the will, the dreams, and the prayers of the men, women, and children who surround us on the spectrum of history.

Davidleh understood, like Ronny Reich, the emotional impact of bringing tourists through the tunnel to connect with the destruction and the return. The National Parks Authority felt the same way. Both for this reason and the importance of connecting the site to the Old City, the decision was made to put the Pilgrimage Road on hold and continue to excavate the tunnel.

This proved to be a pivotal decision.

There was only one issue. Given the tight conditions, and the lack of airflow, another entrance to the tunnel had to be made in order to remove the bags of fill more easily and give the workers more fresh air.

The answer to this came, of all places, from beneath the Givati Parking Lot.

At first, the parking lot was an unassuming piece of property, approximately one acre in size, lying directly between the City of David and the Old City. It hardly seemed worth the millions of dollars we had to raise to buy it. But little did we know it would turn out to be one of the most important excavation sites in Israel.

An Arab family initially owned the parking lot. In the mid-1990s, the original Arab owner had been in negotiations with Davidleh to buy the property for $350,000, but Davidleh couldn't raise enough funds and was forced to let the property go.

In the late 1990s, the lot was bought by two Jewish developers from Tel Aviv. While they waited for the value of the land to increase, they allowed cars and buses to use it as a free parking lot for people coming to visit the Western Wall. When Davidleh heard that two Jewish developers had bought the property for apparently much more than $350,000, he breathed a sigh of relief. Since it was now in Jewish hands, the property would certainly not be used toward anything that would harm Israeli interests in the area.

Or so he thought.

As the excavations on the City of David were starting to get underway, the two Jewish developers began to see some value in the property.

On the afternoon of August 10, 2000, Yehuda Maly, one of the cofounders of the City of David, was walking back from the Western Wall after praying.

That year, the tenth of August happened to be the ninth day of the month of Av in the Jewish calendar. Tisha B'Av, as it's known in Hebrew, is a day of mourning and fasting that originally commemorated the destruction of Solomon's Temple by the Babylonians, as well as the destruction of the Second Temple by the Romans on the very same Hebrew calendar date. Over the centuries it became a day to fast and reflect on some of the other major calamities that have happened to the Jewish people, events like the expulsion from England in 1290, the expulsion from France in 1306, the expulsion from Spain in 1492, and of course the Holocaust.

As Yehuda Maly walked by the parking lot, which ordinarily would have been empty on a fast day, he saw workers installing an electric gate at the entrance. When he asked them what was going on, they said the parking lot was under new ownership and the new owners had decided to fence off the property. It was widely known that the site was owned by the two Jewish developers, and Yehuda didn't remember hearing that they had sold it. When he asked who the new owners were, the workers offered only a silent look in return, obviously eager to end the conversation.

Before leaving, Yehuda looked at the building plans the workers were holding and noticed that they were written in Arabic. This was very out of the ordinary. All building plans in Israel are in Hebrew whether the contractors are Arab or Jewish.

After Yehuda reported on what he saw, a few of the longtime Arab workers at the site went to investigate the issue. They came back with a bombshell: The two Jewish developers had agreed to sell the property to the Palestinian Authority.

What they heard was that the Palestinian Authority had offered the Jewish developers eight times what they had paid for the property just a few years before, in addition to other incentives. A copy of the building plans showed that the Palestinian Authority was planning on building a Center for the Legacy of the Palestinian People adjacent to the Al Aqsa Mosque, directly over the Givati Parking Lot. A road was also proposed that would cut directly through the City of David and link the new center with the Palestinian parliament building, just over the Green Line around a mile and a half away.

In other words, the center would de-facto divide Jerusalem, and cut the City of David off completely from any access to the Old City.

It was a bold move and one that would relegate the City of David ultimately to the hands of the people who had carried out the largest archaeological destruction in Israel's history at the Temple Mount just a few miles away.

The two Jewish developers had apparently hit hard financial times on some of their other real-estate deals and had agreed to sell it to the Palestinian Authority.

This posed a major risk to the City of David, and to Israel's sovereignty in Jerusalem as a whole.

Our investigations revealed that the Palestinian Authority had not yet put the final ink on the deal. In their haste to try and take over the property and assert possession, they had simply jumped on things and had the workers gate off the parking lot.

It was their haste that gave their plans away.

Davidleh turned to one of the original supporters of the City of David, the very person who had originally encouraged him to work on it: Prime Minister Ariel Sharon. Sharon listened to the story and agreed it would be a terrible turn of events for the area. Furthermore, Sharon said, it would put both the Western Wall and the City of David at risk. Sharon agreed to contact the two developers and encourage them to meet with Davidleh at the soonest opportunity.

A day later, a meeting was arranged to take place at the property.

But on the day of the meeting, only one of the two developers showed up. The owner who didn't show up also didn't answer any phone calls from his partner. Apparently, the meeting would have to be postponed. Davidleh told the developer that had come to sign the contract, that as long as he had already driven to the site, he might as well take a brief tour to see what the City of David was all about. The developer was hesitant, but Davidleh won him over. The brief tour turned into three and a half hours. Like many visitors to the City of David, the developer couldn't believe what he was seeing. He was shocked that as an Israeli, he had never visited the site. He said that every Israeli would have to come and see it to understand why they were living in the State of Israel. At the end of the tour, Davidleh stopped at the Givati Parking Lot. He pointed up to the Old City and the Jewish Quarter and explained that if the parking lot fell into the hands of the Palestinian Authority, the City of David would forever be severed from the Old City.

"Who will visit here," Davidleh asked, "if the site is sold to the Palestinian Authority?"

The owner looked at Davidleh and told him that he wanted to sell the property to the City of David and that he would go and speak with his partner and get back to Davidleh in a day or two.

Davidleh heard nothing for four weeks.

Even calls from the prime minister's office went unreturned by both partners. Davidleh began to think that in the end they had caved in and sold the property to the Palestinian Authority.

Then, a month later, the first developer called Davidleh and said he'd gotten his partner to agree to sell to the City of David—for a high but not extortionate price, and he would come the next day to sign the deal.

"Get your finances lined up, and your lawyer ready, so we can get this done quickly," he told Davidleh.

Davidleh urgently called a few loyal supporters of the City of

David who agreed to buy the property in the name of the City of David.

The next day both partners came. The second one had a very glum look on his face and signed the document with barely a word. After the deal was done, Davidleh asked him if he wanted to tour the site. He shrugged off the suggestion and drove off without a further word.

The original partner then proceeded to recount everything that had transpired over the previous month.

While the first partner had been with Davidleh on the tour, the second partner had been meeting with the Palestinian Authority.

Once the Palestinian Authority learned that we were nearing a deal on the property, they offered the other partner several million dollars more, along with additional "benefits," including a substantial sum of cash deposited in offshore foreign bank accounts. After the second partner admitted this, the first partner told him, "We are not going to sell this property, one of the most important properties in the State of Israel, to the Palestinian Authority, an organization that supports terrorism and does everything it can to sever the ties between the Jewish people and Jerusalem."

For more than a month, they met every morning and argued about the deal. A few days before the closing, the second partner told the first partner, "I'm selling my half to the Palestinians, and you can sell your half to whoever you want."

He added, "That is my final decision."

The first partner told us that he told his friend and partner of many years that he simply wouldn't allow the property to be sold to the Palestinian Authority. "This will haunt us for all of our days," he told his friend. "We betrayed the State of Israel and the Jewish people."

Then, looking his partner directly in the eyes, he said, "Over my dead body. I will not let this happen." The implication was clear: it wasn't just over one dead body, but over both of theirs. He told us it was at that point that his old friend and partner realized how serious he was, and it was at that moment that he relented.

When we bought the parking lot, we thought we were just buying a very expensive piece of property to ensure the connection between the City of David and the Old City. The site, while never excavated, was thought to be outside the original boundaries of the biblical city, and probably would not contain any major discoveries. Once the deal was made and word got out that it was owned on behalf of the City of David, a group of archaeologists visited the site and said that they believed the parking lot was not outside the boundaries of the biblical city, but rather that it was the northwest corner of the city, possibly very near the site where the people would have walked from the City of David to the Temple Mount.

"If you dig down," they said, "you're likely going to find an incredible amount of archaeology."

Around a year later, a Russian team came and did the first MRI underground radar study of an archaeological site in Jerusalem. They came up with a digital archaeological scan that showed numerous ancient walls beneath the ground, and other surprising and significant findings. Most important, the scan showed bodies of water trapped beneath the ground in what we understood were ancient cisterns that had been buried over the millennia.

Based on what they told us, we were able to ascertain that approximately six different civilizations had inhabited the site at different times. Hebrew University launched a full dig in 2008 led by Dr. Doron ben Ami. The site is still being excavated by Tel Aviv

University, and to date, the archaeological record has proven there are more than eleven civilizations located beneath the parking lot. The findings begin with the more recent late Muslim Period and extend back through history to the time of the Bible.

The entire timeline of Jerusalem can be seen, preserved beneath the ground of the Givati Parking Lot, one more example of setting the historical record straight.

Today, millions of people from around the world have come to see the archaeological story of ancient Jerusalem unfold before their eyes. As they descend beneath the parking lot, they pass layer after layer of discoveries, as if turning the pages of a book. A massive Roman Byzantine palace was found at the site, the largest ever unearthed in this area of Jerusalem. Then, while digging inside the palace a volunteer from the United Kingdom named Nadine Ross made world news when she uncovered the largest cache of gold coins ever found in Jerusalem. Beneath this layer, archaeologists unearthed the vaulted foyer of an earlier palace likely belonging to a Second Temple Jewish queen named Helena of Adiabene; and finally, down to the earliest layer found to date, a series of homes dating all the way back to the time of the Bible. In one of the rooms, names were discovered on clay seals such as that of the servant Natan Melech, who is mentioned in the Bible as a courtier of King Josiah. The walls of the homes are burnt, still covered with ashes that have been dated to the destruction of the First Temple in 586 BCE.

Can we imagine what would have become of these archaeological treasures had the Palestinian Authority discovered what lay beneath the ground?

I think we can.

The site would have been reduced to piles of rubble, much like the wreckage we sifted through from the destruction of the Temple Mount.

We were able to uncover these treasures—this history, this Jewish history—only because, in their greed, the Palestinian Authority built their fence too soon.

By the time the Supreme Court decision had come out, only a handful of people knew that the diggers along the drainage channel had reached all the way to the northern edge of the Givati Parking Lot, directly in front of the Old City walls of today.

The decision was made to excavate an entrance down into the drainage channel from the corner of the parking lot. Trying to keep politics and tabloids away from the excavation, the entrance into the underground water system was hidden inside a storage shed at the site. From the outside, the shed simply looked like a place where the diggers collected their tools at the beginning of the day and deposited them at the end of their shifts. Inside, however, was a staircase that descended deep beneath the parking lot excavation to the drainage channel. Only someone with a trained eye could see that more than twenty people went into the shed in the morning, only to emerge hours later covered with archaeological dirt.

Over the next two months following the decision, the excavators entered the tunnel via the tool shed and continued clearing the tunnel north underneath the Ophel Road that separates the Givati Parking Lot from the Old City walls.

It was at this time that the digger from the evening crew discovered the tunnel opening—the same one we crawled through with Eli Shukron—and that brought us face-to-face with the two diamond-shaped stones Charles Warren had uncovered and depicted in his drawing. Before turning back and crawling out, we noticed a small tunnel branching off to the side—likely dug by Warren in a last-ditch effort to uncover treasure before abandoning the excavation. We decided to explore just a little farther on.

After around twenty feet, the tunnel abruptly ended. Disappointed, we were about to turn around when Davidleh put out his hand and began to lightly brush some of the silt away with his fingers. Within seconds, he revealed a rough limestone texture. As he revealed more, we could see that we had reached a wall.

Davidleh turned to me with a smile on his face. "This," he said, "is the Western Wall."

We had reached the foundation stones of the Western Wall, deep beneath the ground.

Chapter 11

Rupert Murdoch and
the Foundation Stones

Once we reached the foundation stones of the Western Wall in the tunnel, we knew this marked a turning point for the City of David. We had demonstrated that the City of David was directly and physically connected to the Old City of Jerusalem, the Western Wall, and the Temple Mount—restoring its ancient and profound link to these iconic sites.

But the path that tunnel took carried significant implications. It was directly under an area adjacent to one of the most sensitive structures in the entire world. Although it did not extend beneath the Temple Mount itself, we knew that if rumors began to circulate that there was an excavation taking place this close to Al-Aqsa and the Dome of the Rock, it could easily be construed that we were underneath the Temple Mount itself. Those who were constantly claiming that the Temple Mount was in danger would see this as a ripe opportunity to inflame the Arab world into fiery protests.

Or worse.

In fact, in 1996, when a tunnel had been opened leading from the Western Wall into the Arab Quarter, such a claim had been made. While it had not been true then, it ignited a massive clash between Israelis and rioting Palestinians that lasted for four days and left seventeen Israelis and fifty-nine Palestinians dead.

Now that we had connected the City of David to the Western Wall of the Temple Mount, we entered the realm of geopolitics. We would have to be incredibly careful to make sure that our momentous discovery did not cause the same reaction.

We all agreed that until further notice, no one was to breathe a word that we had reached the Temple Mount.

Together with the heads of the Israel Antiquities Authority, we discussed the excavation and how to release the story to the public. We agreed that reporters would see the intrigue around archaeologists uncovering an ancient tunnel that connected the City of David to the Western Wall for the first time in two thousand years as a front-page story. The issue was that there is a general rule in the media—"if it bleeds, it leads"—and that in the eyes of most reporters, the more intrigue, drama, and potentially explosive nature to a story, the more likely it is to gain headlines.

Despite how enticing it was to ignite the world's imagination and curiosity over the dig with front-page headlines, we all agreed that this was not the responsible approach. Instead, our goal was to inform them of the facts, relate the historic discovery, and to the best of our ability, diffuse any potential rumors that could come out.

The question was, who could we trust with the information that could help us?

We included in the circle one of the closest allies of the City of David, the then-mayor of Jerusalem, Nir Barkat. Nir was a young, high-tech entrepreneur who had been an early investor in Checkpoint, an Israeli cybersecurity company. Following this, he took on the weighty task of transforming Jerusalem into a modern-ancient city in competition with Rome, Barcelona, and Paris. From the very beginning, Nir saw the City of David as a key to the future tourism of the city, and as the most important historic site proving the deep relationship of Jews to Israel overall.

Nir was excited about what we had uncovered and foresaw that opening the pilgrimage from the Pool of Siloam to the Old City would draw millions of tourists to Jerusalem from around the world. He said that he was on board, and wanted to put some thought into how we should proceed from a PR perspective.

The next day, Davidleh had to fly to the States, and Nir called me to his office at City Hall.

Nir wanted us to know that he had just come from a meeting with senior security officials, whom he had an obligation to inform about the discovery. They were concerned and warned him about a repetition of the bloodshed that had happened when the Western Wall tunnel had been opened in 1996.

Most politicians would have looked for a way to distance themselves from the project after receiving such a warning, to find plausible deniability should anything happen. But to Nir's enormous credit, he did not look for either. He told the security services that this was a historic opportunity for Jerusalem and all its residents, both Jewish and Arab, and that he was going to stand behind it. Their job was to make sure that when trouble did happen, they did everything possible to make sure that it was contained.

Nir and I knew we had to move fast and agreed on a plan.

A few years before, Nir Barkat had brought Rupert Murdoch to the City of David for a tour, along with his senior executive Gary Ginsberg. Murdoch's News Corp operated more than 150 networks and newspapers worldwide, including Fox News and the *Wall Street Journal.* Remembering their positive visit, we thought that if we could get them on board, they would be good partners to do a simultaneous print and video exclusive release of the discovery.

We telephoned Davidleh overseas to get his opinion. He agreed, as did the Israel Antiquities Authority, and we moved forward.

The News Corp team understood both the sensitivity and the integrity that would be needed, and they recommended two reporters they were confident would do a thorough and accurate piece: Eric Gibson from the *Wall Street Journal* and David Lee Miller from Fox News would fly out to do the story as soon as we could make the site accessible.

Three weeks later, we had cleared enough of the fill from the tunnel so that we could make our way through it while ducking down and not having to crawl. The two reporters were due a few days later. I breathed a sigh of relief. The excavation had been kept quiet and soon we would be able to release it to the public without the rumors leading the headlines.

Then, something happened that upped the ante of what we were dealing with.

I was sitting in my office when the phone rang from a private number. I answered, and it was Ron Dermer, Prime Minister Netanyahu's most trusted and senior adviser, and someone for whom I had the utmost respect. Ron made *aliyah* from the United States and is one of the wisest foreign policy advisers in the State of Israel. He is also a Torah-observant Jew who sees the modern State of Israel as a continuation of the epic of the Jewish people.

Ron is probably one of the busiest people I know. So, when he called me in the middle of the workday and asked me how my family was, I knew something much bigger was up. "Hey," he said, "I heard you guys may have made a recent discovery, or something."

Just then, Udi Ragones, the City of David's spokesman, showed up at my door and let me know that he was simultaneously on the phone with someone from the prime minister's office. They had called as well, asking about a discovery, when he overheard my conversation from the next room.

I didn't know who Udi was talking to. However, if the issue of our connection to the Temple Mount had drawn the attention of the prime minister, I knew we would need Ron on our side.

"Look Ron, we found something, something significant...I would really like you to come down here and see it with your own eyes."

Ron said he would be over—within the hour.

After I hung up, Udi told me that his phone call had been from another adviser in the prime minister's office, and his call had been much less cordial than mine: The adviser who called him told Udi they had heard we had found a tunnel and that digging had to stop immediately, until further instructions.

Udi and I met Ron just outside the Givati excavation, where his driver dropped him off. He was wearing a black suit with his signature red tie. Trying to lighten up the atmosphere, I laughed and told him, "You've come dressed for Camp David, not the City of David."

That, at least, got a smile from Ron.

We took Ron to the bungalow covering the concealed staircase in the Givati Parking Lot. I grabbed a white coverall from the shelf and handed it to Ron. Once Ron stepped inside, suit and all, we zipped him up and stood back and looked at him. The scene was truly hilarious. Ron said he looked like the pictures of Mahmoud Ahmadinejad, the president of Iran, when he showed off the Iranian nuclear reactor.

We descended with Ron underground and wound our way through the tunnel until we reached the foundation stones of the Western Wall, a large section of which we had now exposed. When Ron saw the wall, he was very moved. We bent down on the ground, and I showed him the very bottom row of stones that were sitting upon the jagged bedrock of the mountain.

I explained that this was the bedrock of Mount Moriah, the very mountain upon which Abraham had bound Isaac. It was only here, in this underground place, that we could touch the bedrock of Mount Moriah with our hands and feel the first stones that had been laid by our ancestors on top of it as part of the Temple's construction.

Ron quietly put his hand out and touched the foundation stones, deep in thought. We showed him where we wanted to make an exit from the subterranean area, up and onto the ground level. The Nature and National Parks Authority would need to approve this along with other government entities, but if the prime minister wasn't behind it, the idea would be dead in the water.

We led Ron out of the tunnel, watched as he removed the white coverall, and escorted him to his waiting car.

He turned to us before getting into the car.

"I am going to tell Prime Minister Netanyahu how important this is. He knows more about history than most people and he will understand the importance of what you've found."

With these final words, Ron left us: "You don't have to worry."

A day later Ron phoned to let me know that, despite others who were pressuring the PM to stop the excavation to avoid any potential fallout, he was going to stand strong and get behind this. Ron expected, however, that we would be very smart in how we released this to the public: no bells and whistles, simply an archaeological discovery.

Two days later the reporters from Fox News and the *Wall Street Journal* arrived. They spent time with archaeologists, learning the intricacies of the excavations. They documented what they needed to on film, and headed back to the States, where the final editing of the two stories would be done.

On January 25, 2011, Fox News released the story.[1] The *Wall Street Journal* story followed a few days later.[2]

The Fox news piece showed reporter David Lee Miller following Professor Ronny Reich as they wound their way through the underground tunnel. The visuals were spectacular, and Ronny focused on the archaeological importance of the discovery as contributing to our understanding of Jewish life in the city going back two thousand years. The piece briefly mentioned the 1996 riots and that they were based on a false accusation of digging under the Temple Mount. Finally, Mayor Barkat appeared and invited tourists from around the world to come and see the discovery, which he stressed did not go under the Temple Mount.

The piece ran multiple times and was positive and unchallenged.

The *Wall Street Journal* piece was even more unassuming and ran as a "Leisure and Arts" piece. The article featured beautiful pictures and a map that clearly showed that the excavation bypassed the Temple Mount and did not go underneath it. The article focused on how important water was to life in the ancient city, and how water tunnels played a major role in the ancient City of David.

The reporter also mentioned the riots that had taken place in 1996, quickly adding that regarding the drainage channel, "Politics seems far off as a group of journalists bend, squeeze, and shuffle through the underground passage."

The piece hit the mark. It put the discovery into the public sphere as just one of other historic discoveries made in the ancient city. It also gently let the air out of a dangerous balloon: We preempted it being taken out of proportion or misconstrued by the Palestinians, as they had done fifteen years earlier with the opening of the tunnel.

As we hoped, the Israeli press, who are often guilty of sensationalizing even the least important of events, picked up the story and ran it as a nice archaeological discovery that would have a positive impact on tourism in the capital.

We then waited for the Arab papers. This was the true test, to see if we had avoided igniting the always flammable tensions, and if our decision to forgo the headlines to take a more measured approach had been justified.

The next day there were a few small items here and there in Arabic about Jews digging near the area, but they came and went without triggering a public outcry that anything was happening to endanger the Temple Mount.

We had overcome an important and dangerous hurdle—the media.

As a military spokesman in the IDF Reserves, I am the person that people search out when they want to vent their frustrations with Israel's public relations. I can certainly understand where they are coming from. I also see the countless pictures of crying mothers in Gaza, with almost no mention that the reason for the tears in Gaza and in Israel is Hamas or Hezbollah carrying out an unprovoked attack against Israel in the first place.

And, as a person often operating on the inside of our military media, I am no less critical.

Without going into a full analysis of Israel's public-relations efforts, I believe that there are a number of reasons for the media disparity: The first is an existing anti-Israel bias that is rooted in anti-Semitism, which hides behind "legitimate" condemnation of Israel.

Everything we say is subject to skepticism by most reporters. In the recent war in Gaza, it took some major media outlets months to acknowledge that Israeli women had been raped[3], despite our showing them clear evidence. When reports came out that Israeli newborn babies had been found with their heads severed from their bodies during the massacre on October 7, the reporters would refuse eyewitness testimonies and insisted on seeing actual proof.

Eventually, despite the sensitivity around revealing such pictures and the potential pain to the families, Israel showed the pictures to senior US officials, who confirmed the story.[4]

Only then were the press somewhat satisfied.

On the other hand, the claims made by the Palestinians in Gaza are taken as absolute fact and not even subject to examination. The most absurd example is the number of civilians that have purportedly been killed in Gaza. These numbers are given out by the "Gazan Health Ministry," which is a wholly owned agency of Hamas itself. In reality, it takes many hours, if not days, to assess how many people have been injured or killed in any single event in war—and which of these are terrorists and which are uninvolved civilians. Within minutes of an explosion, Hamas announces numbers of how many civilians were killed, and almost never is there any mention of terrorists. According to them, it is as if the IDF has managed to kill only civilians and never terrorists. The international media community repeats these numbers again, again, and again.

The other source of information used by news agencies is workers in the so-called international aid agencies, the largest of which is the United Nations Relief and Works Agency, UNRWA. Since before the war began, Israel had been charging that UNRWA, along with many of the smaller aid agencies, has links to Hamas, and cannot be trusted as a reliable source of information. It took the United Nations until August 5, 2024, three hundred days after the October 7th attack, to finally admit that there was evidence that nine of their workers had taken part in the October 7 slaughter. UNRWA operates 183 schools throughout the Gaza Strip and employs tens of thousands of Gazans in its facilities. During Israel's campaign in Gaza, searches in these schools and in UNRWA facilities found Hamas terror tunnels inside school grounds; vehicles and equipment used in the October 7 attack; and thousands of weapons, rockets, and mortars. United States citizens' tax dollars, along with European citizens' tax dollars, fund UNRWA. This is where Western news reporters are getting their information.

The second reason for the media disparity is that on the backdrop of the already fertile anti-Israel playing field, Israel seems to miss many of the opportunities available to show Hamas culpability in many of the deaths they blame on Israel.

During the American Revolution, the British Army marched in straight military formations on their way to the battlefront against the Americans. The American army commanders, realizing they would have to part with formality if they were to beat a much bigger and highly trained British army, hid behind the enemy lines in strategic locations and picked off the marching British soldiers before they could even reach the battle.

When it comes to the media, Israel is like the British Army, marching into the PR battlefield with large, bureaucratic government media offices that often lack the agility and the clout necessary to quickly get to the facts and report them before the other side spreads unchecked lies and the uncorrected story is printed.

Case in point is the Al Ahli hospital bombing that occurred on October 17, 2023, in northern Gaza. Hamas immediately blamed Israel and claimed five hundred people had been killed. It took the IDF over five hours to verify that it was an Islamic Jihad misfired rocket that had landed in Gaza and caused the devastation.[5]

Although the virulently anti-Israel and anti-West Al Jazeera media station had filmed the misfire live and in detail, by the time we confirmed the facts, we had lost the fight.

Today, the State of Israel understands the role the media plays in our wars. There is a new generation of leadership in the IDF that is working to narrow the gap, especially in the Spokespersons' Unit. The stakes are high. When one side can make almost any claim unchallenged, it is up to the IDF to prove it wrong before it goes viral. Even the slightest delay to conduct "inquiries" relegates our version of what actually went down to the fourteenth page of some newspaper.

Regarding the opening of the water channel, we were facing a similar dilemma to the one the IDF often faces. We knew in advance that we were going to be announcing the discovery in a possibly hostile environment. What made the difference was we had the ability to work together as a small group and come up with a well-messaged campaign that supported the facts. We were able to release it before the other side could steal the story away and create an explosive conflict based on distortions and incendiary claims.

While not everything is in our hands, I believe this provides an important insight, albeit limited in scope, into what can be achieved from a public relations perspective in the areas under our control. At the end of the day, the most significant discovery in the modern history of the City of David—and one of the most important archaeological developments in decades for Jerusalem—was successfully brought to public knowledge without any explosions or public recriminations.

From the very beginning, we were clear on the goal: Focus on the long run, when millions of people would be able to experience the Pilgrimage Journey. Had we allowed our egos to rule us and opted for a quick headline in the short run, it very well could be that the tunnel would still be closed to this day.

Having passed the media obstacle, the excavation teams continued to carefully remove the archaeological fill in the tunnel and prepare it for tourists. The foundation stones of the Western Wall, resting on the bedrock of Mount Moriah, were now revealed in all their grandeur. The engineering teams were building a metal staircase that would enable visitors to ascend from the foundation stones all the way up to the plaza over our heads, where we had originally heard the tour guide speaking to his group about Robinson's arch, the remains of which can be seen jutting out of the upper stones of the Temple Mount.

Just before the Passover holidays in March 2011, the teams had completed their work. The Israel Antiquities Authority and the National Parks Authority gave the go-ahead to open the tunnel, which now led from the City of David all the way to the foundation stones of the Western Wall, where visitors could exit. It was just a question of when we would allow the first tourists into the water channel and have them exit the site on the other side. The timing was once again important. Just above the exit there were windows built into the upper walls of the Temple Mount, from which members of the Waqf could peer out on the plaza. We had come this far; we didn't want to take any chances to draw unnecessary attention to the opening. We waited for an opportune time when there would be other distractions to divert attention away from the site.

The time came during the Passover holiday. The Old City was full of tourists and people milling around. There were plenty of tourist attractions going on—festivals, music, and people eating their matza-crusted pizzas in outdoor restaurants. The first few groups that exited the Pilgrimage Road would hopefully just blend into the many crowds touring around the city. By the end of the week of Passover, the exit would seem like just another tourism feature in Jerusalem.

I was guiding Raanan, one of the original people who had helped get the word out about the City of David. I felt it was only right that he be one of the first. We followed Davidleh and Yehuda, who were guiding Ira and Ingeborg Rennert through the tunnel, and by the time we got to the staircase, they had already gone up and through. I moved aside the metal covering and walked up onto the white limestone pavement stones of the Pilgrimage Road, followed by Raanan close behind.

A group was standing there with their guide, who had been describing the Temple Mount. They stared at us open-mouthed. Trying to look nonchalant, I slid the metal covering back over the exit as if it was a normal occurrence to pop out from under the stones of the Old City, and Raanan and I made our way past them.

Just before I thought we were clear, one of them called out to us.

"Hey, where are you guys from?"

Without even missing a step, Raanan called back to them nonchalantly. "We are from long ago..."

We were back in our ancestral home, and for the first time in two thousand years, following in the footsteps of our ancestors, along the route of the same pilgrimage journey they had taken during their Passover holidays, before being exiled from the Land of Israel.

Raanan could not have said it better: *The Jewish people are from long ago.*

Chapter 12

Under Fire: Ted Koppel, Huweida, and the Battle for Truth

The last time I had seen Huweida, we were both attending the University of Michigan, and she and I were cochairs of the Israeli–Arab dialogue and cultural evening on campus.

We were good friends in those days, Huweida and I. I was in charge of a pro-Israel group on campus called the American Movement for Israel, and Huweida became an active member. She even joined me as my guest for shabbat dinners on campus.

Huweida was an Arab Christian with an Israeli Arab father and a Palestinian mother. She understood then that Christian Arabs were under constant threat in other countries in the Middle East and that Israel, by contrast, treated them with respect as citizens. On campus she was a strong advocate for Israel, even more so than many of the Jews that I knew. It even crossed my mind that perhaps she would one day convert to Judaism, given how interested she was in the religion. But after graduation, we lost touch.

The next time I saw Huweida was in Bethlehem, and her life had taken on a radically different path.

In 2002, I was working as a business consultant for a company that introduced Israeli technology into the European market. My thirty-eighth-floor office in Tel Aviv overlooked the Mediterranean Sea, and I was sitting at my desk one day, staring blankly at the Mediterranean. I had been unable to concentrate for days.

A few weeks before, terrorists exploded a bomb in a café around the corner from my home in Jerusalem. I was sitting on my couch when I heard the explosion echoing off the stone walls of the buildings in our neighborhood, followed by car alarms set off by the vibration. As soon as I heard it, I knew what it was; I just didn't know where and how many people had been killed.

Over the past month alone, eighty-one Israelis, including men, women, and children—had been killed in terror attacks in the country.[1] In such a small country, everyone was affected. Every day the news showed the burnt husks of buses that had been attacked with suicide bombers, the broken windows of cafés streaked with blood, and the Passover seder that had ended with bodies of families strewn across the floor. Two of my friends had been killed earlier in the year, when a bomb went off in a cafeteria garbage can at the Hebrew University. Anywhere that innocent people were leading their lives, they were targets.

Perpetrated mostly by the Hamas terror organization and the Fatah military wing of the Palestinian Authority, the goal was to bring Israel to its knees.

I sat at my desk, staring out at the Mediterranean, the half-finished report I was compiling on the Swedish cellular industry sitting off to the side. I felt sick for the innocent lives that had been lost, for the parents of those children, and for the children who were now orphans. I was completely consumed with a desire to do something, to do anything to fight back against the terror.

The news had reported earlier in the day that the Fatah Tanzim and Hamas terror cells that had carried out many of the attacks had been traced to Bethlehem, and IDF soldiers were entering the city in pursuit. The terrorists, on the run, had fled inside the Church of the Nativity, a Christian holy site, taking two hundred hostages captive, including tourists and Greek Orthodox monks.

My phone rang. It was my unit commander. He informed me that I was being activated and was to immediately report to the Military Checkpoint 300 at the entrance to Bethlehem. From there an armored jeep would take me to our military headquarters in the heart of the city controlled by the military wing of the Palestinian Authority Fatah Tanzim.

I quickly gathered my stuff and told my boss that I had received an Order Eight, which was an immediate draft notice without delay. He gave me a hug and wished me to carry out my duty and return safely. As I walked out of the office, I could see other empty desks of fellow servicemen and servicewomen who had been called up as well.

I drove to my apartment in Jerusalem, gathered my gear, and headed to Checkpoint 300. Along the way, I passed empty cafés and restaurants that had once been filled with people at this hour. For months, the booms of artillery fire in the villages bordering Jerusalem such as Beit Jalla, Gilo, and Bethlehem could be heard throughout the day.

Not very inviting for an outdoor cup of cappuccino.

Fifteen minutes later I approached the checkpoint. I parked on the shoulder of the road behind hundreds of cars belonging to reserve soldiers like myself, who had been summoned from their daily routines to report for duty. Israel was a small country, and the fastest way to get to the military front was simply to park your car near a checkpoint and get a ride to the battlefront, usually only a few minutes away.

I joined an armored convoy that brought us to the military

command center in the heart of Bethlehem. It faced Manger Square, which stood before the Church of the Nativity, one of the most important sites for Christian tourists. The square was bordered on all four sides by buildings: To the south stood the Church of the Nativity, and diagonal to the church on the east was our HQ inside the building we had commandeered.

A sign on the entrance to the commandeered building read PAL-ESTINE CENTER FOR PEACE.

The irony could not have been greater.

Two other buildings bordered the square. One housed Hamas snipers and the other housed IDF snipers. That evening, as the sun began to set, the square stood completely empty, except for a few stray cats slinking in the shadows and looking for food.

That first night we slept on thin mattresses on the floor behind steel barriers protecting us from potential sniper fire through the windows. I got to know the forces I was with in the building that night. The Israeli Paratrooper Brigade was overseeing the operation. The commander in charge was Aviv Cochavi, who would one day become the chief of staff of the Israeli Army. Also in the building were special forces, intelligence, negotiators, and a few units in the basement whose identity was off limits even for those of us with security clearance.

I was a captain in the IDF reserves at the time and served as a military spokesman to the foreign press. I was stationed there with my commander—Olivier, a lieutenant colonel originally born in France—along with four other soldiers.

Our small team was responsible for the fight for world opinion.

We would speak to the press and arrange special background briefings. In certain instances, we would take reporters with us into the field to show them our efforts to avoid civilian casualties. Meanwhile, we were battling terrorists who already had blood on their hands and were now shamelessly hiding behind civilians in a church.

And not just any church: the holiest church to billions of Christians worldwide.

The moment a military operation begins, a hypothetical clock begins to tick backward. Once it hits zero, the operation ends and the forces pull back. For the Israeli leadership, the clock is usually based on US support for our military operations. As long as US public opinion was in our favor, the IDF would be free to carry out its objectives to cripple Hamas in Bethlehem and neutralize the terror cell inside the church.

We knew it was only a matter of time before the obsessively hostile members of the United Nations would pressure the Security Council to pass a resolution condemning Israel. The US would most likely veto those resolutions, but as international and domestic pressure grew, American support would erode, and when US public opinion turned against us, the clock would strike zero and the operation would be over.

Our objective was to add as many minutes as possible to the clock by keeping US public opinion on our side for as long as possible. The longer our forces had to act, the greater the likelihood we would accomplish our objectives. It was as simple as that.

Israel had long ago come to expect the sad irony that the United Nations would condemn Israel and not the Hamas terrorists who had killed Israeli civilians and were now holding civilians hostage in a church. In any given year, more than half of all UN General Assembly condemnations are directed toward Israel. The United Nations, established after World War II with the noble objective of preventing tyranny from taking over the world again, had become a corrupt bastion of Israel hatred, so severe it can only be explained by anti-Semitism.

As the sun came up the next morning hundreds of reporters from around the world descended on Bethlehem to cover the story. Despite all our efforts to make the terrorists culpable, the story came to be known as the "Siege on Bethlehem"—and it would be the most watched news item for weeks throughout the United States and much of the world.

A few days later, on May 2, 2002, Ted Koppel, the *ABC Nightline* news anchor and probably the most well-known news personality at the time, went to the city of Ramallah, about an hour away from Bethlehem, to interview Yasser Arafat, the chairman of the Palestinian Authority. In the middle of the interview, a fire broke out at the church in Bethlehem, and a firefight ensued between the IDF and the Hamas terrorists inside the church.[2]

Almost immediately, the terrorists inside claimed that Israel was damaging the holy site and had purposely lit the fire. But not a single IDF unit had fired in the direction of the church or had done anything to light a blaze in the area preceding the fire.

Our assessment was that this was a staged event—an "arson show" put on by the terrorists to sway world opinion to their favor by claiming that Israel was threatening a Christian holy site. This became even more apparent when the IDF fire brigade tried to approach the blaze to put it out.

Hamas gunmen fired on the fire brigade.

The next day after the fire, Ted Koppel was in Bethlehem with our troops. As we skirted the perimeter of our HQ, I explained to him the various troop positions around the square. He seemed irritated that he had missed the action the day before—he had missed an opportunity to show the world that he was bravely standing in a war zone.

The problem for Ted was that since the fire had been extinguished the night before, there had been no fighting. To make matters worse, on May 2 the weather was a beautiful 70 degrees, the skies were clear blue, and the birds were chirping in Manger Square.

This was not the war zone imagery Ted wanted.

As the morning drew on, his annoyance at the lack of "action" shifted to thinly veiled belligerence.

The day before, in Ramallah, Ted had lobbed softball questions during his interview with Yasser Arafat, the leader of the Palestine Liberation Organization, who bumbled his way through the interview, contradicting himself time and again. He said that he found Arafat "reduced to a trembling rage" over the fire in the church, as if the man who had planned numerous terror attacks against Israelis and Americans, including the Ma'alot Massacre in which twenty-five Israelis (twenty-two of whom were children) were killed, could truly be outraged by any form of destruction.

According to Ted, he spoke with Arafat just moments after Arafat had talked to "one of the Palestinian fighters still trapped by other Israeli troops inside the Bethlehem compound." Ted failed to mention that these "fighters" were in fact proven terrorists that had fled to the compound after blowing up buses, killing innocent Israelis.

However, with us, every question seemed to be an accusation. Even after we gave him unheard-of access to a military facility and showed him how our cameras verified the identity of the terrorists before we targeted them, he commented to his viewers that "the Israelis certainly don't share *everything* recorded by *all* of their cameras."

At some point he breathed a sigh of frustration and went up to the IDF commander of the operation, a colonel, and pointed to the middle of the square. He had to broadcast shortly, and he wanted to do so from down there in the middle of Manger Square. Furthermore, he wanted a tank positioned directly behind him to make a more exciting backdrop for his reporting.

Ted wasn't asking; he was insisting.

The colonel had dealt with terrorists and enemies on Israel's borders and had looked death in the eye numerous times and not backed down; however he had never seen an angry reporter before—especially one whom he understood from his superiors was an important man in America. The commander reluctantly agreed.

An hour later I found myself standing in the middle of Manger Square with Ted and his crew. As they set up for the film shoot, an Israeli tank driver came to a stop behind us. I looked around at the dark windows in the Hamas buildings facing the plaza where we were standing. There could be a sniper behind each one, and if they started shooting, we had nowhere to seek cover. Additionally, I was the one wearing a green uniform, which turned me into a green dot on a whiteboard.

I tried to reassure myself that the last thing Hamas would want to do would be to shoot in the direction of a news crew. I hoped that they understood what that might mean for international opinion.

I could only hope...

A few seconds later I heard the familiar words, "Three, two, one, Ted you are on the air."

Ted's voice, as familiar in American homes as a hamburger and fries, filled Manger Square.

He was reporting from the center of Bethlehem, where behind him, just beyond an IDF tank, stood the Church of the Nativity, one of the most sacred places for over a billion Christians. He described the war as "primarily a war of images and perceptions," in which "the soldiers fight the first battles, and then the Public Affairs specialists and the intelligence officers put their spin on what has happened and how they feel the media should report it."[3]

Just as I was processing his casual dismissal of everything we had shown him, a deafening shot rang across the plaza. We all jumped. Ted ducked down near the treads of the tank, hands over his head, with an understandable look of fear on his face. Before I could even reach him to direct him to safety, he and the crew were running for cover inside the IDF headquarters.

Once inside, the same commander who had given in to Ted's

earlier demands to film in the plaza with the tank behind us, met us. He informed us that our forces had been tracking one of the main Hamas terrorists inside the church, waiting for a rare opportunity when he would be alone with no civilians nearby. Using special technology that the commander could not discuss in detail, the army had identified him walking alone down a hallway. The shot we heard was fired the moment the terrorist passed by the window.

"The terrorist was eliminated," he said, "and there were no civilian casualties."

I was blown away as I thought of how difficult it must be to track a terrorist behind the thick stone walls of a fifteenth-century church, and to take him out the second he moved past a window.

Ted and his crew were less enamored.

The colonel, who had been accommodating earlier, spoke with calm authority. "I gave you a tank so you could do your job as a reporter. My job is to win this war against terrorists who have killed innocent Israelis and taken hostages in a church. This is not a film studio."

Minutes later, the ABC film team gathered their gear and left. The soldiers who had been looking on with interest at the exchange went back to their jobs.

Ted had come for war, and he had gotten war. I wasn't so sure he liked it in the end.

It had been an intense morning, and I sat back to enjoy my sandwich looking out at the plaza from behind the bulletproof glass shields we had installed on the ground floor.

That was when I heard the yelling from Manger Square.

The noise didn't sound like the yells of terrorists in Arabic. Rather it sounded like the yells of the crowd rushing the football field at the end of a University of Michigan-Ohio State football game.

I saw a group of around twenty people run past our building in the middle of the plaza heading in the direction of the church. They were carrying shopping bags. I quickly threw on my helmet and bulletproof vest just as a rush of paratroopers ran down the stairs and brushed past me as they ran into the plaza. Not sure if they needed backup support, I followed them.

The group that had passed us could be seen running into the church. A second group was a few steps behind them, and we intercepted them in the middle of the plaza and tackled them to the ground. A few shots rang overhead.

Food spilled from the bags they were holding. There were around fifteen of them—young men and women who looked to be in their early twenties. I could see the names of US and European colleges on some of their shirts. They were clearly from the West.

Once on the ground, they quickly linked arms together and began chanting, "Say no to the occupation! Say no to Israeli violence!"

This happened so quickly that it was clear it had been choreographed in advance. I had a quick look around the plaza to see if anyone was filming. Thankfully it looked like the crews were still sleeping off the late night before.

A young commander stepped forward, and in broken English told the chanting protesters that they had broken into an active military zone. He ordered them to immediately move inside our headquarters building.

But they just kept chanting, even louder, making no attempt to move. The commander grabbed one of the guys on the ground with long sandy blond hair and tried to haul him up and move him toward the building. The guy shook off the commander's arm and went back to chanting on the ground.

The commander moved toward the same guy, ready to haul him up again. We were in a closed military zone with snipers at our back. Our lives were on the line, literally. This time I knew that he wasn't going to let the protester push him away. I still didn't know who had organized the protests, but this was clearly what they had been planning. The next day these college kids, bruised and bloodied, would be on every news station in the world, claiming the IDF had beaten them up during a nonviolent protest.

I knew images like these could be enough to lose support for the entire operation.

I shot my arm out in front of the commander, stopping him in his tracks. He looked at me with raptor's eyes, quickly assessing my rank—equal to his—before muttering, "What?"

I told him he was about to fall into a trap. Everything we did right now would be on the news tomorrow and would be fuel for the terrorists inside the church to bring overwhelming international pressure on Israel. I asked him to let me deal with them.

Looking up at the windows of the Hamas snipers, he told me I had one minute.

I stood before the group and spoke to them in English. They had prepared for Israelis barking orders at them, and as soon as they heard my American accent they looked up. I told them that I was originally from Michigan, and I had plans to get married in June. I said, "There are snipers pointing their guns at my back at this very moment, and I hope to be able to make it to my wedding." I pointed to a girl who was still chanting "Say no to violence! Say no to occupation!" and told them that if they really were against violence as they claimed, they would move peacefully inside our headquarters.

They were taken by surprise. They had prepared for a monster, but not for some American guy from Michigan who wanted to make it to his own wedding. The chants stopped, and they began whispering quietly among themselves. Their whispered words were being directed to a woman who was sitting at the center of the group directly at my feet. She was clearly the leader, on her phone, I later found out, trying to reach someone at the American embassy. As their whispers reached her ears, she looked up.

I saw her face, and I froze.

I couldn't move. I just stared down at her out of my green army helmet. When the commander told me my minute was up, I came out of my daze. I swallowed and called her.

"Huweida!"

She stared at me blankly, not understanding how an IDF soldier could know her name.

I called her name again.

"Huweida, we're not at the University of Michigan anymore, I need you to move inside this building."

She looked up with searching eyes to see who this person behind a heavy bulletproof vest was, with a helmet and a loaded M16. Her eyes widened as recognition dawned on her, and to my surprise, she began to cry. The protesters looked from one to the other in search of some answer as to what was going on.

Seeing the opportunity of a moment of confusion, the IDF commander had his troops gently begin lifting up the members of the group, carrying them inside the building to safety.

Once inside, the group was led to a conference room and given water and food.

A group of senior officers from different branches came to speak with me, wanting to know how I knew Huweida. After telling them the background, they asked if given my past relationship to her and my ability to communicate with them, I would sit with each of the protesters one on one and try to convince them to give us their identities, including names, place of birth, and how they had been contacted and trained.

I had never done this before; however, I told them that if they would guide me through it, I would give it a try.

The first interviews went fairly easily. I told them who I was and that I understood they felt strongly about their beliefs. However, I told them, breaking into a closed military zone and putting themselves and other people at risk was against the law. How would the United States treat them, I asked, if they broke through a military barrier and put US soldiers at risk? What if an IDF soldier, like myself, had been killed because of them?

Most of them hadn't thought of the real implications of what they were doing, and once I explained this, they began to worry. I told them that if they gave us the information we needed, we would be willing to work with their embassies and find out the best way to proceed. Hearing this option, they gave most of their information willingly.

Finally, I came to speak to Huweida.

The IDF by then had figured that she was part of a group that had tried to disrupt IDF actions in the past. They already had a dossier on her. She had publicly called for violent resistance against Israel earlier in the year.

As the leader of the group, she was in her own room and was being questioned by IDF commanders as to how she had organized the group and who was financing them.

She refused to answer any of their questions and wouldn't accept any of their food. She just kept saying that she was in touch with the US ambassador Daniel Kurzer, and they should contact him or his office directly.

I walked into the room. As soon as she saw me, she came right for me, her arms raised in exasperation. I caught her arms and held them firmly in place.

"How could you?" she demanded, her voice shaking, tears streaming down her face. "You joined the occupation army."

I lowered her hands to her sides and slowly let go. I told her, "I once knew a different Huweida. I remember how that Huweida and I once made a vigil on campus for twelve Israelis who were killed by Palestinian terrorists on the evening of the Jewish holiday of Purim in March 1996. I remember how that Huweida stood there and spoke in the central quad at the University of Michigan, holding a candle in their memory. I remember how you spoke on Israel's behalf against extremists on campus."

"That was then," she said quietly. Then, standing up to face me, she said, "I will never stop fighting until the genocide against the Palestinians ends."

"Genocide?" I asked her. "What genocide? The Palestinian population has grown to be at least five times larger since 1948."

"There are different types of genocide," she responded. "We will never stop, you have to know this, until all Palestinian refugees return to their homes that were taken from them by Israel in 1948."

I corrected her: "The refugees that were discussed in the Oslo Accords are not from 1948. They are from 1967, following the Six Day War, when Israel, responding to a coordinated attack by Syria, Egypt, and Jordan, took over the biblical lands of Judea and Samaria."

"No," she replied, "you speak about 1967. The real occupation began in 1948."

I stood, open-mouthed for a second, as her words hit me. Huweida wasn't referring to the disputed territories following the 1967 war, the area that according to the Oslo Accords could be negotiated as a future Palestinian state. Rather she was calling for a return of all Arabs to Israel, a population shift that was not an attempt for Jews and Palestinians to live side by side in two states. She was on the side of those who wanted the destruction of the State of Israel as we know it.

When I told her this, she demurred. She said there would still be a State of Israel, but it would have millions and millions of returned refugees living inside of it.

I reminded her, "In November 1947, Israel accepted the United Nations partition of the land into two states—it was the Arabs who didn't accept this and attacked Israel with seven armies seeking our annihilation. The Arabs who fled to join the attacking armies against Israel were not allowed to return; however, the Arabs who stayed and did not join the attacking armies were welcomed as citizens of the State of Israel and are citizens till this very day.

"Your father," I reminded her, "was one of them"—but she wouldn't have it.

I spent the next hour trying to use logic, history, and the moral cause of the Jews having bought their land before moving to Israel, in vain and futile attempts to reach at least some type of understanding with my old friend.

But, like a broken record, she just kept repeating to me, again and again, "We will never give up until they return to their entire land and the occupation ends."

I looked around the room. A number of the officers who had previously questioned Huweida were listening to what she was saying. They looked stunned. They, like me, were part of a generation that had been educated that the Palestinians wanted a home of their own in the West Bank and Gaza Strip alongside Israel. Although the Palestinians were stubborn negotiators and hadn't yet agreed to what Israel offered, even when Israel risked its own security and agreed to cede the majority of the biblical heartland of Jewish history, we were led to believe that eventually, they would agree. It was just an issue of how much territory would be necessary to seal the deal.

But Huweida was saying something drastically different: She was saying that they were fighting because they wanted *all* of Israel, from the Jordan River to the Mediterranean Sea. For most of us, it was the first time we understood that this would be their demand going forward.

I finally left the room, and a few hours later, Israel reached an agreement with the various embassies. I went back one last time to see Huweida. I grabbed an apple on the way and offered it to her with a bottle of water. She was calm now, and simply waved the apple away, saying, "I won't eat the food of the occupation."

Then she looked at me and said, "If you promise not to wear your uniform of the Zionist occupation, I'll still join you for a shabbat meal, like we've had in the past."

I told her, "Things are not like they used to be. Nor will they ever be again. You bring bags of food to terrorists who have killed innocent Israelis, and I am an IDF soldier defending the Israeli people and my country. If we ever have a meal again, I will know exactly who you are, and you will know who I am."

With that, I walked away.

Her words, however, will never leave me.

Eight days later, under enormous international pressure, Israel agreed to have the terrorists in the church deported to either Cyprus or to Gaza.

In the years that followed, many of those same terrorists returned and carried out terror attacks.

Two days later, I was back in my office, once again staring out at the blue waters of the Mediterranean Sea. Soft music was playing, and I could hear the click of fingers on keyboards around me. People were going about their work as if nothing had changed.

But for me, everything had changed. Huweida's words still echoed in my mind.

Part of me felt like I was still in Bethlehem, like an amputee who still feels the leg they used to have. I could smell the damp stone walls of the Peace Center following the rains, the cold stone floor that we slept on beneath our thin mattresses, the sounds of the muezzin. The shooting and taking cover behind bulletproof glass. And of course, Huweida.

I wanted to talk to her again—to help her see reason.

I had done some background checking and thought I could piece together more or less how she had become so radicalized since I had last seen her. Following graduation, Huweida had joined an organization that promoted itself as supporting dialogue between young Israelis and Palestinians in an outdoor camp setting. While this sounds commendable, the Jews and Israelis active in the organization were often from the extreme fringes of the Israeli political spectrum, some of them virulently critical of the State of Israel. While at the camp, Huweida met her future husband, the organizer of the camp, Adam Shapiro, considered one of the most extreme anti-Israel Jews in the United States.

Five months before she and I met in Bethlehem, only four days after a terror attack in an outdoor mall in Tel Aviv that injured twenty-five people, Huweida and Adam had coauthored an article calling for violent Palestinian resistance against Israel.[4]

It didn't take Hamas or the PA to radicalize Huweida. It was under the influence of self-hating Jews and Israelis that she learned to hate.

In March 2023, Huweida was in the news again.

She had been making numerous public statements supporting terror groups, openly claiming that Israel was committing genocide and ethnic cleansing against the Palestinians. She was a guest speaker on a high-school diversity panel in my native town of West Bloomfield, Michigan, and according to news reports, she went on a "rant against Israel and the Jewish People."[5] The Jewish community demanded a response from the school as to how they could allow young people to be exposed to such hatred of Israel and the Jewish people. Subsequently, the principal and superintendent issued apologies that they were "sorry for the harm that was caused to our community as a result of this speaker's message."

Huweida's group, the International Solidarity Movement, the same ones that organized the "protest" in Bethlehem, has since been declared one of the top-ten anti-Israel organizations in the United States by the Anti-Defamation League. ISM and its members have been accused of sheltering, aiding, and funding terrorists including Hamas.[6]

During the bloodiest days of the Second Intifada, peace talks were still being pursued by the Israeli leadership. Shimon Peres, then Israel's foreign minister, had said he welcomed peace talks with the Arabs just a few weeks earlier.

But it was increasingly clear to me that a peace deal that called for a return to the pre-1967 borders, which reduced Israel to the width of only eleven miles, would never satisfy people like Huweida, who had come to believe that the true occupation of the Palestinians began in 1948.

Why would they ever stop fighting for something they considered so unjust?

And in order to deny the modern historical reality of the State of Israel, they had to deny that the Jewish people had any historic connection to the Land of Israel at any point in history.

And that is why the City of David is so important.

Chapter 13

Obama and UNESCO

Had the coalition of radical advocacy groups not challenged us in the Supreme Court when it did, and had the court not suspended the excavation of the Pilgrimage Road, which resulted in our focusing on the drainage channel, it is likely that the City of David would not be connected to the Western Wall, even today.

Even though the tunnel could never accommodate large groups like the Pilgrimage Road once had, it was proof that the City of David and the Temple Mount were connected in ancient times. It became an irreversible fact-on-the-ground that they were connected once again—if only through a drainage channel.

This fact would become vital in the years to come, as Israel came under enormous international pressure to stop the excavations in the City of David, first by President Obama's administration and then by the United Nations Educational, Scientific, and Cultural Organization (UNESCO).

A carefully coordinated campaign of news features and "reports" pushed a negative narrative about the excavations to diplomats and politicians in both Europe and the United States.

The following guidelines were adhered to in almost every report and article with few exceptions:

- The area would be referred to as either "Silwan" or "Wadi Hilweh" and almost never as "The City of David."
- There would be no mention of the archaeology of ancient Jerusalem or the discoveries made.
- There would be no mention of the historic tie between the Jewish people and the area.
- In the rare event that the phrase "City of David" was mentioned, it would be only to refer to it as an archaeological ploy used to justify expropriating land from Palestinians in an attempt to "Judaize" the areas with government assistance.
- No mention would be made of the millions of dollars in legal real-estate transactions conducted between Jews and Arabs.
- No mention would be made that the merits of these transactions had been upheld in court to be legally binding dozens of times.
- No mention would be made of the death threats against Arabs by either the Palestinian Authority or Hamas for selling their land to non-Muslims.
- No mention would be made of the improved roads, infrastructure, and safety in the area stemming from the City of David's growth.

With no context of the historical importance of the area to Jews, certain foreign government officials were duped, willingly or unwillingly, into believing the narrative that this was nothing more than a militant takeover of an area outside the Old City walls, by lawless Jews at the expense of innocent Palestinians.

The first move came on August 25, 2014, when the United Nations secretary general issued an official report titled, "Israeli

Settlements in the occupied Palestinian Territory, including East Jerusalem, and the occupied Syrian Golan." In the section titled "Archaeological excavations and parks" the report stated, "Observer organizations report that several archaeological projects in the Old City of Jerusalem are being used as a means to consolidate the presence of settlements and settlers in the area." The footnote points out that the "observer organizations" mentioned are none other than Ir Amim—the radical NGO that operates in the neighborhood and that subsists primarily from European funding.[1]

In the same section, another radical NGO called Emek Shaveh claimed that the placement of the excavations and the building of the tourism centers in the City of David "shows that a contiguous line of Israeli settler presence along the entire northern boundary of the Silwan area is being created."[2]

The United Nations report was followed up one month later on September 17 by a Peace Now report that included a map that showed "Settlers Houses" as menacing red dots covering the area of the City of David which is referred to only as "Wadi Hilweh"—with no mention of the importance of the land to the Jewish people.

Echoing the language of the UN report, the Peace Now report referred to "ideological tourist centers established by Elad in Palestinian areas around the Old City of Jerusalem" that are used for "'Israelizing' the area surrounding the Old City."[3]

Not long after, the Peace Now report found its way into the hands of certain officials in the Obama White House.

Throughout 2014, the City of David experienced a tourism boom. It became cleaner and safer, and housing values in the area began to rise. A number of Arab families wanting to take advantage of the increased prices had approached us and sold us their homes. Many of them had gone on to build much bigger homes in other areas in Jerusalem where the prices were still relatively lower. Seeing the courage of these families to stand up against the racist and illegal policies of Hamas and the Palestinian Authority that forbade Muslims from selling their homes to non-Muslims, other Arab families who were happy to sell to Jews and non-Muslims were emboldened to sell as well.

While prices were higher than they had ever been, this was an important opportunity for the City of David Foundation as well. As owners of the property, we could rent out the apartments, while we considered how to utilize the land for the ever-increasing excavations in the future.

On September 30, the day after a group of Arab sellers had moved out of the City of David, I was sitting in the visitors' center as our lawyers went over the paperwork regarding all the land titles when my phone rang.

Ron Dermer's name flashed across the screen. By this time, Ron was Israel's ambassador to the United States, and it was all over the news that Prime Minister Netanyahu and Ron were in DC for a meeting with President Obama. If he was calling me, it meant that once again something was up—and it probably wasn't good.

"Hey, Doron, did you guys just move into some homes in the City of David or something?"

Ron sounded like he was in a rush.

"Hi, Ron, yes, last night. A few families left and we moved into the new properties."

"I have to ask you a question," he said, "just to be absolutely sure: Did you guys do everything according to the letter of the law?"

"Ron, I'm sitting right now in a room with our lawyers. We just went through every one of the documents with a fine-toothed comb. Everything here checks out one hundred percent. You have my word."

Then came the surprise.

"Well," he said, "not everyone likes what you guys are doing over there. I want you to know that tomorrow, the White House is going to issue a statement condemning you guys and the land that you bought."

For a few seconds, I stood there, stunned. Then remembering that Ron seemed to be in a rush, I asked, "Ron, why is the White House interested in a few properties we bought in the City of David?"

"The White House has been getting reports about you guys. Someone contacted the president's senior staff and convinced them that you guys threw a bunch of Palestinians out of their homes last night in Silwan, you're igniting the entire area, and that you are going to bring about a crisis."

I explained to Ron that the families had left quietly and that while there were initial rumblings from a few upstarts in the village, the area had been totally quiet since the morning.

"Listen," he told me. "I spoke to them, and the prime minister spoke to them. I think we can get them to drop the claim about throwing anyone out of their homes. However, I don't think they are going to back down altogether. They are going to issue some type of response."

"What should we do?" I asked.

"I wanted you to know in advance. I also want you to know that the prime minister and I told them that if they do in fact condemn you, we are going to defend you, and do it publicly. Just be ready."

I hung up the phone and updated Davidleh.

The next day, the White House followed through with their condemnation. White House Press Secretary Josh Earnest, speaking on behalf of President Obama, issued the following statement:

The United States condemns the recent occupation of residential buildings in the Palestinian neighborhood of Silwan in East Jerusalem—this is near the Old City—by individuals who are associated with an organization whose agenda, by definition, stokes tensions between Israelis and Palestinians. These provocative acts, these acts by this organization, only serve to escalate tensions at a moment when those tensions have already been high.[4]

After the White House condemnation, Prime Minister Netanyahu had an interview on CBS's *Face the Nation* in which he defended the land transactions between Jews and Arabs in the City of David.

Arabs in Jerusalem are free to purchase apartments in the western [part of the] city and no one is arguing against it. I have no intention of telling Jews they can't buy apartments in East Jerusalem. This is private property and an individual right. There cannot be discrimination—not against Jews and not against Arabs.... This goes against values that the United States also believes in.

Then he added, "Buying a house is a fundamental right...every person is entitled to private property. No one stole those houses or confiscated the property. Arabs are selling houses to Jews and Jews are selling houses to Arabs."[5]

Any transaction between any two people of different ethnicities, in any other city of the world, would never have been questioned by the White House. The only exception is when a Jewish person buys a home from an Arab person—and only here, in Jerusalem. A legal transaction had been made with willing and courageous Arab families who had braved threats from organizations that opposed the sale of real estate by Arabs to Jews.

Instead of issuing a condemnation against the terror organizations threatening the lives of innocent Arabs—a gross violation of the law—the White House was condemning us for buying their homes, which we did according to the letter of the law.

Willingly or unwillingly, the White House had come out on the wrong side of the truth.

Thankfully, Prime Minister Netanyahu and Ambassador Dermer defended us.

Following the prime minister's response, J Street, a radical left-wing US-based NGO that claims to be representative of American Jewry, called on the prime minister "to apologize and withdraw his remarks."

J Street stated it would renew calls on President Obama to "take a tougher stance against settlement expansion, which has gone virtually unchecked for decades and which now threatens to strangle hopes for a two-state solution."[6]

It was clear that the most senior government leaders and other public figures abroad were getting an unchallenged, distorted picture of the site from radical advocacy groups and their proxies abroad. It was imperative that we reveal the coordinated deception that was taking place. It was imperative that we present the true story of the City of David as a site of the highest historical value to the Jewish people and billions of non-Jews who hold Jerusalem sacred.

And it was imperative that we stress the legality of how the land was purchased.

I opened an international-affairs division at the City of David. The goal of the division was clear: We were not to impose our views on anyone or tell them what they should do or believe, but simply to inform them and educate them about the facts regarding the City of David.

The person we chose to lead the division was one of my closest friends, Zeev Orenstein. Zeev had no experience in government or diplomacy, but he was the best teacher and educator I knew: intelligent, sincere, and deeply passionate. I believed people would connect with him and be open to learning from him.

I began by introducing Zeev to a few of my contacts in the Israeli Foreign Ministry and heads of American Jewish and Christian organizations in the States. Zeev gave them tours and then gave tours to their staff. The word soon got out of how informative his tours were, and before long, delegations of groups from abroad began requesting Zeev to guide them as well.

The Foreign Ministry, which hosted delegations of influencers from abroad, quickly realized that after a tour with Zeev in the City of David, not only were participants impacted by the archaeology of the site, but they were also left with a deep intellectual understanding of the importance of the City of David to humanity, as well as the complexities surrounding the site and surrounding Jerusalem as a whole.

Soon, Zeev was guiding government staff and diplomats from Israel and abroad. A number of these were promoted over time to roles of greater importance in their governments. As they became more influential, they took the knowledge they had gained about the City of David with them, and the circle of those interested in the site grew.

One of those foreign officials who visited the site in early 2016 was Ileana Ros-Lehtinen, a Republican member of Congress from Florida. Ileana was taken with the historic importance of the site and was surprised that the tour was not a permanent part of every congressional visit to the country. If Yad Vashem, which documented the Holocaust, was a required part of every visit, Ileana felt, surely the place that documented the Jewish connection to the State of Israel should be as well. While on her tour, one of the sites that most impressed her was the Givati Parking Lot excavation, with its multiple layers of civilizations going back through time. Almost anyone could find some connection in their history to the site.

A few weeks after her visit, one of the archaeologists in the Givati Excavation, digging in a walled stone structure from the sixth century BCE, uncovered a royal seal impression engraved on a semi-precious stone from the First Temple Period. Other such seals had been found before, but this seal was different.

The name on the seal was that of a woman who lived in antiquity. Such a discovery indicated the elevated status of women in ancient Israel during a time when women did not play an influential role in the vast majority of societies throughout the world. What made this find most extraordinary was the first name on the seal: "Ileana the daughter of Gael."[7]

Once the seal was cleared for publication by the Israel Antiquities Authority, Zeev picked up the phone and called Representative Ileana Ros-Lehtinen.

"She has your name!" he told her. Ileana was stunned. Like us, she felt this seemed to be almost too much of a coincidence. From that moment, Ileana felt she had been called to help the City of David.

Many things are hard to relegate to chance in Jerusalem, and this was certainly one of them. Had I not witnessed this unfolding, it would be hard for me to believe.

However, the story of the two Ileanas doesn't end there.

Two weeks later, UNESCO, the United Nations Educational, Scientific, and Cultural Organization, had a preliminary vote on a deeply anti-Semitic and biased proposal submitted by Algeria, Egypt, Lebanon, Morocco, Oman, Qatar, and Sudan.

The declaration called on Israel—the "Occupying Power"—to "immediately cease the persistent excavations in and around the Old City."[8] The phrase "in and around the Old City" was an obvious reference to the City of David excavations, which they wanted to oppose, but which they refused to name because naming it would lend historic importance to the site.

The declaration not only purposefully ignored the City of David, but went one step further: It erased the Jewish connection to additional sites, including the Temple Mount, and the Western Wall. The Temple Mount, the holiest site in Judaism, was referred to solely by its Arabic name: Al-Haram al Sharif.

The Western Wall was referenced in the declaration with quotation marks, implying that the title is unofficial and not based on historic fact. Instead, the Western Wall was referred to only as "Al-Buraq Plaza," an Arabic name for the area based on the Islamic tradition that the Western Wall is the site where the Prophet Muhammad tied his steed, al-Buraq, on his night journey to Jerusalem before ascending to paradise.

The State of Israel was appalled by such a blatant revision of our Jewish history and immediately condemned the proposal. The condemnation was repeated by numerous heads of Jewish organizations in America, although J Street and Peace Now remained silent.

Ileana Ros-Lehtinen was incensed, as were other members of Congress—both Republicans and Democrats. UNESCO was an organization largely supported by the United States, and here it was making grossly anti-Semitic statements that not only denied Jewish history in Jerusalem but, by extension, Christian history as well, the religion of the vast majority of Americans.

Calls began coming in from all over the world asking us for information on discoveries that proved the Jewish connection to

Jerusalem and that exposed the historic injustice that would take place if UNESCO approved the declaration. We immediately put together a booklet of the discoveries with information that clearly showed scientific empirical evidence of the millennia-long Jewish presence in the area that UNESCO's declaration ignored.

Additionally, we included in the book reprinted pages of the guidebook to the Temple Mount published by the Islamic Waqf, the Muslim religious trust that oversees the Dome of the Rock. Published in 1930, the Waqf guidebook stated that regarding the Dome of the Rock, "Its identity with the site of Solomon's Temple is beyond dispute."

The UNESCO resolution was not only denying Jewish history; it was also refuting statements made by Muslims themselves that the Dome of the Rock sat over the site of the Jewish Temple built by King Solomon sixteen hundred years before Islam came to the world.

As the date for the UNESCO vote approached, the US Congress issued a bipartisan letter to the executive members of UNESCO, urging them to oppose the resolution that "would diminish the historic and verified Jewish and Christian ties to the Old City of Jerusalem in an effort to delegitimize Israel."

Ileana wrote the letter with Senator Ted Cruz.[9] Thirty-nine members of Congress signed the letter, one-third of them Democrats. To have bipartisan agreement reached on the issue was no small feat during a time of deep polarization in American politics, during which Democrats and Republicans seemed unable to agree on almost anything.[10]

In condemning the resolution, the letter specifically referred to the City of David, and the evidence of the excavations:

This resolution flies in the face of, among other things, science as recent archaeological excavations, notably in the City of David, have revealed incontrovertible, physical evidence that reaffirms Jewish and Christian ties to the holy city of Jerusalem. Members of the UNESCO Executive Board should vote against this intentional campaign to deny these historical truths, rewrite the history of Jerusalem, and delegitimize Israel.

The next day, October 12, 2016, in what will forever be a stain on what was once hailed as an organization encouraging science and culture throughout the world, UNESCO voted in favor of the resolution 24 to 6—thereby discrediting three thousand years of Jewish history.[11]

The six nations that voted against the resolution were the United States, Great Britain, Lithuania, the Netherlands, Germany, and Estonia.[12]

Saeb Erekat, the secretary general of the Palestine Liberation Organization, hailed the resolution, saying that, "Through an orchestrated campaign, Israel has been using archaeological claims and distortion of facts as a way to legitimize the annexation of occupied east Jerusalem."

The State of Israel immediately stopped cooperating with UNESCO.

Despite the passage of the resolution, and the loud voices in favor, there were a few individual acts of courage that deserve mention. One in particular involved the Mexican ambassador to UNESCO, Andres Roemer. Although Ambassador Roemer was ordered to vote in favor of the resolution, he refused to do so and walked out of the room in protest.

Shortly thereafter, Ambassador Roemer was fired from his position.[13]

Except for Ambassador Roemer's courage, along with that of the sole six countries that voted against the resolution, it looked at first as though UNESCO had succeeded in overturning Jewish history with no consequences. However, it soon became clear that UNESCO had stepped on a land mine.

It was one thing to call for a halt to excavations or even to decry the supposed "throwing of Palestinians out of their homes," but it was another to level an attack on the historical foundations of Jerusalem itself, on which not only fifteen million Jews based their belief, but also one and a half billion Christians worldwide.

In the days after the resolution was passed, it was printed and reprinted thousands of times, making its way into leading newspapers in Israel and abroad. Even new sources typically critical of Israel, like the *Guardian* and the BBC, ran the story.[14]

Public leaders spoke out, including Hillary Clinton, who at the time was a presidential candidate. She dubbed the resolution as "disappointing and wrong" and went on to say that UNESCO was "considering a resolution on Jerusalem that fails to recognize and respect the deep and historic ties of the Jewish people to Jerusalem and its holy sites."

Ban Ki Moon, the secretary general of the United Nations, condemned the resolution as well.[15] A wide range of Jewish and Christian leaders loudly condemned the measure.

Perhaps most incensed by the measure, however, was Congresswoman Ileana Ros-Lehtinen. Speaking from the floor of the House of Representatives about how anti-Semitic attitudes across Europe in the 1920s and 1930s gave rise to Nazism and the Holocaust, she warned the other members about modern trends of growing anti-Semitism, saying:

> What do we need to do? We have to look around at what agencies are doing. The efforts at UNESCO to erase Jewish historical and cultural ties to their ancient homeland, Jerusalem, have been appalling.[16]

Writing now after the October 7 massacre, I cannot help but look back at these events and see them as building blocks upon which the radicalization of Hamas and those who massacred the Jewish people were built. The systematic progression of lies that began with the early founder of the Palestinian movement, Haj Amin al Husseini—Hitler's confidant—spiraled into the Hamas and Palestinian Authority charters in the 1980s. From there, it was echoed not only by radical Islamists, such as Sheikh Ikrima Sabri and Raed Salah, but found its way into the offices of anti-Israel NGOs, including those located in Israel.

From there, echoed by a constant narrative of occupation in the Western media, it ascended to the corridors of institutions that were founded to honor the truth and largely protect mankind from the lies that lead to tyranny. I see that the weakening of these institutions—and the falsehoods that they sanctioned—only added fuel to the fires that burned in the warped minds of those who committed the Holocaust-like horrors on Saturday, October 7.

Equally concerning is that today the denial of the Jewish people's most basic ties to the Land of Israel has spread to educational institutions of higher learning who perpetuate this creed. A shocking number of tenured professors from respected universities were among those who marched in the streets chanting "From the River to the Sea, Palestine Will Be Free," and calling for the elimination of the State of Israel.

Among the crowds, there were also numerous young people who were marching along, either intentionally or ignorantly propagating words that defy history and deny the rights of one people to their land. The degree to which these people bear responsibility for their actions is a matter of debate. What is not up for debate is that if they turn to their most common source of information for the younger generation, social media, they see that the Obama administration, the United Nations, and others believed these lies.

Against this backdrop, I draw strength and hope from three things that I have witnessed: The first is seeing those who have stepped forward, at great personal risk, to challenge these lies. I know there are many in the world who seek the truth. Some have the courage, like the Mexican ambassador, or Congresswoman Ileana Ros-Lehtinen, to speak their truth in front of the world, at the risk of being condemned by the extreme left, misunderstood by their constituents, or even fired from their positions.

The second is that I derive enormous strength from witnessing the unity of the Israeli people, a people often divided by politics, on October 7 and in the ensuing months. The resolve of our nation to put aside our differences and come to our roots, to stand up to defend the country has never been higher.

The third was during a conversation I had with Congresswoman Elise Stefanik during a visit she made to Jerusalem in May 2024 during the height of Israel's war against Hamas. Just a few months earlier, Congresswoman Stefanik made headlines when, during a congressional hearing on anti-Semitism in US universities, she asked the presidents of Harvard, MIT, and the University of Pennsylvania if "calling for the genocide of the Jewish People" violates their rules of bullying and harassment. While disgracefully none of the three presidents answered with a clear "yes" or "no," it was Harvard President Claudia Gay's answer that "it depends on the context" that sent shockwaves through the world. The congresswoman immediately declared, "It does not depend on the context, the answer is 'yes' and this is why you should resign." The hearing revealed that while the rights of minorities are vigorously enforced on campuses, the same apparently does not apply to Jews.

I asked the congresswoman over a dinner in Israel what she thought about the oft-discussed studies that were showing a steep rise of anti-Israel sentiment along with anti-Semitism among eighteen-to-twenty-four-year-olds. It was one thing to deal with university leaders and their policies, but what about the people themselves? She acknowledged the worrying pattern and explained that steps such as banning TikTok, a wellspring of fundamentalist ideas including anti-Jewish propaganda geared at the young generation, were part of the answer. "However," she said, "I can tell you that in my district in northern New York, if you ask any of the farmers, or the manufacturers or the residents, if calling for the genocide of the Jewish people is against the law, they will answer with a clear 'yes.' The vast majority of the American people will answer the same way. Please remember that." I appreciated her answer. She wasn't downplaying that there were worrying trends, however, what she was saying was that average Americans, the ones whose voices you don't hear chanting on the news, have a clear moral sense of right and wrong, and appreciate and support Israel. We are inundated by the news and social media that hyper focus on the naysayers, until it seems as if the whole world is against us. That is likely what those who condemn Israel want us to think. It took Elise Stefanik, a non-Jewish congresswoman from northern New York, who is now serving as the US ambassador to the United Nations, to pierce the echo chamber and remind us that we are not alone.

Following October 7, military conscription was met with over 100 percent attendance. Young Israeli men and women returned from trekking around the world and from jobs overseas. People who had fought in the Yom Kippur War fifty years ago, and were now in their seventies, asked to be enlisted again, and there was hardly a Jewish family in the country—and in a number of cases, non-Jews as well—who were not somehow part of the war effort, making and delivering food and gathering supplies, babysitting children of families whose parents were off serving. We were motivated to defend our homes and the security of our country.

But the nation was also motivated by an attack on our very identity as an ancient people, indigenous to the Land of Israel with a rich history, a history in danger of being destroyed. More than any other people, we know from experience that when we and our identity are demonized, the next step can lead to the events of October 7 and worse. Those who perished, and their families, too, paid an almost unimaginable price; however, their sacrifice was not in vain, for the country has awakened.

Grab almost any Israeli off the streets in Israel today and they will likely tell you: *We are here. We have always been here.*

And we're not going anywhere else.

Part Four

THE CITY OF DAVID
RISES AGAIN

Chapter 14

The Golden Bell

The summer after the tunnel became open to the public, I was sitting at the conference table in the City of David with Davidleh, Yehuda, and some of the other staff. We were deep in a discussion about developing a robotic model that would orient visitors to the City of David by building Jerusalem in front of their eyes—somewhat like assembling ancient pieces of Lego from different time periods.

Suddenly the conference room door burst open, and Eli Shukron walked in. His shoes were covered with mud, and his clothes were covered with a mixture of sweat and dust.

He stood over us, smiling with a mischievous grin, reached out, and put a small translucent bag on the table. He looked like a kid who had found a new toy in the schoolyard and brought it home. Inside was what looked like a dollop of drying mud.

"Who can tell me what this is?" he asked us.

We leaned in closer to have a better look. All I could make out was a shining piece of yellowish metal inside the mud.

Turning to me, he asked half accusingly, "*Nu*, Spielman, what is it?"

Eli gently took it out of the bag and put it in the dusty palm of his hand. The color beneath the mud shined in comparison to his dusty dark hand. He held it before our eyes.

It appeared to be round, and I could see what looked like a small metal clasp protruding from the top of the object. "Is it a ball made of gold?" I asked him hesitantly.

He nodded, his smile widening ever further. Pointing to the little clasp with his hand he said, "This is where it was sewn onto a piece of clothing…"

He gently placed the object in my hands.

I ran my finger delicately over the surface and could feel the smooth metal beneath the mud.

"Shake it," he told me.

Curiously, I gently lifted it up to my ear and shook it.

A faint ringing came from inside the ball.

"Is there a chime inside?" I asked, turning to look up at him.

"There is," he answered. "Now tell me, where do we read about a small gold bell that was sewn onto someone's clothing?"

I looked back at the object in my hand in confusion—and then my eyes widened with understanding.

Around the table, everyone started to murmur—they understood as well.

"Eli, are you telling me that this is the bell"—my voice was filled with awe—"the same bell that was worn by the High Priest in the Temple?"

"I am," he replied. "It is."

A few minutes before, Nissim, the shift supervisor, had seen something partially buried in the dirt, something shining in the light of his headlamp, and had carefully removed it. They speculated that it may have torn off the High Priest's robe while he was either working at the Temple, or perhaps while fleeing the Roman army's advance.

Apparently, it had rolled through a crack in the road and had fallen down into the tunnel below, where it had rested—for two thousand years—until now.

Gently taking the bell back from my hands, Eli held it up again for everyone to see.

"This is the only golden bell ever found in an excavation in Israel with the chime still inside. It was found directly next to the Temple Mount where the High Priest officiated. It is just as the Torah describes."

Eli was referring to an oft-quoted verse from Exodus 28:34 that describes the High Priest's robe:

On its hem make pomegranates of blue, purple, and crimson yarns, all around the hem, with bells of gold between them all around.[1]

If Eli was right, it was one of the most significant discoveries ever made in Jerusalem.

The High Priest was the most central figure in the Temple, and was a direct descendant of Aaron, the brother of Moses. In Hebrew, the High Priest is called the Cohen, still a common surname among Jews, indicating that their family ancestry descends directly from Aaron. This has even been borne out in recent DNA studies of what has been termed the Cohen Gene.[2] Many of the Cohens walking around today descend from the same person who wore that bell.

When the Israel Antiquities Authority released the discovery to the press, it took the world by storm. Hundreds of articles followed, and people streamed from all over Israel to see the place where the bell of the High Priest was found.[3] In fact, so many diplomats and public figures from Israel and abroad asked to see the object that the Israel Antiquities Authority decided to send the object back to the laboratory to be studied and preserved until one day when it will hopefully return to the City of David to be put on display.

Following the bell discovery, dozens of other important

discoveries were made in the drainage channel. Archaeologists continued to dig in the area through the layers of earth dating to the destruction of the Temple. One notable discovery was a sword that originally belonged to a Roman legionnaire of the Tenth Legion—the top strike force of the Roman army. A Roman soldier would never leave his sword behind, which probably meant that this soldier did not make it out alive—a stark reminder of the fierce fighting that took place.

Over the next two years, the excavations continued, and discoveries were announced to the world on an almost monthly basis. As access to the tunnel improved, the National Parks Authority officially incorporated the drainage channel into the City of David Tour.

Hundreds of thousands of tourists a year began walking the drainage channel from the City of David to the Old City of Jerusalem. The prominence of the site began to grow dramatically, both in Israel and abroad. We started to compete with the most visited sites in the country, such as Masada and Caesarea.

A golden bell is not enough to change the minds of people like Huweida, and certainly not enough to hold off the oncoming storm of denial that would issue from the highest quarters in the Western world. This little golden object would, however, inspire the people of Israel, along with Jews and non-Jews throughout the world.

The bell's importance as an object used by the High Priest in the Temple service was invaluable, especially when we consider that archaeological excavations on the Temple Mount are forbidden by the Waqf, and therefore any remains of the Jewish Temples, which would be buried underground, cannot be seen.

Since the discovery of Eilat Mazar's clay seals with the names from the Bible, no other discovery had received such exposure. The small bell, measuring barely half an inch in size, had an almost fantasy-like aura of bringing the days of the Temple back to life.

The discovery of the bell was both a source of pride and a

confirmation of our past connection to the holiest site in the Jewish world, the place where millions of Jews had directed their prayers over the millennia.

The discovery was important for another reason as well. It strengthened the resolve of the Israeli people and our leadership.

We would need that resolve for the challenges to come.

Chapter 15

The Temple Cornerstone

In what was probably her greatest gift to us, Congresswoman Ileana Ros-Lehtinen brought David Friedman, the United States ambassador to the State of Israel, to the City of David. It was the first time a sitting US ambassador had visited the site.

The City of David resonated with Ambassador Friedman deep in his very core. As both a religious Jew and an American statesman, Ambassador Friedman saw the City of David in a unique light, and he proceeded to give voice to a vision that had never been voiced before. The City of David was, to him, the site of the origin story from which the shared values of both the United States and the State of Israel sprung forth. These values bound the two countries together in a way much more profoundly than the military alliance the two countries share.

Expressing this vision in his book *Sledgehammer*, David says:

The Declaration of Independence, perhaps the most profound document since the Bible, contained the guarantee to every person of "unalienable rights" endowed by our Creator.... These unalienable rights endowed by God were His will as revealed in the Bible. And the word of God, as described by the prophet Isaiah, was first expressed in the City of David:

"For out of Zion shall go forth the law and the word of the Lord from Jerusalem." (Isaiah 2:3).

Ambassador Friedman's full name is David Melech Friedman, literally translated as "David King Friedman." The man who bears the name of the ancient king of Israel proceeded to become one of the most important people to grace the site. Ambassador Friedman understood more than anybody else not only that the City of David was the repository of the proof that established the connection between the Jewish people and Jerusalem, but also that the site was the very foundation upon which the divinely given unalienable rights of the American people rested.

In light of this understanding, he saw the UNESCO resolution as not only an attack on Israel, but also an attack on the United States. David pledged to bring every high-level United States official that visited Israel to the site. He resolved to create broad American support for the project, so that its sanctity and importance would never again be ignored by an American administration.

"The City of David," David says in his book, "thus meant as much to me as an American as it did as a Jew, and I was determined to make sure that American political leaders were exposed to this great monument to our Judeo-Christian heritage."[1]

Before David became ambassador, the State Department had fought tooth and nail to keep high-level officials from visiting the site. But during David's term as ambassador, he fulfilled his promise and brought nine sitting cabinet members to the site, along with countless delegations of senators, members of Congress, and high-level officials.

On May 2, 2017, our own David, Davidleh Beeri, was awarded the Israel Prize for Lifetime Achievement, the highest honor bestowed on an individual by the State of Israel. When we had originally come to him in his office to let him know that it had been announced he was being considered for the prize, he said that he did not want it. Davidleh was not building the City of David for a prize. He did not need outside affirmation for pursuing what he felt was the mission he was born for. In fact, Davidleh ran away from honors.

However, we told him it would be good for the City of David and draw positive attention to what he had built. We said this, of course, because on one hand it is true, but also because we who have worked with him side by side knew that no one else in Israel deserved the prize more.

When word got out that Davidleh would be awarded the prize, radical advocacy groups were quick to condemn the decision,[2] and rumors circulated about massive protests outside the ceremony and even disruptions from former prize winners during the event. But in the end, when the day came, there was only one person standing outside the National Assembly Hall, holding a torn sign.

As the recipients of the prize in different categories such as science and music were called, they walked across the stage and received their awards with a friendly handshake from either the president of Israel or the prime minister.

When Davidleh's name was called, the entire room erupted in deafening applause. Prime Minister Netanyahu stood up and saluted him along with Israel's President Reuven Rivlin. Even the head of the Supreme Court, Miriam Naor, a usually reserved and unemotional person, smiled and said she wanted to visit soon.

While this was happening, six former prize winners exited the room in an unnoticed protest.

I looked at Davidleh standing there. He wore his nicely pressed white shirt untucked, just as he did for special occasions and the Sabbath, along with his simple pants and work shoes. The prize commission had called to say that he would have to wear a suit. Davidleh told them he never owned a suit, nor was he going to change who he was for the ceremony. They continued to press him, to which he responded that they could either let him come as he was or keep their prize.

They relented.

As he stood there, next to the prime minister, the president, and the head of the Supreme Court, I felt a deep sense of gratitude to God for bringing me to join this man on the epic journey of the rise of the City of David. There was a sense of completion at that moment, like the circle had come around and finally connected at the tip. I remembered being warned about joining him in the beginning. I remembered seeing him called names, threatened, and almost killed. He had been decried in the papers as a radical, and at the beginning, members of City Hall and even the mayor of Jerusalem had come to protest him.

Today, he was standing on stage receiving the highest-level award offered in Israel. Even more so, while he was the shortest person on stage—and the least formal—I knew then, as I know now, that even though the people handing him the award were great, he was a giant. If that is not yet known, one day I believe it will be.

On May 14, 2018, President Trump made history by courageously moving the United States embassy from Tel Aviv to Jerusalem, Israel's rightful capital.

It took nineteen years after the Jerusalem Embassy Act was passed by Congress and three presidential administrations before this decision was finally implemented, bringing a moment of celebration in Israel.

That day, it would turn out, would be a consequential day also for the City of David. I was at a party that evening celebrating the move. A number of people who had played important roles in the embassy move were also there, including Sheldon Adelson. Sheldon and Miriam Adelson were the Jewish world's greatest benefactors and one of the world's wealthiest couples. Along with countless other projects, they had funded the Birthright project, which had brought hundreds of thousands of Jewish teens to Israel.

Years before I had taken them on a tour of the City of David, and when Sheldon saw me at the embassy celebration, his face lit up.

"You know, Doron," he said, "why haven't you guys asked me for money?"

I smiled, not used to hearing that question from a donor—usually it was the other way around.

I said, "Well, Mr. Adelson, we certainly need your money, especially for the Pilgrimage Road, which is at a critical stage. When would be a good time to discuss it?"

He called over Miriam, and they asked me if Davidleh and I would meet them at the King David Hotel overlooking the Old City the following morning.

The next day, Sheldon and Miriam Adelson made a monumental commitment to the Pilgrimage Road excavation. Matching them, dollar for dollar, was Larry Ellison, the founder of the tech giant Oracle.

With that kind of money, we were able to hire additional crews and construction teams to excavate and prepare a critical leg of the Pilgrimage Road so that the southern section would be accessible to the public. In fact, it was those funds that enabled us to have an opening with the United States government a year later.

Something else happened that day that touched me very deeply. It was while talking with Sheldon and Miriam that I told them that I had just come from a funeral at the Mount of Olives. After my story, Miriam took me aside and asked me if I would be kind enough to show them the Mount of Olives, which I was only too happy to do. I explained the significance of the site in the history of the Jewish people and showed them how part of the cemetery was still undergoing restoration, following the Jordanian destruction of the site.

Sheldon and Miriam decided that they would purchase a section of the cemetery for their family, located directly across from the Temple Mount—a powerful symbol that their family stood together with the Jewish people, not only in the present, but for all of their future generations.

Three years later, Miriam called me in the middle of the night to tell me that Sheldon had passed away and asked if I would officiate over his burial at the family section on the Mount of Olives, with just a few of the family members and close friends.

That was and still is one of the proudest moments of my life.

On February 12, 2019, Zeev Orenstein and I visited Vice President Mike Pence in the White House. The vice president had visited the site when he was still governor of Indiana. Having heard about the progress of the excavations, specifically that of the Pilgrimage Road, he invited us to come to the White House and update him on the progress of the excavations.

Zeev and I visited the VP in his office and presented him with a book that we had prepared just for him that documented our newest discoveries and included an update on the Pilgrimage Road. To our surprise the vice president remembered his tour years before as if it had happened yesterday. He flipped page after page and recognized every discovery at first glance and recited to us its historical background and meaning. He seemed to know almost as much about our discoveries as we did. He told us how he had heard about the progress from every cabinet secretary who had visited the City of David, and they felt the same about the importance of the site.

What interested him most, he said, was the status of our progress on the Pilgrimage Road.

We had relaunched the Pilgrimage Road excavation in 2015 and beautiful broad stairs of the road were being revealed deep underneath the mountain of fill. In the years since we had first started the excavation—before being halted by the Supreme Court—we had developed a new engineering method of creating steel supports in the shape of a wide arch. This new design enabled us to dig a wider section of the road and reveal even more of the historic pathway.

We walked him through the progress and showed him on a map where our teams had reached. We explained that we had two teams excavating simultaneously toward each other from opposite directions. One of the teams was digging from the Pool of Siloam to the north while the second team dug south toward them from a midway station of the road called the Jubilee Station. We hoped the two teams would meet in the next year, which would enable visitors to walk from the Pool of Siloam halfway up the mountain and exit at the Jubilee Station, while our crews then turned to excavate the other half of the road to the north.

We told him that we hoped that members of the United States administration would be with us on the maiden Pilgrimage Journey for a pre-opening that we were planning seven months later in July 2019. The vice president thought this was a great idea, and he and Ambassador Friedman began working on the details of how the United States and Israel could come together to celebrate the opening of the Pilgrimage Road.

Following our meeting, the visit was released to the public and it made the rounds both in the American and Israeli government circles.

The City of David was now important enough that it had been both condemned by one White House and celebrated by another.

Twenty-seven hundred years ago, King Hezekiah's workers had dug a tunnel through the mountain to keep the city's water supply safe from the Assyrian invasion. As recorded by the Siloam Inscription, now in the Istanbul Museum, Hezekiah had two teams of diggers heading toward each other from opposite sides of the mountain. One day, the two teams heard each other through the stone, and with only a slight correction to their trajectory, they met in the middle of the mountain.

In a modern-day replay of that historic event in the City of David, in the spring of 2019, the two excavation teams working to connect the Pilgrimage Road to the Pool of Siloam heard each other digging through the mountain from opposite sides. Two days later, we caught on film the moment when a worker from the northern team put his dusty arm through a small opening and it was grasped by a worker from the southern team.

Workers immediately began to reinforce the area and clear away the wall of earth so the opening could be widened in time for a ceremony on June 30, 2019. The event would commemorate the pilgrimage journey from the Pool of Siloam, halfway up the mountain to the Jubilee Station.

We called Ambassador Friedman with the news, and he was thrilled. He committed to attending and assigned his senior adviser, Aryeh Lightstone, and special assistant, David Milstein, to bring senior administration members to the ceremony. Together, they would help turn it into one of the most significant events, symbolizing the deep bond and shared values between the United States and Israel.

The event would begin at the Pool of Siloam, where I would welcome the guests and introduce the Pilgrimage Journey. Following this, Ambassador Friedman, Yuval Baruch from the Israel Antiquities Authority, Nir Barkat, the Mayor of Jerusalem, and of course Davidleh would give speeches. I was to be the Master of Ceremonies.

Afterward, the group would make their way toward the entrance to the Pilgrimage Road. Instead of the typical ribbon-cutting ceremony, Davidleh, in a stroke of brilliance, felt that we should do something more connected to the City of David.

We decided to open the Pilgrimage Journey with a reenactment of the moment the two teams had met.

Our excavation teams gathered some of the useless dirt that had been cleared out of the tunnel and built a thin wall on top of cardboard at the entrance to the road. The ceremony would begin with our guests carefully lifting up sledgehammers and being given a turn to whack the wall until it all came down. Then, they would begin the journey.

It was a bit kitschy, but then again, so is cutting a ribbon. We thought everyone would love it, and we were right.

After the journey, it was decided that David Friedman, together with Prime Minister Netanyahu, would host a select number of guests for a dinner in the American consulate.

June 30 arrived, and it was a balmy day in Jerusalem. The Pool of Siloam had been converted into a beautiful showcase, with displays of the Pilgrimage Road, antiquities, and a stage with a large screen. However, at its base, we had left the floor just as it was: revealing bare limestone stairs we had first discovered fourteen years before, the stairs that had given birth to the idea of the Pilgrimage Road journey, which had now become the most important excavation site in Jerusalem.

I climbed the stage and looked out at the guests before saying my opening words. I saw heads of Israeli government agencies, Knesset members and ministers, along with numerous United States officials, including ambassadors, senators, and special envoys that Ambassador Friedman had invited.

In the first row sat our donors—that unique group of people who had believed in the dream and vested their trust and their hard-earned money in us to carry it to fruition.

I looked out at Eugene Shvidler among them and thought back to when we crawled through the tunnel and saw the stairs of the Pilgrimage Road over our heads, the beginning of the journey that had led us to this moment. I saw Sheldon and Miriam Adelson, probably the most well-known of all Israel's donors.

I saw Ronnie Chan, who had come all the way from Hong Kong for the opening because he felt a kinship with the Jews, a people as ancient as the Chinese, and Kevin Bermeister, the original investor in Skype who came from Australia. A number of CEOs from Fortune 100 companies were in the crowd, including Safra Catz, the CEO of Oracle, and her husband Gal Tirosh. The next generation of Jewish leaders were there as well, led by Jan Koum, who is younger than I am, and the cofounder of WhatsApp, which he sold to Facebook. He had become one of the most significant donors to the project, and the Jewish world.

What drew all of us together from Israel and around the world had begun with a small underground spring, a miniscule stream of water, poking out between a few rocks on a valley floor. That little spring had brought the first people here in the Stone Age. Later the Canaanites came and built a fortress around the water on the mountain, which turned into a city. King David came and saw the water both as the key to life in the city, and the key to capturing it.

According to the Zohar, the mystical text of Israel, these waters were connected to the Garden of Eden. The modern founding of the City of David had come from Captain Charles Warren walking through these waters, when he discovered the shaft that would be named after him. And now, some of the world's most important people had come together to the very site where the waters gathered in the Pool of Siloam.

I thought about the day we crawled through the tunnel and touched the foundation stones of the Western Wall. I thought of Davidleh, staring out at the Old City walls, seeing the future as if it were already here, telling me that one day we would be inside. I thought of how his vision stands as a beacon for us all as we overcome so many obstacles.

I told the waiting audience about this story, and I pointed to where he and I had stood that day. I told them they were now a part of the story as it continues to unfold.

Ambassador Friedman took the stage, speaking as America's representative to Israel. He told the audience that it was from where we were sitting on the stairs of the Pool of Siloam that America's founders had received their inspiration to pursue life, liberty, and happiness for all, for it was here that the prophets of Israel taught us those lessons. He would later, just before leaving office, make the City of David the first American Heritage Site in Israel. The sign, emblazoned with the American and Israeli flags and commemorating this act, stands prominently on the wall, just next to the entrance to the City of David today.

I invited the guests to enter the Pilgrimage Road, and then followed the group as we walked toward the Old City and the Temple Mount. The full journey would take additional years to excavate, but today we were on the maiden voyage, halfway up the mountain to the Jubilee. We all hoped to meet here again in another five years to complete the journey and exit near the Western Wall.

As we walked up the Pilgrimage Road, I could see the members of the delegation walking in front of me, shoulder to shoulder as they took step after step up the road. They were smiling, talking quietly among themselves, awed by the chance to walk on the same floor stones that the ancients, the world's first monotheists, had walked on, two thousand years before.

I thought about the miracle of my own journey. I had started as an American Jew in a Michigan suburb and left a comfortable life to join my own people's pilgrimage back home to Israel. What gratitude I felt to be a part of this moment in history.

Before reaching the Temple, the Pilgrimage Road narrowed, drawing us closer together like a funnel. I imagined the first travelers on this road thousands of years ago—families from different tribes speaking different dialects—walking side by side with their children, carrying fruit and offerings, and sharing their life experiences as they made their way up to the Temple.

Perhaps the point of the Pilgrimage Road was to unify us as a people before reaching the Temple to pray. The journey, walking in tandem, seeing those in front and behind, making their way up the road, reminds us that every person, whether we see it or not, is on their own pilgrimage, their own journey. Every one of us is learning, and simply doing our best to find our own journey through life and to walk it.

As long as that is so, we might as well walk together.

Israel is not an easy place. It is vibrant, colorful, and full of life, but it is certainly not easy. It is often fractured, like the stairs of the road, broken by the Romans, but it has held itself together, both in the tunnels in the darkness, and in the road in the light.

One day, when the road is rebuilt and people once again rub shoulders on the journey, hopefully the Pilgrimage Road will bring us closer together, unified around the whole story of our people, the story that we are still here, still trying.

I wondered, will the visitors who walk the road in the future have any idea of the struggle we went through now, the struggle to reach this point and open the road for the world?

There must have been countless struggles in ancient Jerusalem, and I am sure only a fraction were recorded in the Bible and remembered.

Most have probably been forgotten over time.

Either way, I realized, it didn't matter. For each moment was connected and formed a chain that continues to bind the Jewish people to Jerusalem.

For those of us who came at the beginning, and those who joined us along the way, we know and we will remember. We made it to this moment because we stood up against the mighty and the powerful with one goal: that our little piece of the chain should remain whole.

Chapter 16

The Battle of the Coins

On the ninth day of the Jewish month of Av, a boiling hot day in mid-August in the year 70 of the Common Era, the Roman Tenth Legion broke into the inner compound of the Temple Mount and set the Temple itself on fire, destroying it.

In so doing, they thought they were destroying the symbol of Jewish hope that had beckoned to the Jewish people for more than a thousand years.

Little did they know that two thousand years later, Jews would still be around, and from wherever they were scattered among the four corners of the earth, they would turn to face the Temple when offering up a prayer.

The Roman Legion rounded up the leaders of the rebellion, along with thousands of other Jews, and brought them to Rome as captives. They were marched through the streets of the city, carrying on their backs the golden menorah from the Temple. The gruesome scene is carved into the Arch of Titus, still standing today in Rome.

Following the Roman victory, Roman Caesar Vespasian issued a coin marking his victory over Judea called the Judea Capta, meaning "Judea has been captured."[1] Minted in bronze, silver, and gold, the image of the defeated Judean Empire made its way through the vast Roman Empire. This was not the first victory coin issued by Rome;

however, it was one of the most widely distributed. Whereas most victory coins were minted in six series, the Judea Capta was minted forty-eight times and over a twenty-five-year period.

On one side of the coin, Caesar Vespasian's profile appears, with his name inscribed in a half circle along the edge. Vespasian now is mostly forgotten as a Roman emperor, remembered only by historians.

It is the obverse side of the coin that I think is most telling and that has followed the Jewish people throughout their exile. Beneath the words "Judea Capta," a victorious Roman soldier stands to one side of a palm tree. On the other side of the tree is the hunched-over figure of a woman who has been defeated. Her hands are bound and she is weeping.

She was the symbol, to the Romans, of the Jewish people's destruction.

So powerful was this symbol of the defeated woman of Judea that it eventually made its way into the Catholic Church. Centuries later it reappeared in the form of a woman called Synagoga, who most often stands opposite another woman called Ecclesia. Ecclesia and Synagoga, Latin for "church and synagogue," are commonly found at the entrance to medieval churches. Ecclesia is a beautiful, crowned woman with an air of confidence about her, while Synagoga is blindfolded, hunched over, and forlorn.

The image symbolizes the church's ascendancy over defeated Judaism.[2]

Throughout the darkness of the exile, it must have been easy for anyone to think that the Jews had been defeated and probably would be forever. When Rome fell and the coins became lost, the image of Synagoga—defeated Judea—persisted. The pogroms followed, and finally the worst pogrom of all, the Holocaust.

Throughout it all empires rose and, one after the other, they fell. Of all these fallen empires, Judea survived. We have paid a price, sometimes a horrible price, but we have survived.

And now, in the State of Israel, with all our challenges, we will survive again.

I first saw an original Judea Capta coin around twenty years ago in the office of George Blumenthal, an enthusiast of Jewish history and antiquities. George placed the Judea Capta in my hands, and I could feel the weight of the bronze. There it was, Vespasian's face staring up at me. When I flipped the coin over and saw the woman of Judea crying, a chill went up my spine. At the end of the meeting, George put the coin back in my hand and closed my fingers around it.

"You have it," he said to me. He felt that it was more important that I have it since I was traveling around the world on behalf of the City of David.

I have taken that coin with me everywhere. In meetings, I pull it out and show it to donors, politicians, and family. After putting the heavy coin in one of their hands, I place in their other hand an original Freedom of Zion coin—the small, lightweight, roughly shaped coins minted by the last Jewish survivors before the exile of the Jewish people.

"Which coin was victorious?" I ask them, and nine out of ten people lift up the Roman coin.

I then ask them, "Did you grow up with people of other backgrounds, people from India, China, or Latin America?" Most of them answer yes.

"Tell me," I then ask them, "did you grow up with any Romans in your classes?"

After that, they usually look at me in silence, until they smile with understanding.

"It has been a hard road for the Jews," I tell them. "Hard almost beyond explanation. But today, we are still here. That is our victory."

This was the message that I would leave people with, on my journeys crisscrossing the world on behalf of the City of David, until one day, when Yehuda Mali called me into his office. His father had recently passed away and while looking through his items, the family had found an original commemorative coin struck by the State of Israel in 1958. This was the first commemorative coin ever made by the State of Israel, and it was minted to commemorate ten years of survival.

Yehuda handed it to me. On one side of the bronze coin there was a depiction of the Judea Capta, with the Roman soldier standing over the crying woman of Judea.

"Turn it over," Yehuda told me.

I flipped it over, and on the opposite side, where the woman had sat mourning, now a Jewish farmer was planting a sapling in the soil. Where the Roman soldier had stood triumphantly now stood a Jewish woman, holding up her newborn baby.

Across the top, written in Hebrew, were the words ISRAEL HAS BEEN LIBERATED.

We were not the first to recognize the significance of the coins. Since the founding of the State of Israel, the first commission tasked with designing its inaugural commemorative coin understood their meaning. They chose to set free the mourning woman of Judea Capta, and with her, to free the Jewish people.

The battle of the coins was finally won.

Epilogue

My Wife's Family:
The Jews Who Never Left

During the bus ride when I met my wife Sarah, she told me that just the day before, she and two of her uncles, Eli and Avraham, had gone together to the village in the Galilee in northern Israel, where her family was originally from. The village is called Peki'in, and her family, the Zenati family, is known to be the oldest Jewish family residing in Israel, having maintained a continuous presence in the village since the Roman destruction of the Temple thousands of years earlier. [1]

Sarah's mother, Esther, had moved to England to pursue a singing career. There, she met Sarah's father and raised her three children. When the children inquired as to their family's roots, Esther told them that she was from an ancient family in Israel, but that she didn't know any more about it. She told the children that if they wanted to know more, they should go to Israel and speak with Esther's older brother, Uncle Avraham, who lived in a small village in the north. On the last week of the summer trip to Israel, just days before we met, Sarah went to her uncle Avraham's home and sat with a notebook as he recounted the family's history.

As I sat next to Sarah on the bus to that wedding, Sarah told me the story of her family.

According to family tradition, the Zenatis trace their ancestry to priests of the Temple in Jerusalem, who fled north with a group of Jews after the Temple's destruction by the Romans in 70 CE. The Talmud recounts this event, noting that Rabbi Yehoshua, a leading rabbi of the time, established a house of study in Peki'in. Unlike many others, the Zenati family never left the Land of Israel during the two-thousand-year Jewish exile. They remained in Peki'in, thus ensuring that there would always be a continuous Jewish presence in the land.[2]

Uncle Avraham remembered as a young boy going to the village to visit relatives before the Passover holiday. He remembered them up on step stools whitewashing their walls before the holiday began, an old Jewish tradition, and he remembered helping them paint. He had returned to the village many times over the years, and recounted to Sarah that the family had a small synagogue in the center of the village, next to a spring of water, which still stands to this day. He told Sarah that he, and his brother Eli, Sarah's other uncle, would take her to see the village and introduce her to Margalit, the last remaining member of the Zenati family living in the village.

The next day, Avraham and Eli led Sarah down a winding path, until they reached a cave with a spring flowing next to it. A sign in front of the cave recounts that it is the same cave in which Rabbi Shimon Bar Yochai wrote the Kabbalah while hiding from Romans for thirteen years and, according to legend, subsisting on nothing but a carob tree and the spring of water.

Sarah recounted to me that she had her uncles squeeze into the cave, and recite together with her the Jewish prayer for forgiveness and healing that Jews recite every evening before going to bed.

In addition to showing Sarah the spring and the synagogue, Avraham introduced her to some of the local Druze residents. He explained to Sarah that over the centuries, members of the Zenati family periodically had to go into hiding from marauders or invading armies, such as the Crusaders, who would systematically kill all the Jews they found. Over the years, the Druze community protected the family, and their Druze descendants are the majority of the residents in the village today. During the bloody uprising of the Arab Revolt of 1938, the local Druze warned the Jews of Peki'in of an impending massacre, and the family again went into hiding, as they had for centuries.

The Zenatis were saved.

I was astounded as Sarah told me this story on that bus ride.

I had learned about the Zenatis when I began studying the history of Israel at the University of Michigan. I was intrigued by the idea that this family was rediscovered by Jews who moved back to the Land of Israel in the mid-1500s after being exiled from Spain and Portugal. These Sephardic Jews must have been astonished to find that there had been Jews living there. The Jews of Peki'in were hard to distinguish from the Druze and Arabs living in the mountains in northern Israel: Wearing similar clothes and speaking Arabic, they stood apart only in their Jewish religion and customs, their proficiency in biblical Hebrew, and the oral history they recounted of their families.

I discovered that in 1525, an early Ottoman census already recorded that there was a thriving Jewish community in this little village nestled in the mountains. Jewish travelers to the area recorded that there was a spring there—and an ancient synagogue.[3] The synagogue was destroyed by an earthquake in 1837, but it was rebuilt in 1873.

Years later, Sarah and I, along with Uncle Avraham, took our children to see the village. We went to that ancient synagogue, still tended by Margalit Zenati, whose home is next door. The walls of the synagogue contain two blocks made of Jerusalem limestone which stand out from the rest. The two stones are believed to have been taken from the rubble of the destroyed Second Temple when the Zenatis and other families escaped from the Romans and came to Peki'in. The stones from the Temple became the symbolic building blocks of the Peki'in synagogue.

Margalit Zenati is an icon in Israel today.

A feisty woman even in her early nineties, Margalit speaks both Hebrew and Arabic fluently. She has always returned to her home in the village, despite all the wars and revolts and riots of the last one hundred years. During the seventieth-anniversary celebrations of the State of Israel, Margalit was asked to light an Independence Eve torch, an honor reserved for only a few of the nation's most important citizens.

Despite her bent-over and feeble body, there is still a strength in her eyes, a strength I see in the eyes of my children.

In the early years of the founding of the State of Israel, the Zenati family was so important that Yitzchak ben Zvi, the president of the State of Israel, purchased the home directly next door and across from the spring. As a historian, he was intrigued with the family's tradition going back to the Second Temple period.

Ben Zvi, like the state's other early founders, also understood the importance of the Zenati family: They showed that the Jews always held on to the land, not only in their daily prayers and holidays in the countries to which they were exiled, but also with a constant physical presence on the soil of Israel. From 1999 until 2017, the one-hundred-shekel bill of the State of Israel featured the Zenati and Ben Zvi homes.[4]

All families have traditions and legends, and those stories are a powerful source of identity, a code that can be looked to for comfort, making us part of a chain of people, a shared history, a tribe, even if we don't recognize ourselves as belonging to that tribe.

The Zenati legacy of settling into a small village next to an ancient synagogue and then hanging on to that land for centuries until other members of the tribe returned—even after two thousand years—is in the realm of such a tradition: a story passed on from generation to generation.

That was the case until 2017, when a limestone pillar, buried in the courtyard of the synagogue, was unearthed by Israel Antiquities Authority archaeologists. The pillar dated back to Roman times, to just after the destruction of the Second Temple.[5] The pillar contained a Hebrew inscription found on the downward facing part, protected for centuries from rain and inclement weather. The inscription contained Jewish names from almost two thousand years ago, the names of the people who had survived the Temple's destruction, and who moved up north to Peki'in, reestablished a Jewish community, and dedicated the synagogue.

What before was only family legend was now a part of history. The synagogue of the Zenati family is in the exact same location as a synagogue that goes back thousands of years. And the site has likely been guarded and tended to by Zenati ancestors—and the ancestors of my wife and children—since sometime in the first century CE, throughout the Roman and Byzantine periods, throughout the time of the Crusades and the Ottoman Empire, and into our present time, throughout two world wars, a war for independence, riots, and intifadas.

The Zenati family is not alone in sharing a deep connection to the Land of Israel. The Jewish people carry within us the stories of two thousand years in exile, in places such as Morocco and Iran, Poland and Lithuania. What has bonded Jews over the millennia, whether across distant seas or while living in different cultures and speaking different languages, is that we know, in the deepest part of our being, that all these stories lead back to the same land, the Land of Israel. When the Jewish people came home, it was with a burning desire, not only because we have no other place on earth to go to, but because this is the only place that is truly our own.

The fallen pillar is now standing again.

The City of David still stands today, nestled on a small hilltop just outside the walls of the Old City of Jerusalem. Despite more than two decades of excavations, a new visitors' center, and attractions that bring these ancient wonders to life, visitors remain astonished to discover that the very origins of ancient Jerusalem—the City of David—lay hidden beneath the earth for so long, only now to be unearthed before their eyes.

We find ourselves in a time when the Jewish connection to Jerusalem and the Land of Israel is under siege, a fragile truth being challenged by those who seek to erase both our history and our presence. Paradoxically, it is only upon returning to our land after two millennia—a return unmatched by any other indigenous people in history—that our detractors have intensified their efforts to sever this ancient bond, echoing the actions of Emperor Hadrian, who sought to erase our identity when he renamed Judea as "Palestina."

Yet, the very stones that bear irrefutable testimony to our connection have become the battleground for those intent on undermining it. It seems as if the City of David—this jewel of history, standing as undeniable proof—was waiting, buried beneath the sands of time, to reemerge at this critical moment when the Jewish people need it most.

We need it, first, to remind ourselves that we, the people living in the modern State of Israel, are continuing the legacy of those who came before us—those who established the moral, spiritual, and legal foundations of civilization, only to be exiled. And we have returned in their place, never allowing the bond to break, even after millennia.

And second, for the many good and reasonable people across the world who see through the layers of propaganda and deception, to understand that we, the Jewish people, are truly an indigenous nation. We still speak the same language, pray to the same God, and have turned our hearts and hopes toward this land for more than two thousand years.

We have finally come home.

The foundation stones of the Western Wall, resting on the bedrock of Mount Moriah, are now fully revealed in their ancient grandeur. When I guide groups through the tunnels, winding deep underground, they are always moved. We bend low to touch the jagged bedrock and the first row of stones our ancestors laid as the Temple's foundation.

A few feet away, we walk along the rough bedrock to the corner where the Western and Southern Walls of the Temple Mount meet. There, I ask them to place a hand on each wall. The Southern Wall, I explain, was once the gateway for Jewish families entering the Temple as free people. The Western Wall, after Jerusalem's destruction, became the only remnant the Romans permitted the exiled Jews to visit—a distant, painful reminder of a shattered dream.

At this place, on the bedrock of Mount Moriah, we recall Abraham and Isaac and the dawn of monotheism—an event that reshaped the world. The cornerstone of the Temple Mount encapsulates the Jewish journey: freedom, exile, and the return to freedom in our own time. Here, on the very bedrock of our origin story, history and faith converge.

Perhaps the greatest victory is that millions from around the world can now walk these ancient stones, connecting deeply to their roots in Jerusalem and experiencing the legacy of the Jewish people—without the hardships of the battle.

But for me, the memory of uncovering this history remains vivid. As we dug through the hard soil of Jerusalem, clearing away centuries of stone, it felt as though the ground was still damp—soaked with the tears of the woman of Judea Capta, shed for generations while she waited for her children to return and for the City of David to rise again.

King David captured it best, three thousand years ago, in Psalm 126: "Those who sow with tears will reap with songs of joy."

And so we have.

For many around the world whose journey began with the Jewish people in Jerusalem, this is your history, too. In standing with us, you, too, have come home.

It is a story that defies logic and transcends history.

But that is the story we hear, when we let the stones speak.

Acknowledgments

With this, my first published work, I now understand how the pages allotted for acknowledgments can never truly suffice. It took a village—at least in my case—to bring this decades-long dream to light.

First and foremost, I want to acknowledge the workers, excavators, diggers, and all the builders of Jerusalem at the City of David. Your tireless efforts, often under tedious and challenging conditions, and your care and respect for uncovering archaeological treasures are the very foundation of this book.

To my wife, Sarah, my mother, Geraldine, and my brother, Danny—you are the pillars that upheld me through this journey. From the book's inception, through drafts and revisions, you gave me the encouragement to believe in this book and the support to return to writing it following months of intense military service in the war.

To my grandmother Beatrice, of blessed memory, who inspired me from a young age to believe in my ability to write—your words have echoed in my heart throughout the years, guiding me to this moment.

I have often said that the most important decision I made, besides writing this book, was choosing Mitchell Ivers as my editor. Mitchell's wisdom and mastery of the craft are unparalleled, and I am profoundly grateful for his investment in a first-time author like me. His guidance and insight are deeply woven into the fabric of this book.

To Keith Urbahn, my agent, and Matt Carlini from Javelin, who recognized the potential in this project and brought it to life—thank you. To Alex Pappas, editorial director at Center Street, for taking the bold step of investing in this work, and to Hailey Juen, Jeff Holt, and the entire team at Hachette Book Group. It is extraordinary how one of the largest publishers in the world gave such personal attention to this book.

To David Friedman and Michael Oren, thank you for your thoughtful insights while reading the manuscript and, even more, for the eloquence and integrity with which you represent Israel and its people.

Yigal Carmon, director of MEMRI, whose life's mission has been to reveal the truth of what is spoken in Arabic by world leaders, bringing it to the attention of an international audience.

To my friend and colleague Shifi Cohen, director of content production at the City of David, and Emunah Ansbacher, who worked tirelessly to locate the perfect images from the City of David archive—thank you for bringing this story to life visually as well as in words.

Aaron Horovitz of the Megalim Institute, Michael Baruchi, vice president of the City of David, and Barnea Sullivan—your archaeological and historical expertise were invaluable in ensuring the accuracy of this work. Special thanks to David Armon, one of the first to review the manuscript and verify its historical accuracy.

To Shalom Kveller, whose artistic talent brought the maps in this book to life, and to Jaime Esshaghian, for your brilliant and meticulous graphic artistry. To Mike Feuer and Zeev Orenstein, for your enduring friendship and countless conversations that sharpened the ideas in this book—thank you.

To Davidleh Beeri and Yehuda Mali, my mentors and friends for more than two decades, your guidance has shaped not only this book but so much of who I am.

To Dawn and Ian Aaron, with heartfelt gratitude for your generous help and encouragement on the Hebrew edition.

To my precious children—Neshama, Yaakov, Ariella, Nachshon, Tzofiya, and Elia—you are the joy of my and Ima's life and my greatest motivation. Your smiles remind me of why this work matters: for the future of Israel and the Jewish people.

And finally, to the Rock of Israel: You called me home and showered me with blessings. For this, and for all things, I am eternally grateful.

Notes

Preface

1. Israel Defense Forces, "Milhamot Yisrael," November 23, 2021, https://www.idf
.il/. (Originally in Hebrew: מלחמות ישראל ל,"צה".)

Introduction

1. MEMRI, "Palestinian President Mahmoud Abbas Denies Jewish Connection to
Israel, Claims Hitler Fought Jews Due to Usury, Not Antisemitism," *MEMRI*,
September 3, 2023, https://www.memri.org/tv/palestinian-president-mahmoud
-abbas-denies-jewish-connection-israel-hitler-fought-jews-usury-not-antisemitism.
2. MEMRI, "He Said It All Already in 2018, and More: 'Jews Poison Wells'—
Mahmoud Abbas's Antisemitism and Holocaust Denial," *MEMRI*, May 7, 2018,
https://www.memri.org/reports/he-said-it-all-already-2018-and-more-jews
-poison-wells-%E2%80%93-mahmoud-abbass-antisemitism-and.
3. *Guardian* Staff, "USA Declares War," *The Guardian*, March 19, 2003, https://
www.theguardian.com/world/2003/mar/19/usa.israel.
4. Reuters Staff, "US Wants Shakeup of Palestinian Authority to Run Gaza After
Hamas," Reuters, December 16, 2023, https://www.reuters.com/world/us-wants
-shakeup-palestinian-authority-run-gaza-after-hamas-2023-12-16/.
5. Anti-Defamation League, "Anti-Semitism in Hamas' Charter: Selected Excerpts,"
September 12, 2014, https://www.adl.org/resources/news/anti-semitism-hamas
-charter-selected-excerpts.
6. Avichai Foundation. *Guttman Avichai Report: A Portrait of Israeli Jews—Beliefs,
Observance, and Values of Israeli Jews, 2012.* Jerusalem: Israel Democracy Institute,
2012. https://en.idi.org.il/media/5439/guttmanavichaireport2012_engfinal.pdf.
7. *Die Welt*, "Die Juden sollen dahin zurückgehen, woher sie kamen," *Die Welt*, January 17, 2001. https://www.welt.de.
8. Aaron Lerner, "PA: No Evidence of Jewish Temple Period in Jerusalem," Independent Media Review Analysis, December 3, 1996, http://imra.org.il/story
.php3?id=1139.
9. Dennis Ross, *The Missing Peace: The Inside Story of the Fight for Middle East Peace*
(New York: Farrar, Straus and Giroux, 2005), 694.
10. *Jerusalem Post* Staff, "Jerusalem vs Tel Aviv and the Battle over Israel's Biblical
Archaeology," *Jerusalem Post*, May 14, 2023, https://www.jpost.com/international
/article-743145.

11. Aren M. Maeir, "Israel and Judah." In *The Encyclopedia of Ancient History* (New York: Blackwell, 2013), 3523–27.

12. Gae Callender, *The Eye of Horus: A History of Ancient Egypt* (Longman Cheshire, 1993), 263.

13. Dvir Raviv and Chaim Ben David, "Cassius Dio's Figures for the Demographic Consequences of the Bar Kokhba War: Exaggeration or Reliable Account?" *Journal of Roman Archaeology* 34, no. 2 (2021): 585–607, https://doi.org/10.1017/S1047759421000271.

14. Clayton Miles Lehmann, "Palestine: History: 135–337: Syria Palaestina and the Tetrarchy," *The On-line Encyclopedia of the Roman Provinces* (University of South Dakota, Summer 1998), accessed October 2, 2024.

Chapter 1

1. William Simpson, *Well of the Steps*, watercolor, 1869, in Underground Jerusalem, Palestine Exploration Fund, accessed December 2, 2024, https://www.pef.org.uk/underground-jerusalem/.

2. A. H. Sayce, ed., *Records of the Past*, 2nd series, vol. 1 (1888), Sacred-texts.com, accessed October 1, 2024.

3. Jewish Publication Society, *Tanakh: The Holy Scriptures* (Philadelphia: Jewish Publication Society, 1985), accessed October 1, 2024, https://www.sefaria.org/II_Chronicles.32.27?lang=bi.

4. "Culture Minister Offers Turkish Mayor Elephants for Ancient Hebrew Inscription," *Times of Israel*, February 10, 2020, https://www.timesofisrael.com/culture-minister-offers-turkish-mayor-elephants-for-ancient-hebrew-inscription/.

Chapter 2

1. Karen Armstrong, *Jerusalem: One City, Three Faiths* (New York: Ballantine Books, 1997), 323–27.

2. British Consulate in Jerusalem, May 1864, Foreign Office Records, 195/808 British National Archives.

3. Dotan Goren, "Go, Explore the Land: The Establishment of the Israel Exploration Society," Israel Exploration Society, accessed December 3, 2024, https://www.israelexplorationsociety.com/copy-of-%D7%9E%D7%90%D7%9E%D7%A8-%D7%90%D7%91%D7%99%D7%A8%D7%9D.

Chapter 3

1. Center for Israel Education, "Jerusalem Timeline," Center for Israel Education, accessed October 8, 2024, https://israeled.org/jerusalem-timeline/.

2. Nadav Shragai, "The Mount of Olives in Jerusalem: Why Continued Israeli Control Is Vital," Jerusalem Center for Public Affairs, accessed December 3, 2024, https://jcpa.org/article/the-mount-of-olives-in-jerusalem-why-continued-israeli-control-is-vital/.

3. United Nations, "The Status of Jerusalem: The UN General Assembly Resolution 181," UNISPAL, December 10, 1949, https://www.un.org/unispal/document/auto-insert-210978/.

4. Nadav Shragai, "The Destruction of the Temple Mount Antiquities," Jerusalem Center for Public Affairs, accessed December 10, 2024, https://jcpa.org/article/the-destruction-of-the-temple-mount-antiquities/.

5. Nadav Shragai, "The Danger to Al-Aksa from Muslim Building Activity in Solomon's Stables," Jerusalem Center for Public Affairs, accessed December 3, 2024, https://jcpa.org/al-aksa-is-in-danger-libel/danger-to-al-aksa-from-muslim-building-in-solomons-stables/.

Chapter 5

1. Haviv Rettig Gur, "Jerusalem vs Tel Aviv, and the Battle over Israel's Biblical Archaeology," *Jerusalem Post*, July 12, 2020, https://www.jpost.com/israel-news/jerusalem-vs-tel-aviv-and-the-battle-over-israels-biblical-archeology-635218.

2. Alec Wilkinson, "In Search of King David's Lost Empire," *New Yorker*, June 29, 2020, https://www.newyorker.com/magazine/2020/06/29/in-search-of-king-davids-lost-empire.

3. Kathleen Kenyon, *Archaeology in the Holy Land* (New York: Praeger Publishers, 1970), 244.

4. "The Jewish Connection to the Land of Israel," Azure, accessed October 9, 2024, https://azure.org.il/article.php?id=170.

5. Isabel Kershner, "King David's Palace Is Found, Archaeologist Says," *New York Times*, August 5, 2005, https://www.nytimes.com/2005/08/05/world/middleeast/king-davids-palace-is-found-archaeologist-says.html.

6. "King David's Lost Empire," *New Yorker*, June 29, 2020.

7. "King David's Lost Empire," *New Yorker*, June 29, 2020.

8. "The Birth and Death of Biblical Minimalism," Armstrong Institute of Biblical Archaeology, accessed October 8, 2024, https://armstronginstitute.org/814-the-birth-and-death-of-biblical-minimalism.

9. Gustav Niebuhr, "The Bible, as History, Flunks New Archaeological Tests," *New York Times*, July 29, 2000, https://archive.nytimes.com/www.nytimes.com/library/arts/072900david-bible.html.

10. Haviv Rettig Gur, "Web of Biblical Cities Depicts King David as Major Ruler, Says Israeli Archaeologist," *Times of Israel*, September 5, 2013, https://www.timesofisrael.com/web-of-biblical-cities-depicts-king-david-as-major-ruler-says-israeli-archaeologist/.

11. Holly Watt, "Researchers Dig Up Controversy in Jerusalem," *Reuters*, March 24, 2010, https://www.reuters.com/article/us-palestininians-israel-jerusalem-digs/researchers-dig-up-controversy-in-jerusalem-idUKTRE62N33D20100324.

12. Isabel Kershner, "King David's Palace Is Found, Archaeologist Says," *New York Times*, August 5, 2005, https://www.nytimes.com/2005/08/05/world/middleeast/king-davids-palace-isfound-archaeologist-says.html.

13. Proceedings of the National Academy of Sciences (PNAS): Finkelstein, Israel, et al., "Radiocarbon Dating and the History of Ancient Israel," *Proceedings of the National Academy of Sciences* 121, no. 6 (2024), https://www.pnas.org/doi/abs/10.1073/pnas.2321024121.

14. Nirit Schulman, "Jerusalem in King David's Time Was Much Larger Than Previously Thought, Researchers Say," *Haaretz*, April 29, 2024, https://www.haaretz .com/archaeology/2024-04-29/ty-article-magazine/jerusalem-in-king-davids -time-was-much-larger-than-previously-thought-researchers-say/0000018f -155d-d2e1-a7df-15ffc4a20000.

15. Ilan Sivan, "Jerusalem in King David's Time Was Much Larger Than Previously Thought, Researchers Say," *Haaretz*, April 29, 2024, https://www.haaretz.com /archaeology/2024-04-29/ty-article-magazine/jerusalem-in-king-davids-time -was-much-larger-than-previously-thought-researchers-say/0000018f-155d -d2e1-a7df-15ffc4a20000.

16. "Die Juden sollen dahin zurückgehen, woher sie kamen," [The Jews should go back where they came from], *Die Welt* (in German), retrieved 2022-07-18.

Chapter 8

1. David Makovsky, "Why Israel Outlawed the Northern Branch of the Islamic Movement," Brookings, December 7, 2015, https://www.brookings.edu/blog /markaz/2015/12/07/why-israel-outlawed-the-northern-branch-of-the-islamic -movement/.

2. Yoram Schweitzer, "The 'Al-Aksa Is in Danger' Libel: Sheikh as Successor of the Mufti," Jerusalem Center for Public Affairs, accessed October 8, 2024, https://jcpa .org/al-aksa-is-in-danger-libel/al-aksa-libel-sheikh-as-successor-of-the-mufti/.

3. *Documents on German Foreign Policy, 1918–1945: From the Archives of the German Foreign Ministry. Series D (1937–1945), Volume XIII: The War Years, June 23–December 11, 1941* (Washington, DC.: United States Government Printing Office, 1954).

4. Arutz Sheva, "In the Wake of the Western Wall Tunnel Opening," Arutz Sheva, September 26, 1996, https://www.inn.co.il/news/158949.

5. "The Week in History: Violence in the Old City as New Tunnel Opens," *Jerusalem Post*, September 26, 2014, https://www.jpost.com/magazine/this-week-in-history -violence-in-the-old-city-as-new-tunnel-opens-376201.

6. "A Spark in a Tinderbox," *The Economist*, February 15, 2007, https://www.economist .com/middle-east-and-africa/2007/02/15/a-spark-in-a-tinderbox.

7. "NGO Profile: Ir Amim," NGO Monitor, accessed October 8, 2024, https:// www.ngo-monitor.org/ngos/ir_amim/.

8. Jonathan Lis and Haaretz News Service, "Salah Calls for Intifada Against Temple Mount Excavation," *Haaretz*, February 16, 2007, accessed September 30, 2024, https://www.haaretz.com/2007-02-16/ty-article/salah-calls-for-intifada-against -temple-mount-excavation/0000017f-dbbc-d3a5-af7f-fbbeda570000.

9. Neil MacFarquhar, "Israel Works at Temple Mount, and Sets Off Alarms," *New York Times*, February 12, 2007, https://www.nytimes.com/2007/02/12/world /middleeast/12cnd-mideast.html.

10. Nadav Shragai, "Israel's Archeological Digs," Jerusalem Center for Public Affairs, accessed October 8, 2024, https://jcpa.org/al-aksa-is-in-danger-libel/al -aksa-libel-archeological-digs/.

11. Ir Amim, "The Mughrabi Gate Access Ramp—A Troubling Development in the Old City," January 1, 2007, accessed September 30, 2024, https://www.ir-amim .org.il/en/report/mugrabi-gate-access-ramp-troubling-development-old-city.

12. Ahiya Raved, "UNESCO: Israel Stalling Mughrabi Bridge," *Ynet News*, April 15, 2016, https://www.ynetnews.com/articles/0,7340,L-4793357,00.html.

13. "Behind the Headlines: Northern Faction of the Islamic Movement Outlawed," Government of Israel, November 17, 2015, https://www.gov.il/en/departments/general /behind-the-headlines-northern-faction-of-the-islamic-movement-organization -outlawed-17-november-2015.

14. "EU-Funded NGOs Promote Palestinian Positions on Jerusalem," *NGO Monitor*, accessed October 8, 2024, https://www.ngo-monitor.org/press-releases/eu _funded_ngos_promote_palestinian_positions_on_jerusalem_/; "Role of NGOs in the Palestinian Political War," *Jerusalem Center for Public Affairs*, accessed October 8, 2024, https://jcpa.org/overview_palestinian_manipulation/role_of_ngos_in_the _palestinian-political_war/.

15. Anna Melamed and Abeer Salman, "Israeli Settlers Rampage through Palestinian Towns," CNN, February 26, 2023, https://edition.cnn.com/2023/02/26 /middleeast/west-bank-violence-intl/index.html.

16. Gassan Mahmud Weshah, "Image of the Jews in the Opinion of Ibn Khaldun," *Academia Arabia*, Islamic University of Giza, accessed December 10, 2024, https://academia-arabia.com/en/reader/2/138051.

17. Naama Goren-Inbar, et al., "Early Evidence of Fire Usage by Hominins," *Nature Communications* 5 (2014): 4835, https://www.nature.com/articles/ncomms5835.

18. NCBI: Zhu, Hu, et al., "Genetic Structure of Populations," *Proceedings of the National Academy of Sciences* 97, no. 13 (2000): 7945–50, https://www.ncbi.nlm .nih.gov/pmc/articles/PMC18733/.

19. Ilan Troen and Carol Troen, "Word Crimes; Reclaiming the Language of the Israeli-Palestinian Conflict," *Israel Studies* 24, no. 2 (Summer 2019): 17–32. Published by Indiana University Press.

20. Troen and Troen, "Word Crimes," 17–32.

21. Troen and Troen, "Word Crimes," 17–32.

22. Bernard Lewis, *Semites and Anti-Semites: An Inquiry into Conflict and Prejudice*, (New York: W. W. Norton & Company, 1999), 49.

23. H.H. Ben-Sasson, *A History of the Jewish People* (Cambridge, MA: Harvard University Press, 1976), 334; Clayton Miles Lehmann, "Palestine: History: 135–337: Syria Palaestina and the Tetrarchy," *The On-line Encyclopedia of the Roman Provinces* (University of South Dakota, Summer 1998), accessed October 2, 2024.

24. Britannica (Philistine): "Philistine," *Britannica*, accessed October 8, 2024, https://www.britannica.com/topic/Philistine-people.

25. Eric M. Meyers, ed., *The Oxford Encyclopedia of Archaeology in the Near East: Volume 4* (Oxford: Oxford University Press, 1997), 313.

26. Britannica (Palestine): "Palestine," *Britannica*, accessed October 8, 2024, https:// www.britannica.com/place/Palestine.

27. Mark Twain, *The Innocents Abroad*, accessed October 8, 2024, http://www
.literaturepage.com/read/twain-innocents-abroad-356.html.

28. Haviv Rettig Gur, "The Year the Arabs Discovered Palestine," *Jerusalem Post*,
February 15, 2022, https://www.jpost.com/jerusalem-report/article-700904.

29. "Origin of 'Palestine,'" *Jewish Virtual Library*, accessed October 8, 2024, https://
www.jewishvirtuallibrary.org/origin-of-quot-palestine-quot.

30. Daniel Pipes, "The Year the Arabs Discovered 'Palestine,'" *Daniel Pipes Middle
East Forum*, September 20, 2011, https://www.danielpipes.org/8025/the-year-the
-arabs-discovered-palestine.

31. "The Year the Arabs Discovered 'Palestine'," *Daniel Pipes*, September 20, 2011.

32. Vice President Sebutinde, Dissenting Opinion, International Court of Justice,
Case 186, July 19, 2024, https://icj-cij.org/sites/default/files/case-related/186/186
-20240719-adv-01-02-encc.pdf.

33. United Nations General Assembly, "A/RES/181(II) of 29 November 1947,"
accessed October 7, 2024, https://undocs.org/A/RES/181(II).

34. Benny Morris, *1948: A History of the First Arab–Israeli War* (Yale University Press,
2008), 187.

35. Khaled Al ʾAzm, *Mudhakarat* (Beirut: al-Dar al Muttahida lil-Nashr, 1972), vol.
1, 386–87.

36. Arieh Avneri, *The Claim of Dispossession*, (NJ: Transaction Books, 1984), 272;
Benjamin Kedar, *The Changing Land Between the Jordan and the Sea* (Israel: Yad
Izhak Ben-Zvi Press, 1999), 206; Paul Johnson, *A History of the Jews* (New York:
Harper & Row, 1987), 529.

37. Central Bureau of Statistics, 2023, "Israel in Numbers—Rosh Hashanah Eve
5784: Selected Data from the 2023 Annual Tables," last modified September 2023,
https://www.cbs.gov.il/en/mediarelease/Pages/2023/Israel-in-Figures-Rosh
-Hashana-Selected-Annual-Data-2023.aspx.

38. "Jewish Refugees Expelled from Arab Lands and from Iran," *Israel Ministry of Foreign
Affairs*, accessed October 8, 2024, https://embassies.gov.il/bern/NewsAndEvents
/Pages/Jewish-refugees-expelled-from-Arab-lands-and-from-Iran.aspx.

39. "Palestine Refugees," *UNRWA*, accessed October 8, 2024, https://www.unrwa
.org/palestine-refugees.

40. Einat Wilf and Adi Schwartz, "UNRWA Has Changed the Definition of Refugee," *Foreign Policy*, August 17, 2018, https://foreignpolicy.com/2018/08/17/unrwa
-has-changed-the-definition-of-refugee/.

41. Jewish Publication Society, *Tanakh: The Holy Scriptures* (Philadelphia: Jewish
Publication Society, 1985), accessed October 1, 2024, https://www.sefaria.org
/Genesis.25.8?ven=Tanakh:_The_Holy_Scriptures,_published_by_JPS&lang=bi
&with=Translations&lang2=en.

Chapter 9

1. Nadav Shragai, "Al-Aksa Libel: Section 9. Israel's Archaeological Digs," *Jerusalem Center for Public Affairs*, accessed October 8, 2024, https://jcpa.org/al-aksa
-is-in-danger-libel/al-aksa-libel-archeological-digs/.

2. Eyāl Benveniśtî, *The International Law of Occupation* (Princeton University Press, 2004), 108.

3. Greer Fay Cashman, "Digging Too Deep," *Jerusalem Post*, accessed October 8, 2024, https://www.jpost.com/local-israel/in-jerusalem/digging-too-deep; Daniel A. Gross, "Archaeological Digs Stoke Conflict in Jerusalem," *The Nation*, February 2, 2016, https://www.thenation.com/article/archive/archaeological-digs-stoke-conflict-jerusalem/.

4. "Jerusalem: Unearthing the Past Amid Conflict," *BBC News*, accessed October 8, 2024, https://www.bbc.com/news/articles/cnvyyz8461yo.

5. "Archaeological Digs Stoke Conflict in Jerusalem," *The Nation*, February 2, 2016.

6. Sylvia Poggioli, "Rome's Subway Expansion Reveals Artifacts from the Ancient Past," NPR, July 22, 2018, https://www.npr.org/2018/07/22/630532760/romes-subway-expansion-reveals-artifacts-from-the-ancient-past.

7. "Blood-Libel Cleric Raed Salah, Who Was Praised by Jeremy Corbyn, Jailed in Israel for Inciting Violence," *The Jewish Chronicle*, February 10, 2020, https://www.thejc.com/news/israel/blood-libel-cleric-raed-salah-who-was-praised-by-jeremy-corbyn-jailed-israel-for-inciting-violence-1.496669.

8. *Nouel Kra'in and 26 Others v. Israel Antiquities Authority*, HCJ 1308/08 (2009); *Muhammad Attallah Siam v. Israel Antiquities Authority*, HCJ 1308/08 (2009).

9. Nadav Shragai, "Al-Aksa Libel: Section Nine. Israel's Archaeological Digs," Jerusalem Center for Public Affairs, accessed October 8, 2024, https://jcpa.org/al-aksa-is-in-danger-libel/al-aksa-libel-archeological-digs/.

10. "Controversy in Jerusalem: The City of David," CBS News, October 14, 2010, https://www.cbsnews.com/news/controversy-in-jerusalem-the-city-of-david-14-10-2010/.

11. "Details About the Tensions in Silwan," *Silwanic*, accessed October 8, 2024, https://www.silwanic.net/index.php/article/news/45571.

12. "Silwan: A Document on the Tensions and Challenges in the Region," *Silwanic*, accessed October 8, 2024, https://www.silwanic.net/writable/uploads/silwanic.pdf.

13. "CBS *60 Minutes* Rebroadcasts Jerusalem Propaganda Piece," CAMERA, accessed October 8, 2024, https://www.camera.org/article/cbs-60-minutes-rebroadcasts-jerusalem-propaganda-piece/.

Chapter 11

1. David Lee Miller, "City of David Archaeological Discoveries," Special Report with Bret Baier, Fox News, January 25, 2011, https://archive.org/details/FOXNEWS_20110125_090000_Special_Report_With_Bret_Baier/start/720/end/780.

2. Charles Levinson and Eric Gibson, "Jerusalem Underground: Secrets of an Ancient City," *Wall Street Journal*, January 22, 2011, https://www.wsj.com/articles/SB10001424052748704698004576104320263685168.

3. "The *Washington Post* Isn't Sure Hamas Engaged in Mass Rape," *Jewish News Syndicate (JNS)*, October 6, 2023, https://www.jns.org/the-washington-post-isnt-sure-hamas-engaged-in-mass-rape/.

4. Tzvi Joffre, "Photos of Babies Being Burnt, Decapitated Confirmed," *Jerusalem Post*, October 12, 2023, https://www.jpost.com/breaking-news/article-767951.
5. Israel Defense Forces (IDF), "Al-Ahli Al-Ma'amadani Hospital: Initial IDF Aftermath Report, October 18, 2023," *IDF*, https://www.idf.il/en/mini-sites /israel-at-war/all-articles/al-ahli-al-ma-amadani-hospital-initial-idf-aftermath -report-october-18-2023/.

Chapter 12

1. "Suicide and Other Bombing Attacks in Israel Since 1993," *Israel Ministry of Foreign Affairs*, accessed October 8, 2024, https://embassies.gov.il/MFA /FOREIGNPOLICY/Terrorism/Palestinian/Pages/Suicide%20and%20 Other%20Bombing%20Attacks%20in%20Israel%20Since.aspx.
2. "Inside the Terror Web," *ABC News Nightline*, August 19, 2004, https://abcnews .go.com/Nightline/story?id=128578&page=1.
3. "Nightline: The Holy Land," *ABC News*, May 2, 2002, https://tvnews.vanderbilt .edu/siteindex/2002-5.
4. "Israel's War on the Palestinians: A New Perspective," *Palestine Chronicle*, January 29, 2002, archived at the Wayback Machine, https://web.archive.org/web /20070929131948/http://palestinechronicle.com/story-20020129050221695.htm.
5. "Michigan High School Apologizes for Inviting Anti-Israel Activist to Diversity Assembly," Fox News, October 5, 2023, https://www.foxnews.com/politics /michigan-high-school-apologizes-anti-israel-activist-diversity-assembly.
6. Jonathan Tobin, "Preaching Peace Using Violence: The International Solidarity Movement's Activism," *Honest Reporting*, last modified October 4, 2023, https:// honestreporting.com/preaching-peace-using-violence-the-international-solidarity -movements-activism/.

Chapter 13

1. United Nations, *The Question of Palestine: The Palestinian People's Right to Self-Determination* (New York: United Nations, 2014), accessed October 9, 2024, https://digitallibrary.un.org/record/780153?ln=en&v=pdf.
2. United Nations, *The Question of Palestine* (New York: United Nations, 2014).
3. "The Appeals Committee Cancelled Construction Permit Granted to Elad at Hashalom Forest," Peace Now, last modified October 4, 2023, https://peacenow .org.il/en/the-appeals-committee-cancelled-construction-permit-granted-to-elad -at-hashalom-forest.
4. Josh Earnest, "Press Briefing by Press Secretary Josh Earnest, 10/1/2014," The White House, October 1, 2014, https://obamawhitehouse.archives.gov/the -press-office/2014/10/01/press-briefing-press-secretary-josh-earnest-1012014.
5. Barak Ravid, "Netanyahu Rejects U.S. Criticism Over E. Jerusalem," *Haaretz*, October 2, 2014, https://www.haaretz.com/2014-10-02/ty-article/.premium/netanyahu -rejects-u-s-criticism-over-e-jlem/0000017f-e4b0-d568-ad7f-f7fb48550000.
6. "Netanyahu Should Withdraw Statement That Opposing Settlements Is Un-American," J Street, last modified October 1, 2014, https://jstreet.org/press-releases

/netanyahu-should-withdraw-statement-that-opposing-settlements-is-unamerican
-_1/.

7. Daniel K. Eisenbud, "Rare 2,500-Year-Old Woman's Seal from First Temple
Period Unearthed in Jerusalem," *The Jerusalem Post*, October 4, 2016, https://www
.jpost.com/Israel-News/Rare-2500-year-old-womans-seal-from-First-Temple
-period-unearthed-in-Jerusalem-447113?fbclid=IwAR0UxAlqSDVYkK6bHV0
OqAPfrsAF2wZpLeWxlGf6bs3ZRn-IrKdC_tXJJmU.

8. United Nations, "The Question of Palestine," UNISPAL, 2017, https://www
.un.org/unispal/document/auto-insert-203201/.

9. Ted Cruz, "Sen. Cruz, Rep. Ros-Lehtinen Lead Bipartisan Letter to UNESCO
Member States: Do Not Rewrite Jerusalem's History," Senator Ted Cruz, last
modified October 3, 2017, accessed December 10, 2024, https://www.cruz.senate
.gov/newsroom/press-releases/sen-cruz-rep-ros-lehtinen-lead-bipartisan-letter
-to-unesco-member-states-do-not-rewrite-jerusalem-and-rsquos-history.

10. Jerry Nadler, "Nadler Statement on the New York State Legislature's Passage
of Legislation to Protect Palestinian Rights," Representative Jerry Nadler, last
modified July 5, 2017, accessed March 20, 2023, https://nadler.house.gov/news
/documentsingle.aspx?DocumentID=391375.

11. UNESCO, *The 1975 UNESCO General Conference Resolution on Palestine* (Paris:
UNESCO, 2019), accessed October 9, 2024, https://unesdoc.unesco.org/ark:/48223
/pf0000246215.

12. "UNESCO: No Connection Between Temple Mount and Judaism," *The Jerusalem Post*, October 13, 2016, https://www.jpost.com/breaking-news/unesco-no
-connection-between-temple-mount-and-judaism-470050.

13. Raphael Ahren, "PM Meets Mexican Diplomat Fired for Challenging UNESCO
Jerusalem Vote," *Times of Israel*, October 5, 2016, https://www.timesofisrael.com
/pm-meets-mexican-diplomat-fired-for-challenging-unesco-jerusalem-vote/.

14. Peter Beaumont, "Israel Suspends UNESCO Ties after Resolution on Jerusalem Holy Sites," *The Guardian*, October 14, 2016, https://www.theguardian.com
/world/2016/oct/14/israel-unesco-resolution-jerusalem-palestine.

15. "UNESCO Chief 'Received Death Threats' for Opposing Jerusalem Motion,"
Times of Israel, October 17, 2016, https://www.timesofisrael.com/unesco-chief
-received-death-threats-for-opposing-jerusalem-motion/.

16. "U.S. House Meets for Morning Hour," C-SPAN, December 5, 2018, https://
www.c-span.org/video/?426189-1/us-house-meets-morning-hour.

Chapter 14

1. Jewish Publication Society, *Tanakh: The Holy Scriptures* (Philadelphia: Jewish
Publication Society, 1985), https://www.sefaria.org/Exodus.28.34?ven=Tanakh
:_The_Holy_Scriptures,_published_by_JPS&lang=bi&aliyot=0.

2. DM Behar, L Saag, M Karmin, MG Gover, JD Wexler, LF Sanchez, et al.,
"The Genetic Variation in the R1a Clade Among the Ashkenazi Levites' Y
Chromosome," *Scientific Reports* 7 (November 2017): Article 40447. https://doi
.org/10.1038/s41598-017-14761-7.

3. Judah Ari Gross, "2,000-Year-Old Golden Bell Discovered in Jerusalem," *The Jerusalem Post*, October 5, 2023, https://www.jpost.com/national-news/2000 -year-old-golden-bell-discovered-in-jerusalem#:~:text=A%20golden%20bell%20 ornament%20that,Thursday%2C%20the%20Antiquities%20Authority%20 announced.

Chapter 15

1. David Friedman, *Sledgehammer: How Breaking with the Past Brought Peace to the Middle East* (New York: Broadside Books, 2022), 4.
2. Yaakov Lappin, "Left-Wing NGO Denounces Israel Prize Laureate David Beeri," *The Jerusalem Post*, April 11, 2017, https://www.jpost.com/israel-news/left -wing-ngo-denounces-israel-prize-laureate-david-beeri-484610.0

Chapter 16

1. "Commemorative Coins," Israel Mint, accessed October 9, 2024, https:// en.israelmint.com/default/33190027.html.
2. "Ecclesia et Synagoga," Jewish Virtual Library, accessed October 9, 2024, https:// www.jewishvirtuallibrary.org/ecclesia-et-synagoga.

Epilogue

1. Zvi Bar'el, "Racing to Record a Druze Village's Last Jew," *Haaretz*, July 25, 2012, https://www.haaretz.com/2012-07-25/ty-article/racing-to-record-a-druze -villages-last-jew/0000017f-eefa-d8a1-a5ff-fefae4930000.
2. *Talmud, Tractate Chagigah 3a*, accessed October 9, 2024, https://www.sefaria .org/Chagigah.3a.15?vhe=William_Davidson_Edition_-_Vocalized_Aramaic& lang=bi.
3. Moshe Bassola, *Journeys in the Land of Israel* (Jerusalem: The Hebrew Society for the Study of the Land of Israel and its Antiquities with the assistance of the Bialik Foundation, affiliated with the Jewish Agency for Israel, 1938).
4. Bank of Israel, "Second Series of the New Israeli Shekel," accessed October 7, 2024. https://www.boi.org.il/en/economic-roles/banknotes-and-coins/second-series -nis/.
5. Zvi Bar'el, "1,800-Year-Old Hebrew Donor Plaques Found in Synagogue in Israel," *Haaretz*, February 22, 2017, https://www.haaretz.com/archaeology /2017-02-22/ty-article/.premium/1-800-year-old-hebrew-donor-plaques-found -in-synagogue-in-israel/0000017f-e717-d97e-a37f-f777e6b50000?lts=1710179 141848.

Index

About the Author

Born and educated in the United States, Doron Spielman moved to Israel in 2000, where he serves as an international spokesperson in the Israel Defense Forces reserves with the rank of major. For more than two decades, he has worked to transform the City of David into one of the world's most significant archaeological and historical sites. He is a graduate of the Churchill National Security Program, a senior fellow at the Herut Center in Jerusalem, and a graduate of the University of Michigan.